WATERFOWL CARVING
BLUE RIBBON TECHNIQUES

WATERFOWL CARVING
BLUE RIBBON TECHNIQUES

by William Veasey
with Cary Schuler Hull

Schiffer Publishing Ltd

Box E, Exton, Pennsylvania 19341

Dedication

This work is dedicated to my wife Dotty for always giving me the freedom and the space to grow in whatever I chose to do.

Designed by Ellen J. Taylor

Front jacket photo: Wood ducks by William Veasey. Photo by Tricia Veasey. Collection of Don Griffith.

Printed in the United States of America.
ISBN 0-916838-67-6
Published by Schiffer Publishing LTD.

Table of Contents

Acknowledgments

Photography
Tricia Veasey
Cary Hull

Artwork
Debra Norvell

Project Preparation
Paul Suarez

I would like to give special recognition to all those who have been students over the years. You are the people who taught me.

Thanks to Bob Biddle for involving me in this beautiful madness, my brother Don for believing, Bill Purnell for having the guts to tell me I had done a lousy job of carving and then telling me how to improve, and Gunter Sunkler for believing my carvings were saleable.

Also, I wish to give special notice to all the unnamed people who work so hard in producing the carving shows which have showcased all our works.

A special thanks to all the teachers who have taught in my studio and at seminars: Pat Biddle, Jan Calvert, Rosalind Daisey, Doug Eppes, Gregg Ewell, Sina Pat Kurman, Penny Mace, Debra Norvell, Don Osborne, Lisa Schuler, Paul Suarez, Robert Tito, and Tricia Veasey.

William Veasey

Introduction

"Hold fast to dreams
for if dreams die,
life is a broken
winged bird that
cannot fly."

--Langston Hughes

Winning a blue ribbon in a carving competition is a thrilling achievement. Like any personal achievement, it begins with a dream. I always knew I was a dreamer, but it never occurred to me that I could be an artist. To take a block of wood and turn it into a beautiful sculpture with life and personality is an art. This is what I do. More importantly, this is what I teach others to do.

My initiation into the fascinating world of hunting, carving and collecting came about through a good friend who also happened to be my brother-in-law, Bob Biddle. Bob was so enthusiatic about all this that in the winter of 1969 he talked me into going duck hunting with him. At that time I felt anyone was an absolute idiot who got up at 4 a.m. to sit in the freezing cold just for the opportunity of shooting at a duck (and probably missing).

I still feel that way. I still miss whenever I shoot; however, I love going into the marshes or on a river to "layout" shoot. Mostly, I like the company of the people I hunt with and I like to observe waterfowl in their natural habitat.

After that first hunting season I could recognize a Mallard (drake only) and a "Canadian" goose. (I later learned the proper name is Canada goose.)

During that same winter, on a visit to Bob's workshop, I was encouraged to try carving a miniature flying Mallard. "An impossible task," I thought. I was sure I could not make anything artistic with my hands; I certainly could not do anything with a knife.

I was wrong. I had forgotten, since my high school woodworking days, how good it felt to work with wood and make something. So when Bob suggested that as "something to do in our spare time" we attend a few beginners' carving classes with Harry Waite in West Chester, Pa., I willingly went along.

After about three months of carving, I attended my very first carving show. I was so overwhelmed by what I saw--the beautiful work being done--that I felt I should throw away my knife and forget about carving. However, close on the heels of that thought came an even stronger and more compelling determination. If all those people could do it, so could I!

Because I always believed that you are what you say you are, the first thing I did after that show was to have cards printed that read: WILLIAM VEASEY — WOOD CARVER. Having announced to myself and the world my status as a carver, it was incumbent on me to become one.

Where to start was a major problem. I needed information. I knew little about waterfowl, less about carving. At that time there was not much written about carving ducks. There were a few reference works on birds written for bird-watchers and ornithologists but nothing that could be used as a guide for would-be carvers. The search was on. As I sought out other carvers for help, I realized I did not know enough even to know what to ask. I found people who were helpful and people who were reluctant to share their knowledge. I read everything I could find. I went to all the carving shows, watched the judging carefully, and later asked judges what they looked for in a carving. I scrutinized the carvings as well as live birds and mounts.

Since my business was seasonal, I had a good deal of time to devote to the compilation of information and to carving. I carved birds one after another after another and began to realize that the "art of carving" is indeed developmental. You don't carve a bird and all at once become an "artist". It takes time. It takes doing it over and over…learning…experimenting…carving…improving…carving……… carving. People start to notice your progress and begin referring to you as an artist, but you know you are still developing your art. Then finally one day you finish a piece. You look at it and you can not believe that *you* really did it. You look at it and you know--you *are* an artist.

After a few years, people began coming to me with questions, so eventually I started teaching classes. It was a modest beginning with four students in my garage. Today, 11 years later, I am a full-time carver and carving teacher.

Teaching is an extension of myself and my art. I take great pride in teaching--in giving my students basic instructions and standing back to watch them develop. It is an incredible high to teach them how to carve and see them go on to win a blue ribbon. Most people never think about competing when they first start carving. But as their talent develops, they become eager to see how their carvings match up against others. I have had students of all ages, including eight-year-old children and 73-year-old women, win the blue, and many of them have also won best of show. I am so proud of my students that in preparing this book I decided that the carvings that would be included in it would be some of theirs, instead of mine.

My own experience proves that anyone can become a fine bird carver--an artist. Most people say, "I can't do that, I'm not artistic." I said the same thing. The truth is, you *can* do it; all you need is the dream, time to learn, and access to good information.

You obviously have the dream and feel the need for good information.

In writing this book, it is my intention to give you the basic information you need to learn to carve waterfowl. It is not my intention to be the last word on carving. I hope there never will be a last word. I encourage you to learn, to experiment, to carve, to compete, and ultimately to contribute to the field of carving by never placing limitations on it or yourself, thereby creating an ever-expanding art.

Go for the blue.

William Veasey
Elkton, Maryland
March 1982

9

Words of Wisdom
from some of the World's Great Carvers

Knute Bartrug. Chairman Emeritus of the Ward Foundation who has worked untiringly on the behalf of carvers and carving--one of the main reasons why carving has become known throughout the country. "Carvers need their work critiqued and that is why contests are the backbone of the carving world."

Don Bridell. Very fine carver who studied at the feet of the master, Lem Ward. "In the words of Lem Ward--'Be Reckless.' "

Tan Brunet. The "Cajun Carver" and World Champion three times in the floating decorative pairs division. "Be broad-minded. Accept criticism with an open mind. Discipline is the key word. Remember to take advice from the Old Pros and put a little class in your carving."

Paul Burdette. Canadian, World Champion, teacher. "A good head can carry a weak body, but a good body can not carry a weak head."

Al Glassford. One of Canada's great carvers. "Don't be too ambitious with your first efforts. Keep it simple."

Pat Godin. Canadian, World Champion. "Maintain originality. Study live subjects. Stress simplicity and develop a painting strategy while planning the carving."

John Scheeler. Champion of Champions. World Champion six times in twelve years. I've heard it said by someone winning the World Championships that the only reason why he won was because John Scheeler wasn't competing. Another World Champion attributed his winning to the help that John Scheeler had given him. "No one is any better than his source material."

William Schultz. World Champion. "The mechanics of translating a living bird into wood are demanding and exciting. Certainly, the creation of an exquisitely textured wing or well-turned bill is a worthy achievement. But it is all too easy to become lost in the fine points of craftsmanship. This is true if the finished carving is no more than a mere photographic image of a bird--a static image that does not convey that avian essence of life and character each individual species represents. Perhaps, a revision of the old folk admonition is appropriate for carvings that sacrifice character for technique--the bird in the bush, in these instances, will always be worth more than the bird in the hand."

Jimmy Vizier. One of America's great carving teachers. A teacher of champions, one of whom was Tan Brunet. "Take care in selecting a good block of wood. Have well-sharpened tools. Of utmost importance is observation and research."

George Walker. In the times Walker was competing, he probably won more ribbons than anyone else who has ever competed. He is credited with many innovations in the world of bird carving, such as carving tools and materials to use. "An artist is no better than his tools."

Gary L. Yoder. World Champion who works mostly in miniature sizes. "Study your subject. Knowledge is the basis for any good carving."

Becoming a Bird Carver

When I was learning how to carve, most carvers were making hunting decoys or smooth-bodied birds. These were very simple carvings made realistic with paint. Today, bird carvings are textured to be realistic. Everything is in the wood before the carving is painted.

This evolution occurred through experimentation among large numbers of people and through an interchange of ideas. Over the years, carvers thought of some new technique to try; if it worked, they'd incorporate it into their carvings. Other carvers observed this new technique and made their carvings that way. Then someone experimented with another method, and so on. Thus, bird carvings have evolved from hunting decoys to smooth decorative decoys to rough-textured decoys to lightly textured decoys, and finally, to today's highly detailed, decorative and floating decorative birds. The general public still refers to them as decoys, but they are actually decorative wood sculptures.

Today's bird carvings are realistic and lifelike. The carver takes a block of wood and turns it into a sculpture, something with life, that says "touch me". Everyone viewing the carving should have the impulse to reach out and touch it to feel what looks so exactly like a live bird. The most often heard response from the public is, "Oh! They look just like real feathers!"

We've taken bird carving where it's never been before. It has become fine art and is being recognized as such by the art establishment today. This has been a very difficult step to achieve and is the result of work by such groups as the Ward Foundation and the Easton Waterfowl Festival Association. These people work hard because they believe in the development of bird carving, even though they may not be carvers themselves.

The joy of bird carving is that it's not a narrow art form. Once a carver learns the basic techniques, he can take his carving as far as he likes. He never has to grow bored. There's no end to the learning he can do if he chooses. He can take up photography and take pictures of live waterfowl for reference. He can experiment with all kinds of painting methods. He can learn all there is to know about wood. The list of possibilities goes on and on from sawmill to art gallery.

Where does a new carver begin? Perhaps by learning basic facts about waterfowl.

WATERFOWL BASICS

To be able to carve a realistic duck, you should know its basic anatomy. Study figure 1. Really look at each part of the duck and learn what each one is called. Observe how these parts come together. Look at the way feathers are layered, with the rump feathers on the bottom of the layer. Feathers come smoothly out from the body with no bends. Look at the quills and barbs of the feathers. Study the feathers on the wings to see how they are layered. (Figure 2) Note that there are no harsh, sharp lines in nature. There is always a smooth transition from one color to another, from one feather to another, etc. The more you understand about waterfowl, the better your carvings will be.

By definition, only ducks, geese and swans are waterfowl, or members of the duck family. But there are many other birds, such as marsh birds, shorebirds and seabirds, that live in or around the water that are often loosely referred to as waterfowl and are generally accomodated in the wildfowl competitions in separate categories.

Ducks, geese and swans have several characteristics in common that a bird

Fig. 1. BASIC BIRD ANATOMY

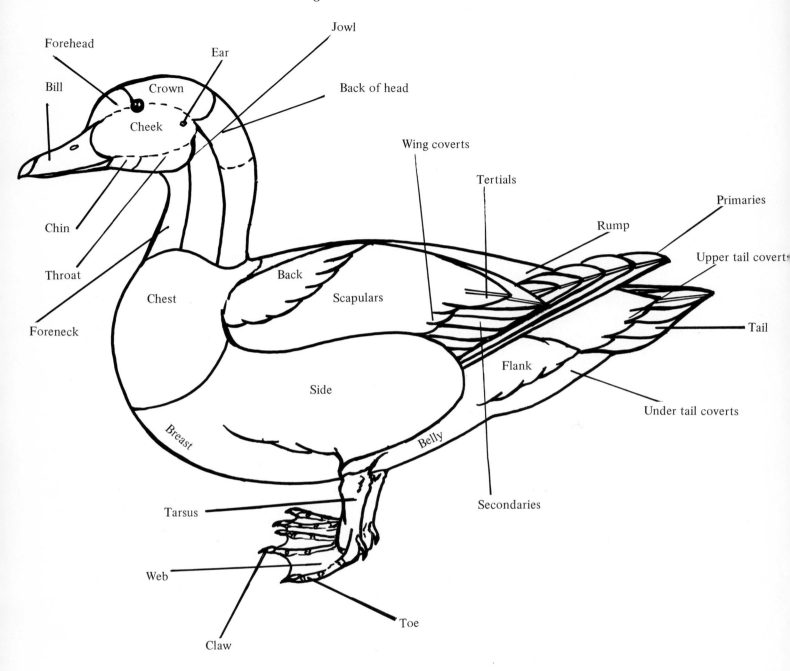

Forehead

Jowl

Bill

Ear

Crown

Back of head

Cheek

Wing coverts

Chin

Tertials

Primaries

Throat

Rump

Back

Upper tail coverts

Scapulars

Chest

Foreneck

Tail

Side

Flank

Breast

Belly

Under tail coverts

Secondaries

Tarsus

Web

Claw

Toe

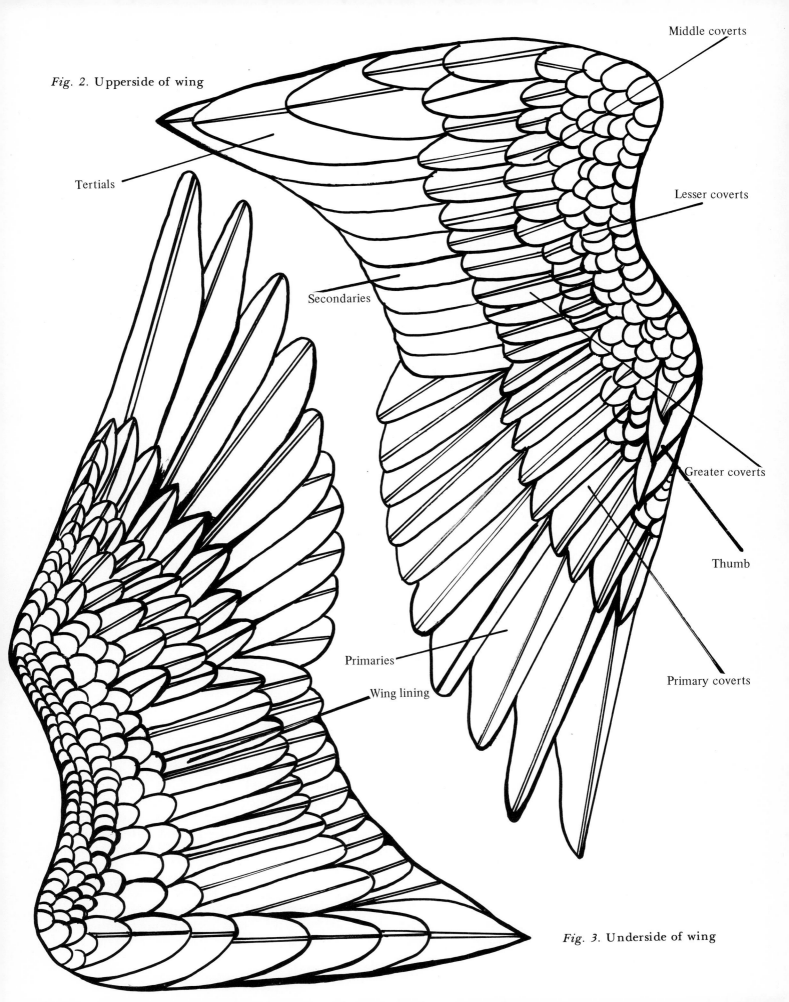

Fig. 2. Upperside of wing

Middle coverts

Tertials

Lesser coverts

Secondaries

Greater coverts

Thumb

Primaries

Wing lining

Primary coverts

Fig. 3. Underside of wing

carver should know. Their feet have three webbed front toes and a small and separate fourth toe set farther up the back of the leg. Their bills are relatively soft with a hard "nail" at the tip of both mandibles. In the lower mandible, there is a skin-like membrane that serves as a pump to get rid of the water taken in with food; the water goes out through serrations along the mandible edges. Their tongues generally are rectangular, thick and fleshy. Their wings are narrow and pointed and sometimes the secondary flight feathers are brightly colored. After breeding, the males of many species molt and grow a drab, female-like plumage, called eclipse plumage. At the same time they lose their flight feathers so they must hide from their enemies among the marsh plants or under water. Females go into a similar molt, but not until the end of the nesting season. The eclipse plumage lasts just a month or two. Waterfowl also have in common the shape of their tertial feathers. As a means of identification, we have included some drawings showing their tertials. (Figures 4 — 10)

Swans. Swans are the largest of all the duck family. Four species are found in North America, all of them white in color. Male swans are larger than females. Swans' necks are usually longer than their bodies and their legs are short.

Geese. There are nine species of geese in North America. They are smaller than swans and larger than ducks. The males are larger than the females. Their necks are shorter than those of swans but longer than ducks. Their bodies are more rounded than duck bodies. Geese walk on land with more balance than swans and ducks because their legs are further forward under their bodies. Geese are often seen flying across the sky in V's or long lines with a very regular wing beat.

Dabbling ducks. Dabbling ducks are also commonly referred to as marsh or puddle ducks. They are the best known of the duck family with 39 species in the world. Fourteen of these live in North America. Their name refers to the fact that they generally live among the cattails and reeds of lakes and ponds and feed in the shallow water by reaching just below the surface for food. When they sit on the water, their tails generally are high off it.

The bodies of dabbling ducks have been adapted to living in such restricted areas. They are long and streamlined and their wings are large so they can spring immediately off the water into flight. Because they do not have to dive under water for food, their feet are usually smaller than those of other ducks and have no lobe on the hind toe. Their legs are also short and placed near the sides of their bodies, so they walk with a definite waddle. Dabbling ducks generally have an iridescent patch of color on the secondary flight feathers.

Diving ducks. Of the 20 species of diving ducks in the world, six are found in North America. They are so called because they generally dive deep underwater for their food. Their large feet and short legs placed near the rear of their bodies simplify diving and underwater swimming, but make them more awkward on land. Their hind toes are lobed.

Diving ducks are usually shorter and broader in their bodies than dabbling ducks, with shorter and broader wings. They must run along the water surface, paddling their feet and beating their wings, to become airborne. When sitting on the water, their tails are generally on or slightly under the surface. They do not have the brightly colored patch on their wings that dabbling ducks have.

There are a couple of other small groups of ducks. **Whistling or tree ducks** are between geese and dabbling ducks in size. They get their name from the whistling noise their feathers make in flight and because a very few make their nest in trees. **Stiff-tailed ducks,** such as the Ruddy duck, are more aquatic than any other ducks. Their long, stiff tail feathers act as a rudder in underwater swimming and their legs are set very far back.

Mergansers. There are four species of Mergansers in North America. Their ability to maneuver under water and to pursue fish is aided by their streamlined, slender bodies and their large, broadly webbed feet and lobed hind toes. Their bills are long and narrow with very prominent serrations along the edges that help them grab and hold fish.

Other waterbirds include members of the Rail family, Loons and Grebes. These are often entered in carving competitions. **Rails** have adapted to living among dense marsh grasses. Their bodies are narrow, their wings are flexible, their toes are strong, and their plumage is brown, gray or reddish. Their feet are not webbed but some have large lobes protruding from

Fig. 4—10 TYPICAL TERTIAL GROUPINGS

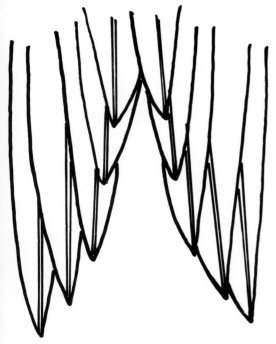

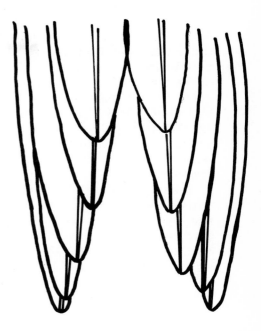

Fig. 4. Drake--Shoveler, Cinnamon Teal, Blue-winged Teal, Green-winged Teal, Gadwall, Pintail, Baldpate

Fig. 5. Hen--Shoveler, Cinnamon Teal, Blue-winged Teal, Green-winged Teal, Gadwall, Baldpate

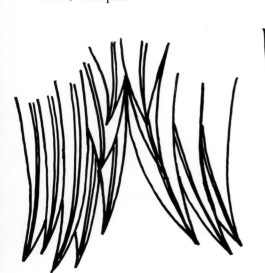

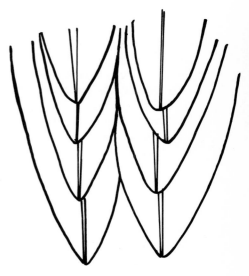

Fig. 6. Hooded Merganser

Fig. 7. Divers, Red-breasted Merganser, American Merganser

Fig. 8. Black duck, Mallard, Pintail hen

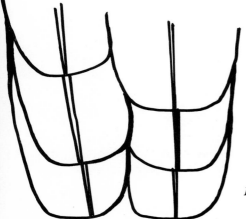

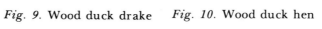

Fig. 9. Wood duck drake   *Fig. 10.* Wood duck hen

each toe. Coots are Rails that do more swimming in open water than hiding in the marshes.

Grebes are the size of small ducks--with the exception of the Western Grebe, which is a large bird. Their bills are slender and pointed. Their feet, which are lobed with partial webs, and their stream-lined bodies enable them to be rapid underwater swimmers. Their tail feathers are very short and hairlike.

Loons generally are large birds but the Artic Loon and the Ruby-throated Loon are small. They have thick necks, pointed bills, smallish, pointed wings and short tails. They are extremely powerful swimmers that are able to dive very deep. Their bodies are streamlined and their feet are webbed and set far back on their bodies.

DO'S AND DON'TS ABOUT CARVING

Another thing a person needs to begin carving is a list of general hints to refer back to whenever he gets frustrated, discouraged or confused.

Do   realize that there's no way you can create a real bird. You're always limited by the medium.

Don't say I can't.

Do   listen to and observe the masters.

Do   take the masters' constructive criticism.

Don't take what the masters say as absolute because what works for them may not work for you; yet some things that work well for you may not work well for them.

Do   observe the real thing in life and in mounts.

Do   go to shows and observe.

Don't try to learn everything at once.

Do   realize there are gifted people.

Don't be discouraged by gifted people. Most of us have to work and study hard and long to accomplish small gains.

Do   remember that mastery of an art develops slowly.

Do   work every day. It helps develop your eye-hand coordination.

Do   experiment with new techniques, new or different tools, etc.

Don't buy materials and tools just because they are there. Buy only what you need.

Do   collect a body of literature.

Do   ask questions.

Do   use all available data when working on a subject.

Do   share your knowledge and expertise with someone else; it will reinforce what you know.

Don't get discouraged if you are stuck on a particular step. Get help or work on something else for a while.

Don't look for absolutes in carving. Since carving is an art and not a science, the terms "always" and "never" mean "mostly"!

Do   learn where, how and what to simplify so your carving doesn't become too busy.

Do   remember it's only a piece of wood until it's done.

Do   remember everyone has been exactly where you are at any given point.

Don't sell yourself short!

Do   strive for smooth transitions from one thing to the next in your carvings.

Don't work without safety precautions.

Do   approach each carving project as a learning project. You should learn something new every time you carve.

Don't try to duplicate a carving you've already done. Each one should stand alone. Admire and critique your carving, but use the live bird as your model each time--not your carving.

Do   form a carving group or become a part of one.

Do   become a member of the Ward Foundation, the most dominant force in the world of carving.

Do   become a member of Ducks Unlimited to help promote and restore nesting habitats for waterfowl.

Do   remember it is fun!

Project One

Your first project is a miniature flying Canada goose. It is a very simple, smooth-bodied bird carving. It is carved with only one tool, an X-acto knife, and is sanded by hand. It can be painted with a minimum of anxiety. The skills you will learn in this project are elementary and are the basis for more advanced skills that will come later.

Chapter 1
Introductory Carving Techniques

Introductory carving projects can be accomplished with one basic carving tool--an X-acto knife. This is the ideal tool for the beginning carver to make small and simple carvings. It can also be used in more advanced projects, but as you progress you're likely to want to use tools that make the work go faster.

The X-acto knife is easy to use and inexpensive. It comes either in a kit with a variety of blades or singly. I prefer the old blade #24 because it's larger than the new #24, which means it works better. Order it through X-acto, 4535 Van Damm Street, Long Island City, N.Y. 11101.

There are two acceptable methods of carving with a knife. One is to draw the blade toward you as if you're using a paring knife in the kitchen. (Figure 12) (Put a bandaid on your thumb before you begin carving so you won't cut yourself.) Use the other method when you push the blade away from you. In this case, the thumb of the hand holding the wood becomes the fulcrum (pushing support) on the ferrule (metal between the blade and handle) of the knife. (Figure 13) Both of these methods provide the control you need over the knife.

Note: Never "whittle" in a carving project. In whittling a stick, you push the blade away from you without placing any additional support on the knife. (Figure 14)

Unless you're otherwise instructed, when you carve with the X-acto knife you should keep the blade as flat to the wood as possible so you don't gouge it. There are two reasons for this: (1) You have better control in developing the symmetry of the bird body and (2) you're using the knife as if it's a plane, so you'll have a much easier time sanding the wood. This is referred to as shaving the wood.

Sometimes you have to make scooping cuts with the knife. You still should keep the knife as flat to the wood as possible, but you have to cut deeper into the wood. You may have to shave an area repeatedly in order to scoop out some wood.

Sometimes you will use the knife blade to trace a penciled line, making several passes over the line to cut into it. Next you will hold the knife at a 90° angle to back-cut to the line, thus relieving a tiny sliver of wood. (Figure 15)

UNDERSTANDING THE WOOD GRAIN

In all your carving projects it is very important to understand the flow of the wood grain. Before you lay your pattern on a piece of wood, study the grain flow. It is imperative that the thin areas of the pattern, such as the bill and tail, lie on the wood in line with the grain to give strength to the carving. When you cut wood across the grain, it doesn't have the necessary strength and probably will break.

Always carve with the grain (Figure 16) particularly if you're working with a loose-grained wood such as pine. If you cut against the grain of pine, a piece of wood may pop out. Your first indication that you're working against the grain will be that your knife seems to drag. Immediately change the direction of your cut. The drawings for the first three projects in this book are marked to indicate the grain flow so you will learn when to change the direction of your cut.

USING GUIDELINES

When you draw the pattern of your carving project on a block of wood, always be careful you've traced the pattern correctly. When you cut it out on the bandsaw, cut right on the traced lines. These are finite points of reference because they give the exact shape of the bird. Some

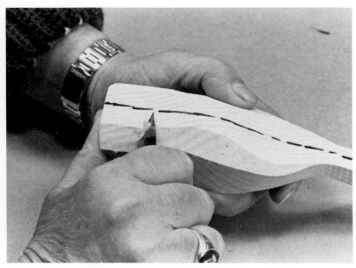

Fig. 12. Pull knife blade toward you as you do with a paring knife.

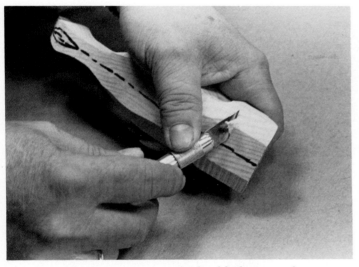

Fig. 13. If you must push the blade away from you, use thumb as fulcrum on ferrule of knife.

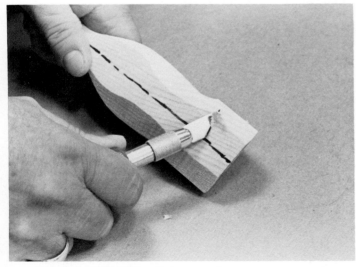

Fig. 14. "Whittling" is not the way to carve because you do not have the necessary control over your knife.

carvers rough out a carving larger than it is supposed to be to leave themselves margin for error. I feel that thinking is incorrect. I've found that if people expect to make an error, they will; but if they don't have room for errors, they are less likely to make any.

Always draw a centerline down the length of the body on the top and underside of the bandsawed block (blank). The centerline is extremely important. It is always to be maintained on any carving. Never cut it out because it is the exact profile and the high point of the bird.

Trace any guidelines supplied by a carving project on your blank. Guidelines will help you keep your carving symmetrical. Do not trust your eye until you have gained some carving experience. Over a period of time you will develop a good eye-hand coordination, at which point you may eliminate the use of some of the guidelines, but you'll never eliminate all of them.

When you carve, you may sometimes think something looks unbalanced. Your eye will be pulled to that area, so you'll assume that is where it's unbalanced. I've found that if you consciously look at the area directly opposite the first one, chances are you will find where your carving needs to be corrected for balance. This seems to be some built-in inversion of vision.

SUPPLIES FOR INTRODUCTORY CARVING

Besides the X-acto knife, there are supplies you'll need for this project that will be used in all carving projects.

Sandpaper. For fine hand-sanding, one-inch-wide strips of fabric-backed coated abrasive are preferable to the more common square pieces of sandpaper. A strip gives more control than a square. It's easy to draw around the curvature of the bird, and as you do so, the bird is quickly shaped. (Figure 17) I use 120-grit, Bear brand strip coated abrasive made by Norton Coated Abrasive Division. If you can't find it, cut any piece of 120-grit, cloth-backed coated abrasive into inch-wide strips about 12 inches long.

Wood plastic and acetone. Wood plastic is used for filling seams, holes and cracks in wood. I prefer the brand made by Duratite, called Wood Dough, because it has a finer consistency than wood plastic. When I use it, I saturate it with acetone, which breaks down the air bubbles in the dough and makes a tighter fill. (Figure

18) Wood Dough can be textured or burned or sanded and left smooth.

5-minute epoxy glue. I use 5-minute epoxy almost exclusively whenever I need glue because it sets up fast and can be counted on to really hold. It is a superior glue. I use the brands made by Duro and Devcon but prefer the better quality consistency of Devcon's epoxy. Caution: Epoxy is a skin irritant, so always wash your hands immediately after using it, especially before going to the bathroom.

Brads. Brads of various sizes are used for setting wings or to hold something in place while glue dries.

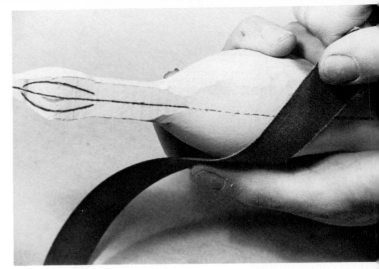

Fig. 17. A strip of coated abrasive helps shape the curvature of the bird.

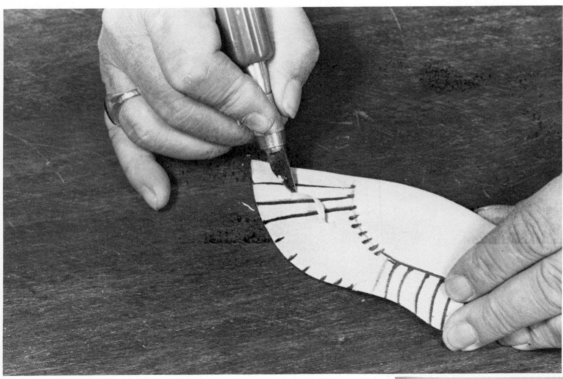

Fig. 15. Sometimes use knife to backcut at a 90° angle to a line to relieve a tiny sliver of wood.

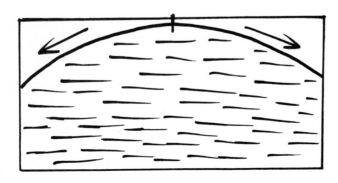

Fig. 16. Grain flows downhill from high point, so always carve with the grain.

20

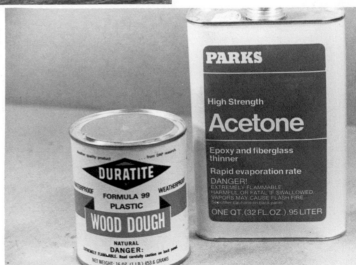

Fig. 18. Wood Dough, bathed with acetone, is used to fill gaps and seams in every carving project.

Chapter 2
Introductory Painting Techniques

Many fine carvers find painting an especially difficult step to master. It *is* difficult; it takes time and practice to paint a carving well. You'll never get enough experience if you paint only your own carvings. When I learned how to carve, I was advised to buy machine-made birds and paint them over and over again to become truly proficient at painting. This was, and still is, excellent advice.

Because the Canada goose in this project is a smooth-bodied bird, it is painted relatively easily. You need not worry unduly about it. You'll only have to practice one painting technique.

PAINTING SUPPLIES

The supplies called for in this project are a few of the ones that will be used in future projects.

Paint. I prefer acrylic artists' paints to oil paints. They have a much better consistency of color than oils. (Oils vary too much from one tube to the next and from manufacturer to manufacturer.) They are easy to paint over. You can blend jagged edges of two colors of acrylics easily. They are water-soluble so they're simpler to work with and to clean up than oil paints. They dry quickly and they are odorless. I prefer Hyplar paints by Grumbacher because they are consistently superior in quality.

Gesso. Gesso is a white painting base sold in art supply stores. It is very thick and is used straight from the can as the undercoat on smooth-bodied birds.

Sealer. Krylon 1301 is an acrylic spray that serves as a soft sealer. I always use it before painting a carving to seal the wood so it doesn't burr up under water-base paint. If you can not find it, use a clear ceramic spray or a matte acrylic spray designed for flat work. Some people prefer a hard surface so they use a sealer such as a sanding sealer. I advise against hard sealers

because, in my experience, the build-up of acrylic washes tends to lift off a hard surface.

Alcohol and white shellac. Mix denatured alcohol and white shellac in equal proportions to make a sealer for any Wood Dough used in the carving. If you seal Wood Dough with Krylon 1301, it will become mushy under the acrylic paint washes; consequently, a harder sealer is necessary.

Gloss medium. This varnish product gives a carved bird's bill a soft sheen. It can be mixed with the paint or applied on top of the paint either straight from the can or diluted with water.

Brushes. In this project you need only two brushes. "Wash" brushes are used to apply thin washes of base colors to the carving. I recommend a ¾-inch or 1-inch-wide wash brush. Robert Simmons' Skyscraper 755 or 955 wash brushes are very good.

To paint feather edgings, you need one round red sable brush, #7 or #8. Two good brands are Grumbacher 190 series and Windsor Newton series 7. Another good brush for edging cupped feathers is the Langnickel cat's paw brush that is rounded at the tip. Order it from: Beebe Hopper, 731 Beach Avenue, Chula Vista, CA 92010.

Chalk. The novice carver may find it easier to draw the outlines of the feathers on a bird with a piece of chalk prior to painting them. If any chalk gets on the brush, it is easily washed off. Wash the chalk outlines off the bird when you've finished painting.

Palettes. You need at least two palettes because working with two is easier than using only one. Buy permanent or disposable palette pads, or use a piece of glass or waxed paper. When you've finished painting, wash the wet paint off the palette or let it dry and then scrape it off with a putty knife.

Water containers. You need several coffee cans filled with water for rinsing out your brush or for getting a drop of water on it. If you have several water containers, you will keep from contaminating one can with all the paint colors. You'd be surprised how a drop of dirty water can change a paint color. If you fill the cans to about one inch from the top, the water is easier to use. Anchor your palette with one can to keep it from sliding when you get paint on your brush. Anchoring is one of those silly-sounding rules that really makes a big difference.

Pliers. Have a pair of pliers handy to loosen the caps of paint tubes.

Hair dryer. Use a hair dryer to speed up paint drying. Operate it on low heat and hold it about 10 to 12 inches from the carving. Don't let the paint get too hot.

Paper towels. Have a supply of paper towels folded near your work area to use for stroking out excess paint and water from your brush.

BASIC PAINTING POINTERS

Base paint. Whenever you paint the base colors of a carving, dilute your acrylic paints with water to the thin consistency of whole milk. Apply anywhere from 8 to 10 washes. The color builds up in intensity while the water evaporates and develops a soft sheen. If you use thick paint, the bird will be too shiny.

Note: This rule applies to painting all bird carvings and will not always be repeated in the painting instructions.

Trimmed brush. Brushes are generally designed to come to a needle point. If you flatten out a brush, it has little jagged edges. If you trim it with a knife, as shown in figure 19, you give it a flat edge. This method just seems to work better than buying a flat brush in the first place. Note: Under no conditions should you trim more than that shown in the diagram because you will get too far up into the brush and it will be ruined.

Feather edging. The paint for feather edging is of a thicker consistency than the base washes--more like heavy cream. It should be semi-dry in the brush. Use only a very little bit at a time. It is better to make feather edgings several times over than to put on a blob of paint.

There are two types of feather edging. One type--the "cupped" feather--will be

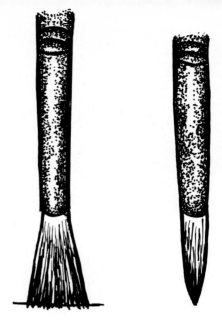

Fig. 19. Trim round red sable brush to give it a flat edge.

Fig. 20. To make a cupped brush, bend bristles 90° on palette and twist handle. Use water container to anchor your palette at all times.

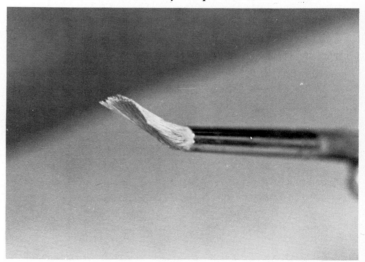

Fig. 21. A cupped brush will paint curved feather edgings on bird.

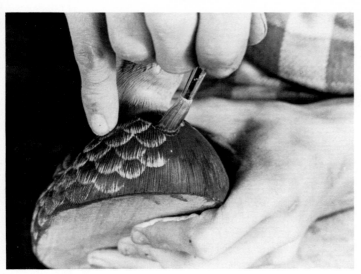

Fig. 22. Place cup on bird, anchoring hand with pinky to have control of brush, and paint rows in a fish scale pattern.

done in this project. Use a cupped brush to paint it. Bend the bristles of your trimmed round red sable brush about 90° on the palette and twist the handle. When the brush is lifted from the palette, it has a natural cup. Place the cup on the bird at a 90° angle, anchoring your hand with your pinky somewhere on the bird to give you control over the brush.

Cupped feathers should be arranged in rows across an expanse. Do one row; then the next row should follow a fish-scale or brick layering idea. That is, place the feathers between the ones in the previous row. Always start from the bottom and work up (this more closely duplicates the way feathers are overlapped on a bird.) Draw arcs with chalk on the bird to outline where you will paint the cupped feathers. Eventually as you gain experience you will loosen up and make your cupped feathers a little more random, as they are in life.

Practice making cupped feathers on a board that is sealed and undercoated with several thin washes of burnt umber. When you are confident of your ability, do them on the carving itself.

If you make a blob of paint on a feather, soften it with a very thin wash of burnt umber and redo the cupping. If the cupping is much too thick and heavy, apply two or three washes of the base paint mixture and start again.

Jagged edges. On the Canada goose there are patches of white painted on top of the black body and head paint. These patches should not be painted with perfectly straight edges, but with jagged edges so they look more like feathers. This is done in one of two ways. Use the brush with a straight edge, place it perpendicular to the bird and pull and lift. This leaves a jagged edge. Alternatively, you can turn the brush so it has a knife-like edge and actually paint a jagged edge.

Toning wash. When a carving is all painted and dry, a toning wash is applied to tone down and blend the colors. The wash is made by thinning burnt umber until it resembles dirty water. It is very important that the wash is very thin. Novice carvers generally use too much paint and then have to start all over. So, when you think you've made a toning wash of the right consistency, take a teaspoonful of it and add it to ¼ cup of water, and use that mixture as your toning wash.

WHEN YOU PAINT

Always work in a well-lighted area. The best artificial light is a combination of incandescent and fluorescent lighting. Don't wear tinted glasses of any sort because they'll distort the paint colors.

Acrylic paints dry very quickly, so you should never put down your wet paint brush--not even for a few minutes--without cleaning it because the paint will harden in the bristles. This is particularly true if the heat or air-conditioning is on. The danger here is that if you're painting detail, such as feathers, the paint in the top of the bristles may dry without your realizing it. If this happens, the brush must be cleaned in a harsh acrylic cleaner which will break down the bristle fibers.

When you finish painting for the day, wash your brush in a lukewarm mild detergent solution, rinse it in clear water and sling out most of the water. Never leave a brush in a can of water overnight because it puts a strain on the bristles and bloats them. Turn the brush upside down to dry.

Chapter 3
Carving a Canada Goose

When I started teaching I realized that the best way to introduce my students to the basic techniques of bird carving was with a very simple project of a familiar bird. I chose the Canada goose because it is so well known and liked and because it can be simplified in carving and painting more attractively and easily than any other bird. I devised a project for a miniature Canada goose. This is a nice size to handle, quick and easy to make, and designed for standard 2-inch stock that is no problem to acquire.

My students make four Canada geese all at the same time. The first week they learn how to carve and sand the body and they repeat these steps on all four bodies. The second week they work on the necks and heads. The third week they progress to the wings, and so on. Thus, they are learning simple techniques on the easier parts of the bird first and repeating the steps over and over until they become ingrained.

MAKING ROUGH CUT

The rough cut, or the blank, of a carving is done on a bandsaw. As you proceed in your growth as a carver you may want to own a bandsaw, but at this point, while you are just learning, I assume you do not own one. You will have to locate someone with a bandsaw who is willing to rough out your bird. If you have a pattern shop or a vocational-technical school in your area you will probably be able to get the bird roughed out there.

Buy a couple of board feet of 2-inch stock sugar pine at a lumberyard. If you can not find it, Northern white pine will suffice, but it is a little harder.

Trace the profile view of the Canada goose, as shown in figure 23, on the wood, laying the bill in line with the wood grain.

Note: The drawings for this project, as well as almost all the other projects in this book, are drawn in the exact size that you should carve. This will greatly simplify your work. In addition, I've found that to

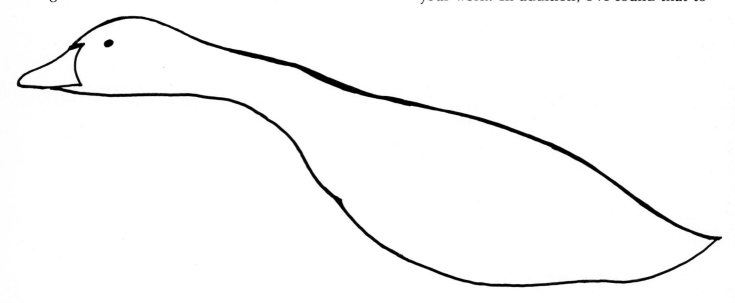

Fig. 23. Profile of Canada goose.

enlarge or reduce a pattern, modifications always need to be done.

Have the bird cut out on the bandsaw. (Figure 25) Turn it over so that the belly side of the bird is up. Trace the drawing in figure 27 on this side of the block. Cut it out on the bandsaw.

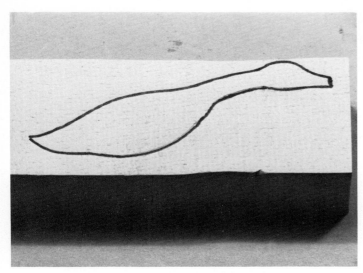

Fig. 24. Draw the profile view of Canada goose on 2-inch stock sugar pine.

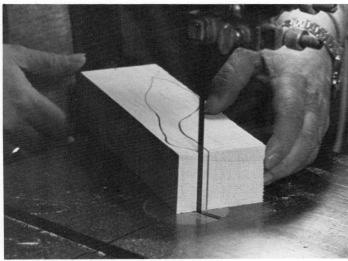

Fig. 25. On bandsaw, cut out the profile view following lines exactly.

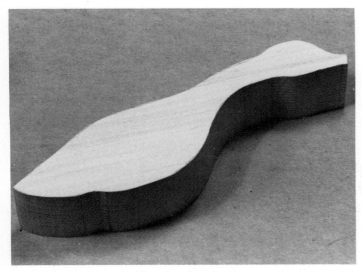

Fig. 26. The profile view has been cut out.

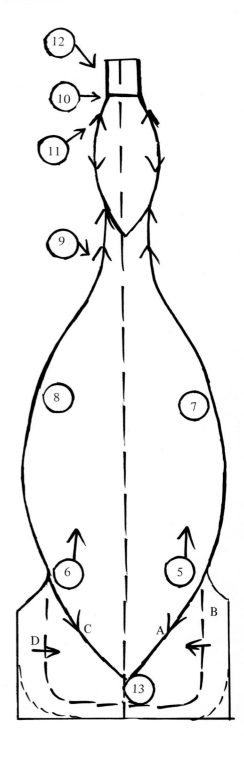

Fig. 27. Plan view of Canada goose (underside of bird).

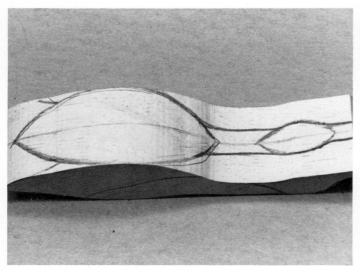

Fig. 28. Draw the underside of the Canada goose on the block. This is the plan view.

Fig. 29. On the bandsaw, cut out the plan view of bird.

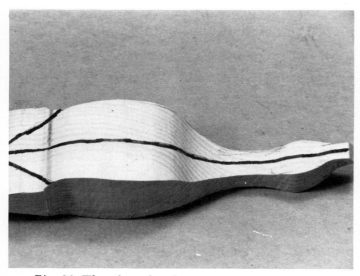

Fig. 30. The plan view is now cut out and ready to be trimmed.

Fig. 31. With bandsaw table tilted, trim excess wood from edges of top side of bird.

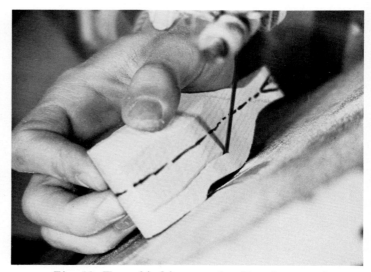

Fig. 32. Turn bird in opposite direction to trim excess wood from other side of bird.

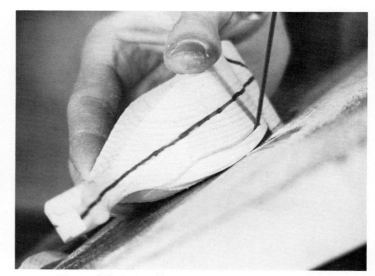

Fig. 33. Trim wood from side edges of underside of bird.

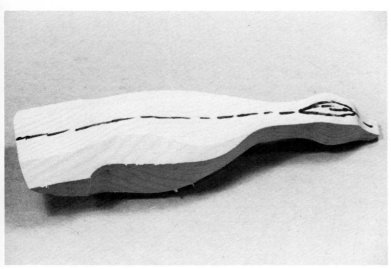

Fig. 34. Excess wood is now trimmed from top of bird.

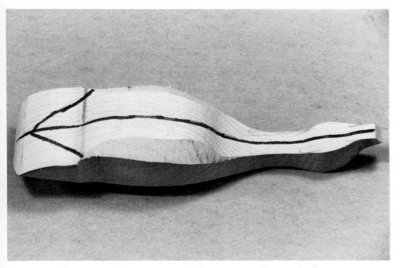

Fig. 35. Excess wood is now trimmed from underside of bird.

Ask the bandsaw operator to tilt the table of the bandsaw in order to trim excess wood from the bird body. (Tilting the table is the only recommended way to safely trim wood at a 45° angle on the bandsaw because the wood still rests on a flat surface.) On the back of the bird, trim the two side edges from the neck down to the tail. (Figures 31 & 32) On the underside of the bird, trim the two edges from the "shoulders" down to the indentation for the tail. (Figure 33) The reason for trimming these edges is that, even though you now have two edges where there once was just one, the body will be easier to round. (If you can't get this done on the bandsaw, you can do it with your knife, but it takes longer.)

Draw two plan views of the wing (Figure 36) on the wood. (You actually will have enough wood to make wings for four birds, but because you are a novice, it is easier to make one wing per drawing.) Cut out the plan views on the bandsaw.

Now draw the profile view of the wing. This is done by turning both blocks on their sides so that the leading edge (top of the wing) faces you so the tertial feathers are butted together. They now look like a right and left wing. Draw a straight line across this side of one block, ½ — ¾-inch down from the top. Now draw an arc (Figure 37) that extends from the ends of the line up to the center of the top of the block. (Figure 39) Cut along this arced line on the bandsaw, thus preparing the curved surface. Draw (scribe) a new arc 1/4 — 3/8-inch down from the first arc line and cut it out on the bandsaw. This is your wing. Repeat on the other wing block.

CARVING THE BODY

Draw on the body block the numbered points shown in the diagrams (Figures 27 & 43). They denote the relative areas of the grain flow and indicate that you should start to carve in a different direction. These points also help you keep the bird symmetrical.

Begin carving at point 1, drawing the knife in a gentle scooping or curving action in the direction of the arrow. (Figure 42) As you carve, work from the centerline to the end of the bird, being always careful not to disturb the centerline. Use the rounded line on the outside edge of the underside of the tail as your guideline in carving all the way down the back. You should not remove a great deal of wood because that would make your bird too thin. You're supposed to remove just enough wood to get rid of the squared edges. Remember, there are no flat areas on a bird; their bodies are gently curved and rounded, so your carving should be, too.

At point 2 repeat the same procedure, being sure to balance it with point 1 to begin forming the symmetry of the bird. (Figure 44)

At points 3 and 4 begin to round off the edges, keeping in mind that the grain reverses in this area.

Turn the bird over. At points 5 and 6 shave the wood in the direction of the arrows and gently round the sides to the back of the bird. At points 7 and 8 round

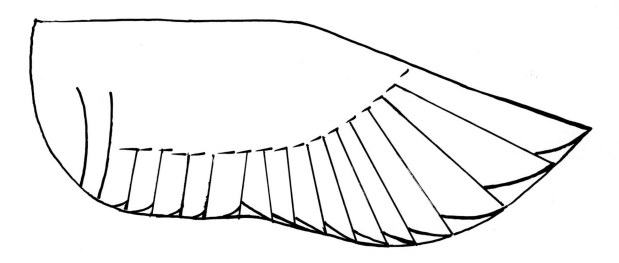

Fig. 36. Plan view of wing

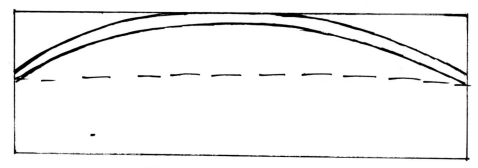

Fig. 37. Arced profile of wing

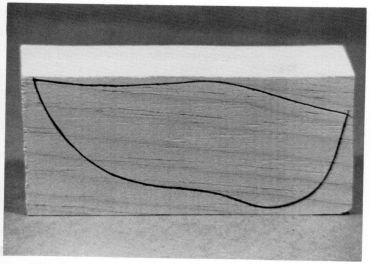

Fig. 38. Draw pattern view of wing on block to be cut out on bandsaw.

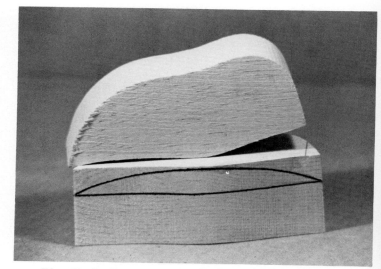

Fig. 39. Scribe an arc on leading edge of wing block for first cut of wing profile.

Fig. 40. On bandsaw, make cut to prepare the curved surface of wing.

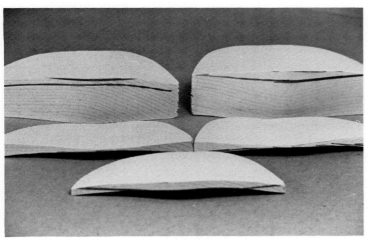

Fig. 41. The two wing blocks in rear have had initial flat cut taken; finished wing is in front.

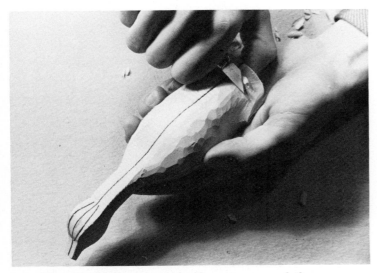

Fig. 42. With X-acto knife, scoop wood from point 1 down through the tail of bird.

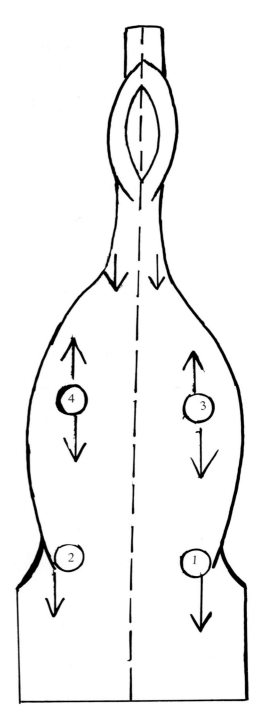

Fig. 43. Back of bird

off the edges to the back. (Figure 46)

The underside of the tail, point 13 in figure 27, simulates the under-rump of a bird and the tail feathers coming out of the rump. Insert the point of your knife at the beginning of line A. Following the arrow, push the knife blade along the line to the centerline, with your thumb as the fulcrum on the ferrule of the knife. (Figure 48) Repeat several times in order to make a deep cut. Turn the bird in the other direction. At the beginning of line B make a deep, scooping cut, drawing the blade toward you, until you reach the centerline. (Figure 49) This will make a channel that starts narrow, widens to about ½-inch and narrows again. (Figure 50) Repeat the

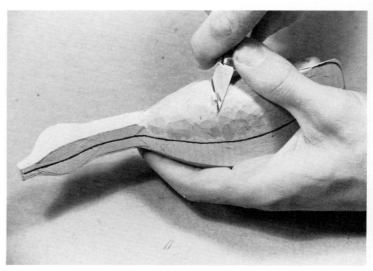

Fig. 46. Round sides of bird from belly to back.

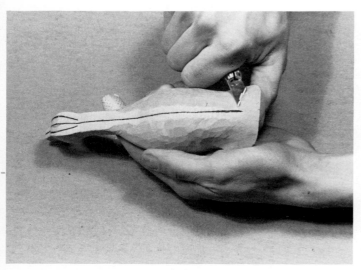

Fig. 44. On back of bird, maintain centerline and be sure to keep both sides symmetrical.

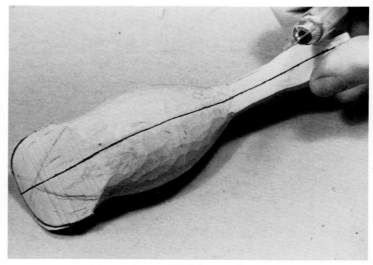

Fig. 47. Belly is completed when it is symmetrical and rounded to back of bird.

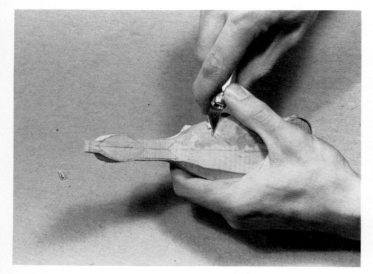

Fig. 45. On underside, shave wood following the grain. Note position of thumb on knife.

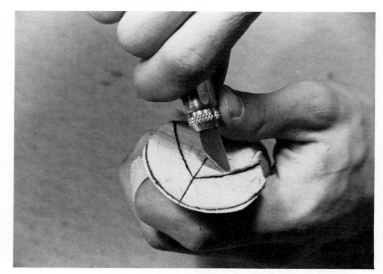

Fig. 48. With point of knife trace line A on under-rump of bird.

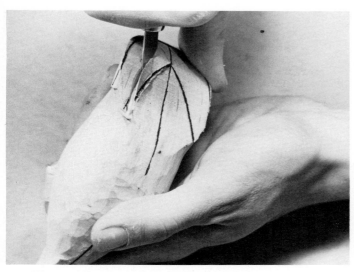

Fig. 49. Scoop out wood between B and A.

Fig. 50. You've made a channel on one side of the under-rump.

Fig. 51. Channel is now cut on both sides.

Fig. 52. Shave some wood from belly to make a smooth transition from belly to tail.

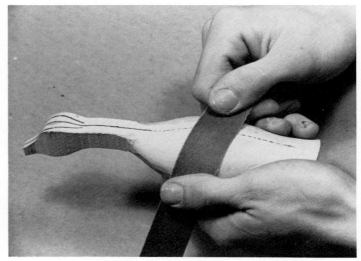

Fig. 53. Hold strip of coated abrasive between thumb and forefinger and drag it under other thumb across the grain.

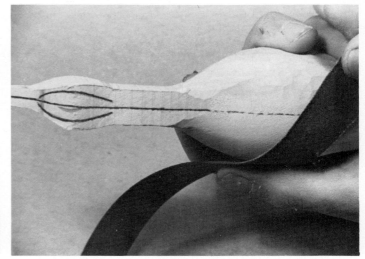

Fig. 54. You have finished sanding when no dark or high spots can be seen.

process on lines C and D. Shave some wood from the belly where it meets the tail so there's not a sharp drop off.

You have now finished carving the body of the Canada goose. It will not yet be smooth, but it will have basically the correct shape. For more practice, if you wish, repeat all these steps on a second bird.

The next step in my classes is sanding the body. Hold one end of the coated abrasive between the thumb and forefinger and drag the paper across the grain under the other thumb (of the hand holding the bird). (Figures 53 & 54) Do not apply much pressure for you'll create flat spots and ridges. All you want to do is smooth out all the marks left by carving. The bird is sanded when all the dark spots are removed. You'll note that where the coated abrasive has been is lighter in tone and color than the areas that are carved. You may sand the centerline at this time. In some areas you won't be able to use this drag-under-thumb method, so just sand in the conventional method.

CARVING HEAD AND NECK

Now proceed to the underside of the neck. Carve toward the head, following the arrows at point 9 in figure 27. At point 10, cut a slight notch between the head and the bill so that when you're carving the neck the bill won't split out. (Figure 56) At point 11, note the direction of the arrows and carve, following these arrows, to round the underside of the head. At point 12,

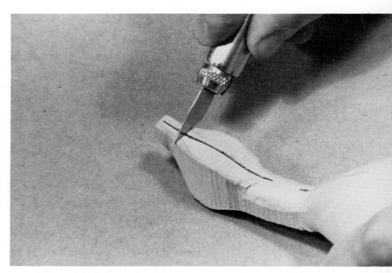

Fig. 56. With underside of neck carved at point 9, make notch between head and bill.

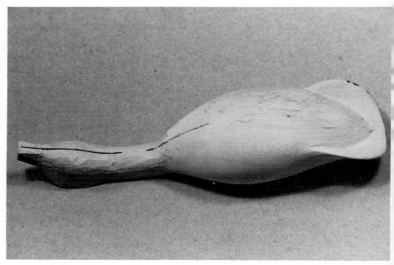

Fig. 57. Round the sides of head and shave sides of bill.

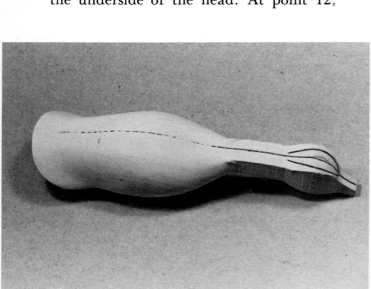

Fig. 55. When back and belly are smooth and rounded, go on to the neck.

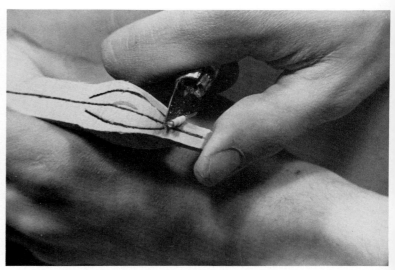

Fig. 58. Lightly carve from peak of crown down to the bill.

32

slightly shave the sides of the bill to simulate tucking the lower mandible under the upper mandible.

Turn the bird over. Following the direction of the arrows in figure 60, lightly carve from the peak of the crown down to the bill and down the neck. Draw the dotted line on the cheeks as indicated in the same drawing. Gently scoop from the crown to these dotted lines to make the eye channels. (Figure 61) Then, knock the corner off the lines to round them off.

Sand the head and neck.

Following the diagram, figure 63, draw the line between the head and the bill. Cut into that line with the point of the

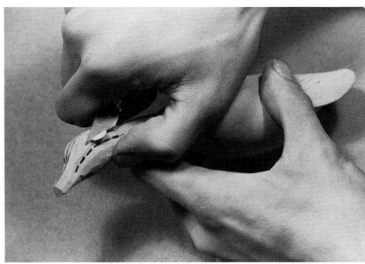

Fig. 61. Gently scoop from crown to dotted lines on cheeks to create eye channels.

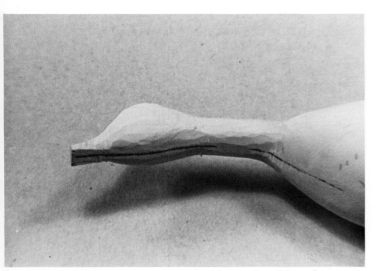

Fig. 59. Carve from the crown down the sides of neck.

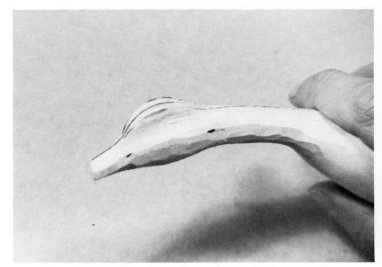

Fig. 62. Head and neck are completely carved and ready to sand.

Fig. 60. Lightly carve head following direction of arrows. Scoop from crown to dotted line to create eye channel.

Fig. 63. Draw line on sanded head between head and bill.

33

knife. (Figure 65) Next, back cut at a 90° angle to the line to relieve a tiny sliver from the bill, thus forming a ledge, but don't remove the line of delineation between bill and head. Sand the cheeks smooth.

Check that the end of the bill is rounded, as indicated in Figure 68. You may have already accomplished this as you sanded the head. If not, do so now, and sand smooth.

CARVING THE WINGS

Your roughed-out wings are 1/4—3/8-inch thick. Round the leading edge by shaving off some of the wood with your X-acto knife, figure 68A. Taper the trailing edge to about 1/16-inch thick, starting in the center of the wing and working gradually outward. (Figures 69 & 70) Find

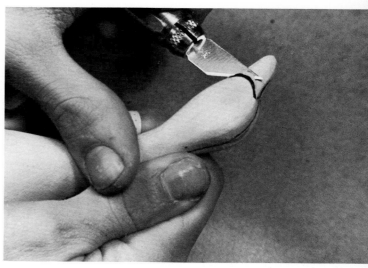

Fig. 66. Back cut into line to relieve tiny sliver from bill.

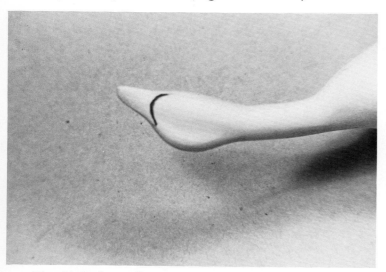

Fig. 64. Refer to figure 63 as you draw the line between the head and bill.

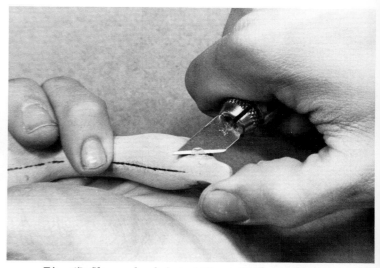

Fig. 67. Shave cheek into bill to eliminate ledge, and sand smooth.

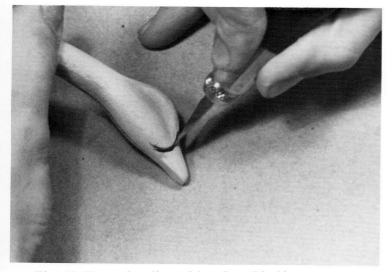

Fig. 65. Trace that line with point of knife.

Fig. 68. End of bill should be rounded.

the edges of the wings that fit into the body. Taper them all the way down to the leading edge, working from the underside, so that they will fit smoothly into the body. (Figure 71)

Sand both sides of the wings smooth.

Draw the primaries, secondaries and tertials on the wings as illustrated in figure 73. With your knife, cut the wing tips on the drawn lines.

With the point of the knife, trace all the lines from the trailing edge to line AB, plus the tertial lines. (Figure 74) It is important that you trace the lines inwards from the trailing edge because if you work in the opposite direction you might snap the wing tip off.

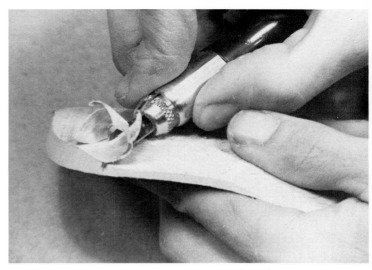
Fig. 70. When grain flow changes, taper trailing edge in opposite direction.

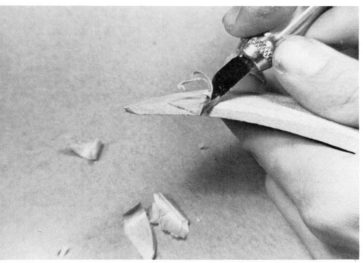
Fig. 68A. Shave wood from leading edge of wing to round it.

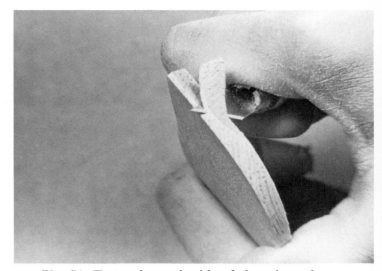
Fig. 71. Taper the underside of the wing edge that fits onto the body.

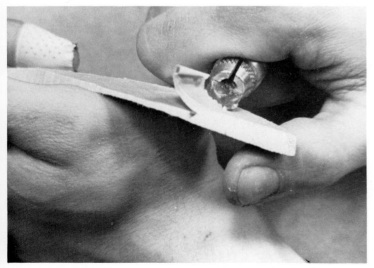
Fig. 69. Taper trailing edge of wing to 1/16-inch thick.

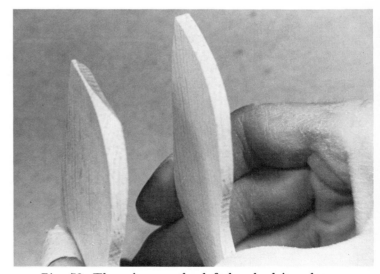
Fig. 72. The wing on the left has had its edge tapered prior to being attached to body.

35

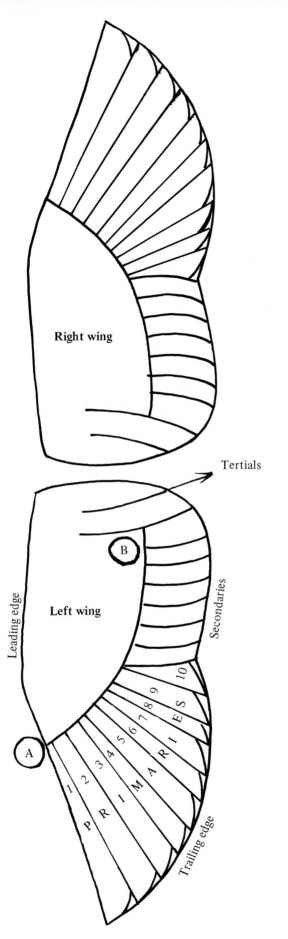

Beginning on the feather numbered 1 at line AB, turn the knife at an angle to the traced line and relieve a tiny sliver all the way down the line. Repeat on feathers #2 through #6. (Figure 76) At about this point the grain reverses, so begin your relieving cuts at the trailing edge and work towards line AB. Repeat on the other primaries and also on the secondaries. Relieve a slice along the tertial lines, working from the trailing edge toward the leading edge.

Fold a strip of coated abrasive and sand all the lines you cut.

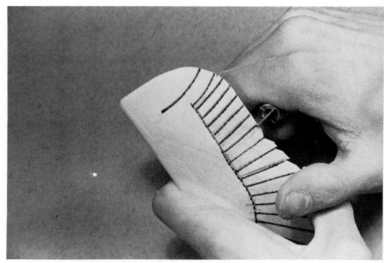

Fig. 74. With feathers drawn on wing, cut wing tips.

Fig. 75. Trace primary edges from trailing edge to line AB with point of knife.

Fig. 73. Carve layout of primaries, secondaries and tertials into wings.

36

Fig. 76. Beginning at line AB, relieve a tiny sliver from the edges of primaries through #6.

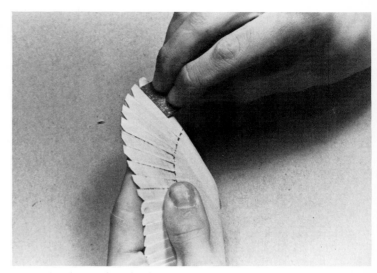

Fig. 78. With folded coated abrasive, sand the relieved feathers.

Fig. 77. Work from trailing edge to line AB as you relieve secondaries and tertials.

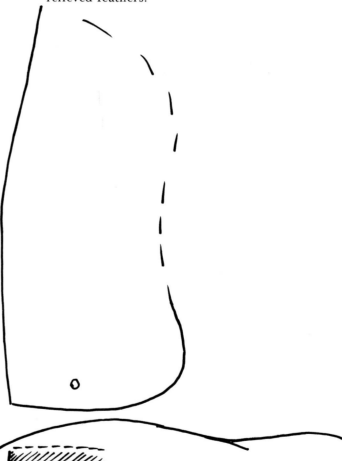

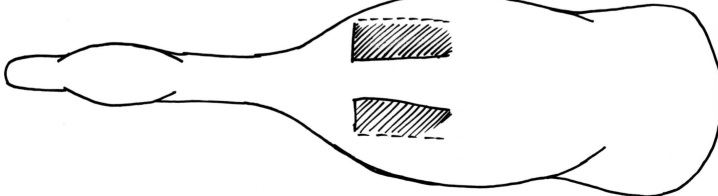

Fig. 79. Cut notches into back of bird for wings.

JOINING THE WINGS AND BODY

Hold the edge of the wings on the back of the body at the point illustrated in figure 79. With a pencil, trace these lines with your knife (Figure 80) and make a flat cut to create a notch in the body to fit the edge of the wing. (Figure 82) When the wings are in the correct position, they will be level with the back of the bird and their tips will be slightly down. If you want the wings to arc down further, move your notches out to the sides of the bird. If you want the wings to be up, cut a narrow notch in the back of the bird and set the ends of the wings into it.

Mix 5-minute epoxy and drop a little into each notch. Place the wings in the notches and hold them in place with a #17 or #18 ¾-inch brad while the epoxy hardens. Lacking a brad, you must hold the wing in place by hand.

Remove the brads or drive them into the surface of the wing and countersink them. In either case, fill the holes with Wood Dough. At the same time you must also fill the gaps around the wing joints. Use the Wood Dough straight from the can. Spread a small amount on the holes or gaps. Wet a small brush with acetone and brush it over the Wood Dough to saturate it thoroughly. Repeat until all the gaps are filled and smooth. Let the Wood Dough dry completely.

Sand the Wood Dough smooth and feather the edges into the wood so there are no ridges left on the back.

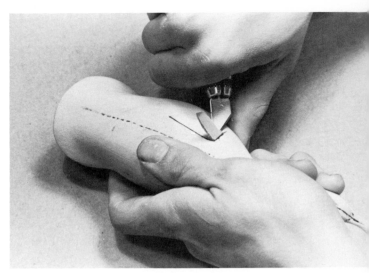

Fig. 81. Make flat cut at line to create a notch.

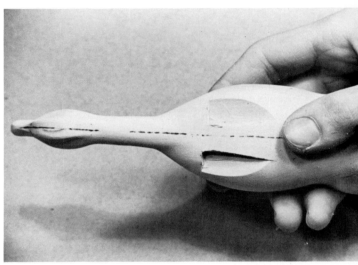

Fig. 82. Notches should be deep enough to hold wing.

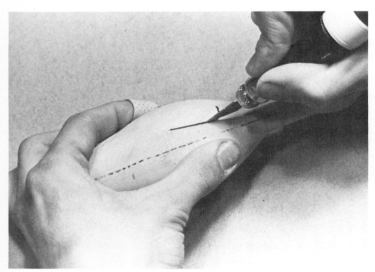

Fig. 80. Trace wing edge with pencil and then with point of knife.

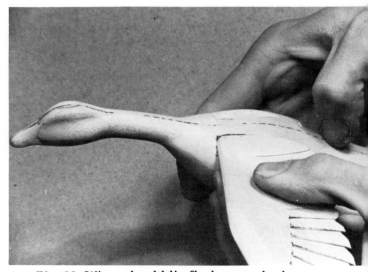

Fig. 83. Wings should lie flush across back.

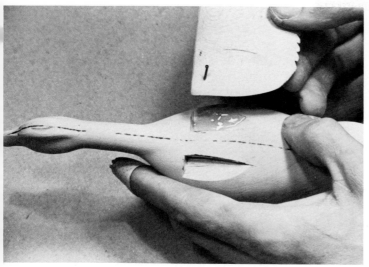

Fig. 84. Fill notch with 5-minute epoxy.

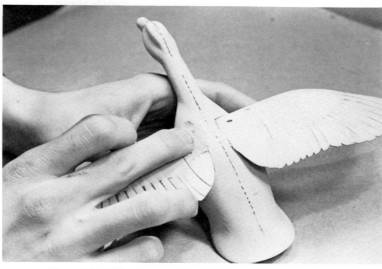

Fig. 87. Fill gaps and brad holes with Wood Dough.

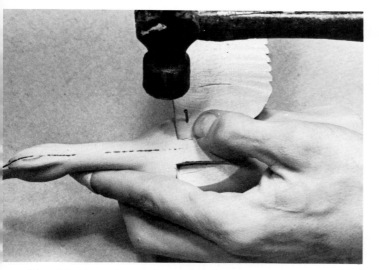

Fig. 85. Drive brad through wing into back to hold wing while glue dries.

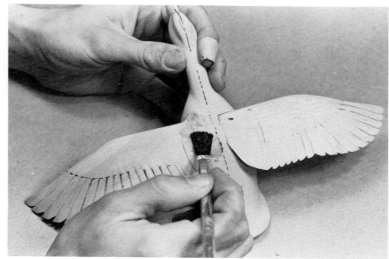

Fig. 88. Saturate Wood Dough with acetone to break down air bubbles.

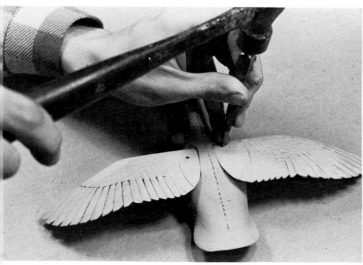

Fig. 86. Countersink brads into wing when glue is dry.

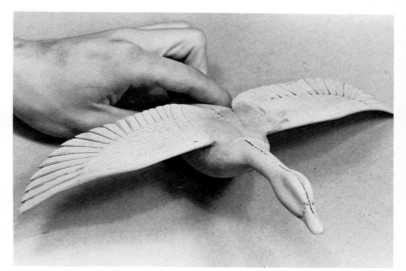

Fig. 89. Wood Dough smooths out gaps where wings are attached to body.

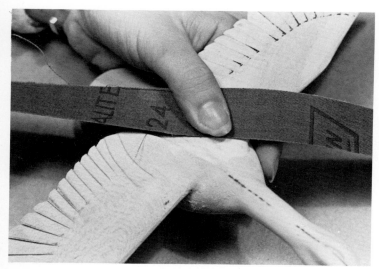

Fig. 90. Sand Wood Dough completely smooth.

Fig. 91. Spray bird with Krylon 1301 to seal wood prior to painting.

PAINTING

Seal the wood with Krylon 1301. One coat is sufficient. Mix alcohol and white shellac and brush it on the Wood Dough to seal it. Paint a thick coat of gesso, straight from the can, all over the bird. Allow it to dry. Then lightly sand with 180 or 220-grit sandpaper until the surface is smooth.

To paint the Canada goose you need tubes of acrylic artists' paint in black, white, burnt umber and raw sienna.

Follow the illustration, figure 93, that shows the paint patterns. With the wash brush, begin with a thin wash of burnt umber on the back and upper wings. Let it dry, apply a second wash, and repeat until the paint has built up in depth and has a soft sheen.

Paint the head and neck, top and underside, and the wing tips with thin washes of black paint.

Paint the belly of the bird whitish by adding a tiny bit of burnt umber to white paint.

Paint the undersides of the wings and the sides of the bird a medium dusky gray, which is made from a mixture of black, white and a little burnt umber. When it is dry, paint the underside of the tail black. All these colors are applied as washes, so they must be very thin and applied 8 to 10 times.

The feather edgings are done next in white with a little raw sienna added. First draw the outlines for the feathers with chalk, being sure that they have a fish-scale effect. (Figure 99) With a cupped brush, edge the feathers on the back and work forward. On the wings, start at a far point on the wing and work inward and upward.

When the feather edgings are dry, apply a toning wash of burnt umber. This is an ultra-thin wash resembling dirty water. Redo the feather edgings if you think they need it and apply a second toning wash.

Paint the white patches on the underside of the head and on the top of the rump, making jagged edges with your brush. You may want to draw the chalk outlines of these stripes before you paint.

Paint a little diluted gloss medium on the bill to give it a soft sheen.

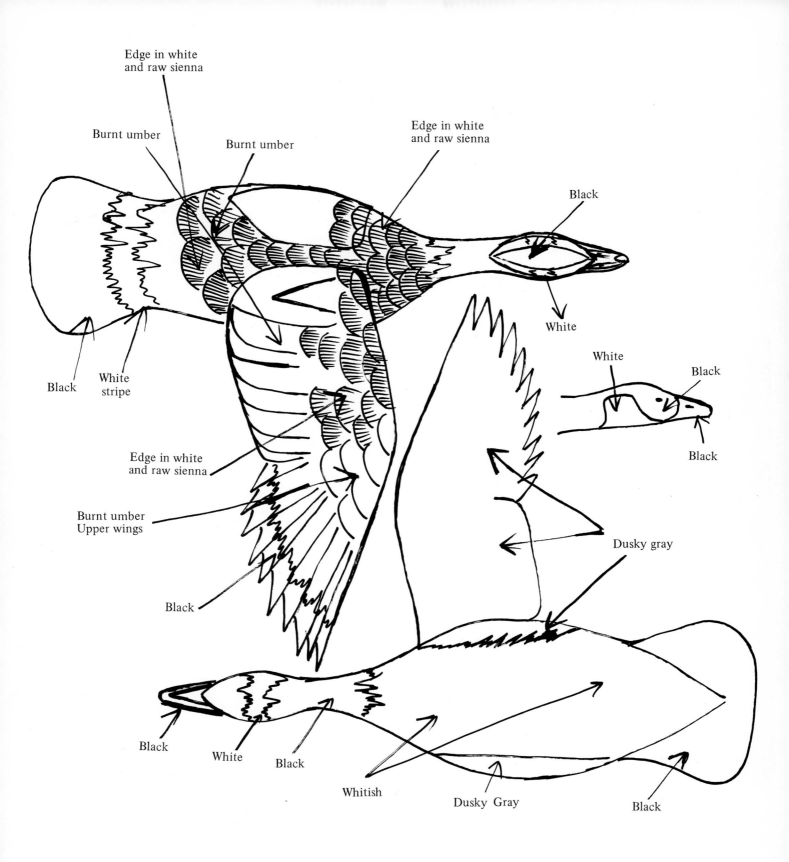

Edge in white
and raw sienna

Burnt umber

Burnt umber

Edge in white
and raw sienna

Black

White

White

Black

Black

Black

White
stripe

Edge in white
and raw sienna

Burnt umber
Upper wings

Black

Dusky gray

Black

White

Black

Whitish

Dusky Gray

Black

Fig. 92. **PAINTING OF CANADA GOOSE**

41

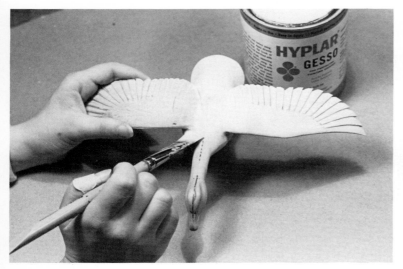

Fig. 93. Paint one coat of gesso onto bird as a paint base.

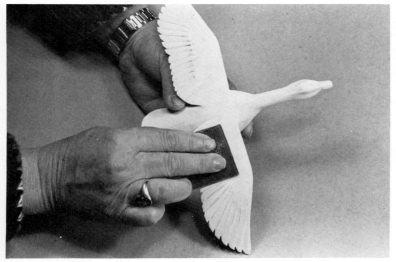

Fig. 94. Sand the dried gesso with fine grit sandpaper.

Fig. 95. Apply several thin washes of burnt umber to the back and upper wings.

Fig. 96. Paint the top and underside of head and neck, wing tips and tail black.

Fig. 97. Paint the belly whitish, using a mixture of white and a little burnt umber.

Fig. 98. Paint undersides of wings and sides of belly medium dusky gray and underside of tail black.

42

Fig. 99. Place cup on bird at 90° angle, anchoring hand on bird with pinky.

Fig. 100. Draw chalk outlines, if desired, to aid in painting cupped feathers.

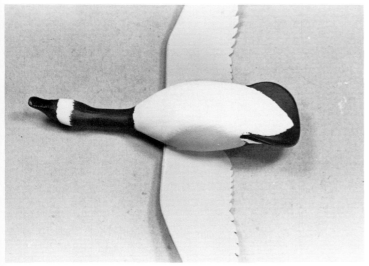

Fig. 101. Paint white patch on neck of bird with slightly jagged edges.

Fig. 102. Paint white patch on rump with jagged edges.

MOUNTING

There are several points to keep in mind about mounting carvings in general. First, a mounting should never overpower a carving but complement it. Experiment with several different mountings to find one that looks the right size. Second, remember that to create a sense of motion you need opposing motion--in other words, the mounting should point in the opposite direction from the carving. Third, if you are mounting a pair of birds, avoid having them in absolute parallel because this tends to make your design look very stiff and unrealistic.

Any mounting you like is fine. There are no absolutes. I often choose different mounts for this carving. The one on page 17 is on a different mount than the one in color plate 60. You'll probably need a small piece of driftwood and a wood base. If the base is hardwood, finish it with wax or polyurethane or any way you like. If it is softwood, consider coating it with glue and sprinkling it with sand to resemble a sandy beach. It can also be stained, painted, waxed, or whatever. Spray the driftwood with insect spray to get rid of any insects living in it.

Drill a hole through the base into the driftwood. Insert a wood screw (several if necessary) and countersink it into the bottom of the base so it won't scratch a table. Glue a piece of felt to the bottom with white glue or purchase paste-on felt dots.

Hold the bird up to the driftwood to choose a position for it. Drill a hole into the body and then into the driftwood. Determine the length of the wire needed to hold the bird on the driftwood. Use a piece of light gauge wire, or even a coat hanger or welding rod. The rod should not show any more than necessary. I insert it in both holes, dotting both ends with 5-minute epoxy so it will stay in place.

If you make two birds, they may be mounted together, using the same method as above.

The Canada goose can also be mounted on a piece of driftwood and hung on a wall. In that case, attach the goose to the driftwood and fasten a hanging device to the back of the driftwood.

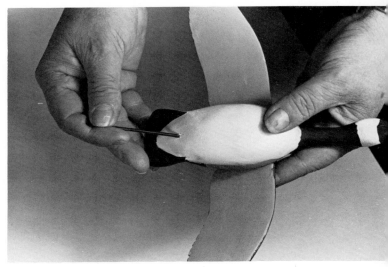

Fig. 103. Insert wire into drilled hole in belly prior to mounting.

Fig. 104. Canada geese may also be mounted as a pair.

Project Two

The Canada goose from Project One has been reduced in size for Project Two. It is carved and shaped in the same way, but because it is smaller, it is more difficult to do. You will proceed in your development as a carver by learning how to texture the carving with a burning pen, insert eyes and do more involved painting.

Chapter 4
Burning in Texture

Now that you've learned how to shape a block of wood into a smooth-bodied bird, it's time you learn how to texture a bird to make it more realistic.

Burning is one of two ways of texturing a bird carving. It is the most practical method to teach a beginning carver because a burning pen is low in cost. It has more advantages than cost, however. Some professional carvers consider burning the best way to texture because it can be done much more tightly and finely than any other kind of texturing. It is also considered the most desirable way to texture carvings entered into competition.

The disadvantage of burning is that it is very tedious and time-consuming. If you're interested in selling your carvings, it will probably not be an economically worthwhile texturing method. Some carvers also think it produces a too-perfect texture.

Whatever your opinion, buy a burning pen and learn how to use it. Even if you don't use it to texture the entire carving, you'll have to use it once in a while.

I recommend the Hot Tool as the basic burning pen for carvers. It is a pen-like instrument used for wood burning by hobbyists as well as bird carvers. I like the Hot Tool for its quality, its short tip that lets me hold it close to the work area, and its consistency of heat. I like being able to replace just the tip whenever it wears out and to use different size tips when I wish. It is the most logical tool for the wood carver to own because it will always be useful as an adjunct to more sophisticated burning systems.

Experiment with the Hot Tool on a scrap of wood. Wear a magnifier of some sort so you can see your work clearly. Always draw the Hot Tool toward you in order to give the utmost control over it.

First practice texturing with it. Make very narrow and fine lines that are tight together with no white areas between them. These lines are burned with the sharp edge of the pen. This is the method you'll use to texture the bird bodies in this project. (Figure 107)

Another type of texturing simulates the pin feathers on the bird's head. Place the top of the burning pen at the forward edge of the feather. Hesitate briefly to make a deep burn before drawing the pen toward you. I call this the indent-and-pull method. On the bird's under-rump the feathers are layered and longer. Duplicate these by burning lines that are a little broader, longer and farther apart than the head feathers.

See what else you can do with the burning pen.

The burning system is also used to outline some details. To delineate a feather, trace it with the point of the pen, then go around the outside of the line with the flat edge of the pen. (Figure 111) This creates a layered effect, simulating the way feathers lie on top of the body and one another. Do not make a ridge inside the feathers. Keep each feather coming flat out from under the one in front of it.

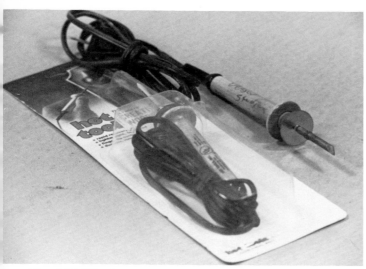

Fig. 106. The Hot Tool is a good burning system for the novice carver.

Fig. 109. Experiment some more with the Hot Tool.

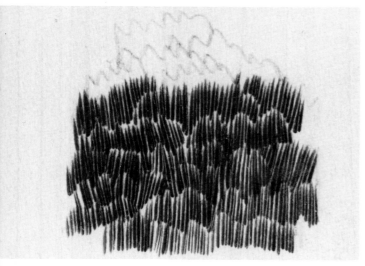

Fig. 107. Practice burning very narrow and fine lines with the Hot Tool.

Fig. 110. This is another type of texturing you can do with a burning pen.

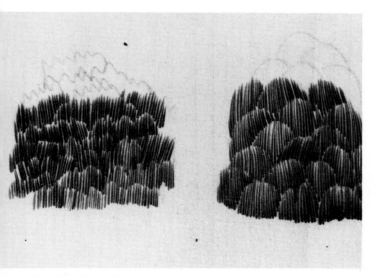

Fig. 108. Practice burning feather patterns with the Hot Tool.

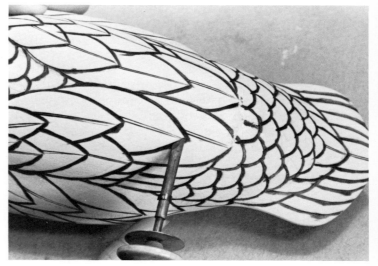

Fig. 111. Delineate a feather by going around the traced line with the flat edge of the Hot Tool.

To raise a feather quill, burn two very thin lines down the center of the feather and join them at a point at the trailing edge of the feather. Then run the flat edge of the pen down the lines; this raises the quill. (Figure 112)

Study the feathers of a bird and try to duplicate them with the burning pen. The more you experiment, the more proficient you'll be. Finally, try out your skills on the carving itself. If you make a mistake, sand and start again. If you made a hole, fill it with Wood Dough, sand, and then burn the Wood Dough.

When using a burning pen, always remember:

1) Don't use it near an air flow because the tip will cool down and you won't get a consistent burn.

2) Always finish shaping and sanding a carving before you burn it.

3) Whenever possible, don't burn an area that has been glued with 5-minute epoxy or superglue because the heat from the burning causes fumes to be released that are very irritating to the mucous membranes.

4) When you need to burn an area that has been Wood-Doughed, burn very quickly and lightly because Wood Dough tends to melt under high heat.

5) Before you paint a burned surface, clean it thoroughly with a fine suede brush to get rid of the char left by burning.

6) After cleaning, spray the surface with Krylon 1301 to seal it. Actually, burning acts as a sealing method, but spots where the wood is not burned will burr under the paint washes, so the Krylon 1301 is simply an extra precaution.

7) When you paint a burned surface, always begin with two thin washes of titanium white acrylic artist's paint before you apply the base paint so the latter doesn't get too dark too quickly. Do not use gesso on a burned surface because it will fill the burning grooves.

ADVANCED BURNING SYSTEMS

The Feather Etcher, the Detailer and the Detail Master are more sophisticated burning systems. Each has a rheostat that controls the heat so it can burn more quickly, deeply and with greater versatility than the Hot Tool. The Feather Etcher can get a little hotter than the Detailer. You can make your own tips for it with nichrome wire.

The Detailer has a more rigid tip than

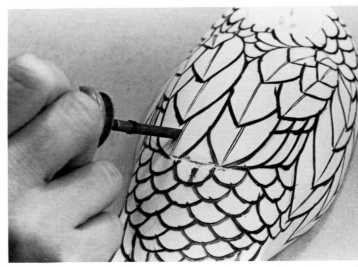

Fig. 112. To raise a feather quill, begin by burning two thin lines with Hot Tool.

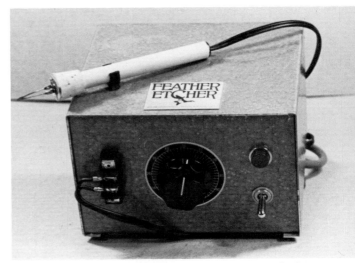

Fig. 113. The Feather Etcher is one of three sophisticated burning systems available to the carver.

Fig. 114. The Feather Etcher has a nichrome wire tip.

48

the Feather Etcher. It has a complete handpiece which needs to be replaced if the tip burns out.

Besides having a rheostat, the Detail Master is a solid-state system for very efficient heat distribution. It has a rigid tip that is contained in a complete handpiece.

As you attempt more advanced carvings you will probably want to purchase one of the above burning systems.

SUPPLIERS

You can get a burning system from:

Annex Manufacturing   (Detail Master)
955 Blue Ball Rd.
Elkton, MD 21921

Chesterfield Craft Shop   (Feather Etcher)
George Walker
P.O. Box 208
Chesterfield, N.J. 08620

Colwood Electronics   (Detailer)
715 Westwood Ave.
Longbranch, N.J. 07740

Hot Tools, Inc.
7 Hawkes St.
P.O. Box 615
Marblehead, Mass. 01945

Fig. 116. The Detailer has a more rigid tip than the Feather Etcher.

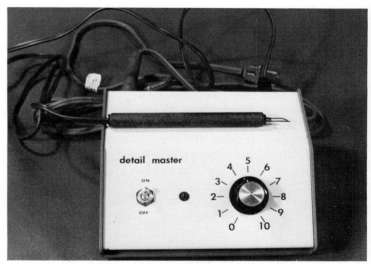

Fig. 117. The Detail Master is a solid-state system for very efficient heat distribution.

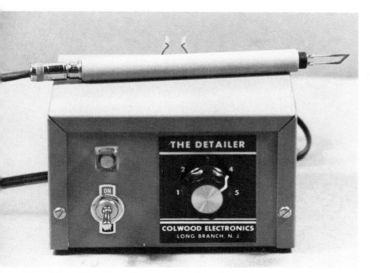

Fig. 115. The Detailer is another burning system available to the wood carver.

Fig. 118. The tip of the Detail Master is rigid and contained in a complete handpiece.

Chapter 5
Eyes

The Canada goose in Project One did not have eyes because it was intended to be a simple, introductory project. Its lack of eyes is not very noticeable. All your other carvings should have eyes, however. The eyes are the feature that bring a bird to life and give it expression.

EYE SIZES AND COLORS

It is essential to use the color and size eyes recommended for each species you carve. Refer to the list at the end of this chapter for waterfowl, song and game bird eye sizes and colors. The sizes given are for lifesize carvings. In most cases I have reduced the size from what is generally called for by taxidermists because most carvings can not accomodate the larger size. The eye size for miniature carvings is any size that you think looks right.

Several grades of eyes are available through taxidermy and carving supply stores. The least expensive, costing around 50 cents a pair, are clear glass with a black pupil. They have poor uniformity so I do not recommend them. Medium-priced eyes are of good quality and are clear or have the color fired in. I prefer to use higher-priced eyes, costing a couple of dollars, because they come fired with color and I can count on their quality.

Don't buy clear eyes unless you want to have a wide variety of eyes available for future carvings. Paint the back of clear eyes the appropriate color, preferably with several thin paint washes. In the chart, most of the yellows mentioned are cadmium yellow, a bright yellow. The straw color is achieved with yellow ochre. The reds are generally bright red, using naptha crimson or cadmium red. Brown generally refers to a reddish-brown or burnt umber. The hazel color can be achieved with burnt umber and a touch of yellow ochre. Fired eyes are available in all these colors.

EYE PLACEMENT

The eye placement is critical because it is totally responsible for the expression of the bird. If you want your bird to look slightly mean or frightened, move the eyes slightly forward. If you move the eyes slightly back, the bird will look sleepier and more gentle. Just moving the eyes a tiny bit one way or another creates subtleties of expression. Experiment with the placement to determine the correct spot for the eyes on your carving.

For most birds the eye channel lies in an arc from the point of the culmen (upper bill) and flows to the back of the head. A common error is to make the channel too shallow or narrow. It must have enough room on the cheek so the eyes can sit straight up and down rather than bug out. (Figures 119 & 120)

MAKING THE EYE CAVITIES

Mark the spots for the eyes, being sure they are perfectly even. In lifesize carvings the eye cavity is drilled with a drill bit. In miniatures, burn the eye cavity with a heated tool the exact diameter of the eye; drilling might break off the top of the head. The eye should fit inside the empty hole. If it is too deep or too wide, use epoxy putty (moldable epoxy) to fill the hole.

After the head is textured, set the eyes. Make a tiny ball of epoxy putty. Press it into the eye cavity to half-fill it. Cut the eyes from their connecting wire and insert one into the filled eye cavity. Press it into the epoxy putty; some of the putty will squeeze out around it. Using a dampened index finger, wipe around the eye to

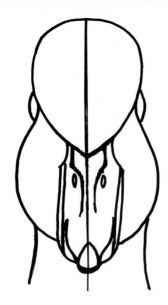
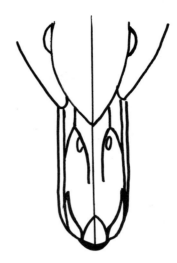

Figs. 119 & 120. Eye channels should have enough room on cheek so eyes can sit straight up and down (drawing on top) rather than bug out (drawing on bottom).

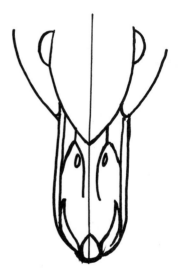

Fig. 121. Partially fill the eye cavity with epoxy putty.

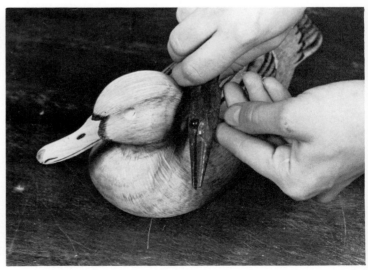

Fig. 122. Cut the eyes from their connecting wire.

Fig. 123. Insert the eye into the cavity on top of the epoxy putty.

feather the epoxy putty into the wood. (Figure 125) The putty should gently round the eye so it appears to have a tiny overhang.

MAKING EYELIDS

Eyes without eyelids are perfectly acceptable for your early carvings. In time, however, you should try to make eyelids to make your carvings truer to life.

Eyes are set in the same way whether they have eyelids or not. Therefore, you can always try to form eyelids after the eyes are set, and if they don't come out well, just remove them.

Roll a very, very thin line of epoxy putty, no longer than one inch, under your fingers. (Figure 127) (Note: A common error in making eyelids is using too much putty. Keep it thin.) Break the piece in

Fig. 124. Press the eye into the epoxy putty with a popsicle stick.

Fig. 125. With damp finger, smooth epoxy putty into the wood around eye.

Fig. 126. Epoxy putty is feathered into wood around the eye.

Fig. 127. Roll the epoxy putty preparatory to making eyelids.

half. Lay one piece along the top of the eye. With a thin metal tool, dampened at one end, crimp the edge of the putty into the wood. Lay the second line of putty along the bottom of the eye, with its ends just overlapping the top eyelid, and crimp it into the wood.

Dampen a soft paint brush and smooth out the crimped edge, feathering it into the wood. This leaves a distinct eyelid around the eyeball. (Figure 132)

If you have more work to do on the bird after the eyes are set, you must cover them with a small piece of masking tape to keep them from being scratched.

When you paint the head, paint right over the eyes. However, you must scrape the white base paint off the eyes before you proceed to your head paint color. If you don't, a white rim of paint will surround the eyeball. Paint the eyelids the same color as the head.

SUPPLIERS

Eyes are available from:

American Taxidermy Studio
Box 71
Dorothy, N.J. 08317

Dolington Woodcrafts
Washington Crossing
Newtown Road
Newtown, PA 18940

Hutch Decoys
7715 Warsaw Ave.
Glen Burnie, MD 21061

Jerry's
9536 W. 7 Mile Road
Northville, Mich. 48167

Van Dykes
Woodsocket, S.D. 57385

Christian J. Hummul Co.
P.O. Box 2877
Baltimore, MD 21225

Fig. 128. On snow goose head, eye is placed into cavity and epoxy putty is smoothed around eye.

Fig. 129. Crimp edge of thin line of putty into wood to make upper eyelid.

Fig. 130. Position line of putty for bottom eyelid and crimp it into wood.

Fig. 131. With damp brush, smooth epoxy putty into wood.

Fig. 132. By working with the brush, you'll make a distinct eyelid around the eye.

Fig. 133. If you have any work to do on head after eyes are set, cover them with masking tape so they don't get scratched.

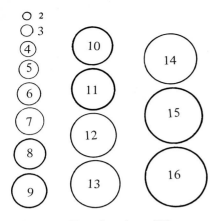

Fig. 134. Eye sizes in millimeters

	COLOR	SIZE/MM		COLOR	SIZE/MM
Bittern	Yellow	10	Ring-necked	Straw	9
Blackbird-Red wing	Brown	5	Ruddy	Brown	9
Rusty	Brown	5	Scaup-Greater	Yellow	10
Brewers	Yellow	6	Scaup-Lesser	Yellow	8
Yellow Headed	Brown	6	Scoter	Yellow	10
Bluebird	Brown	4	Shoveler	Yellow	9
Blue Jay	Hazel	6	Sheld Drake	Red	9
Bobolink	Brown	5	Surf Scoter	White	9
Bob White Quail	Hazel	7	Teal-Blue-winged	Brown	7
Bull Finch	Brown	6	Teal-Cinnamon	Red	7
Buzzard	Brown	12	Teal-Green-winged	Hazel	7
Canary	Brown	3	Widgeon	Yellow	9
Cardinal	Brown	5	Wood Duck	Red	10
Catbird	Brown	5	Eagle-Bald, young	Brown	16
Capperal Cock	Yellow	9	Bald, adult	Yellow	17
(Road Runner)			Golden	Brown	18
Chickadee	Brown	4	Falcon	Brown	12
Chicken-Domestic	Hazel	9	Finches-Various	Brown	4
Coot	Red	9	Flicker	Brown	7
Cuckoo	Brown	6	Goose-Canada	Brown	11
Dove-Mourning	Brown	6	Lesser Snow & Blue	Brown	10
Turtle	Brown	6	White fronted	Brown	11
White Winged	Orange	7	Grackle	Straw	5
Duck-Bald Pate	Yellow	9	Grebe-Long eared	Red	7
Black	Black	9	Horned	Red	6
Blue Bill	Yellow	10	Pie Billed	Red	6
Brant	Dr. brown	9	Grouse-Ruffled	Hazel	9
Bufflehead	Brown	8	Gull-Black Backed	Yellow	12
Canvasback	Red	10	Bonaparte	Brown	9
Eider	Brown	10	Franklin	Brown	9
Florida	Brown	10	Glaucus	Straw	12
Gadwall	Brown	10	Herring	Yellow	10
Golden-eye	Yellow	10	Laughing	Red	9
Harlequin	Brown	10	Ring Bill	Yellow	9
Mallard	Brown	10	Hawk-Chicken	Hazel	14
Merganser-American	Red	10	Cooper	Straw	12
Merganser-Hooded	Yellow	9	Fish (Osprey)	Yellow	14
Merganser-Red Br.	Yellow	10	Goshawk	Hazel	14
Old Squaw	Hazel	9	Hen	Hazel	14
Pintail	Brown	9	Marsh	Yellow	12
Redhead	Yellow	10	Pigeon	Brown	7

	COLOR	SIZE/MM		COLOR	SIZE/MM
Red Tail	Brown	14	Pheasant	Red	10
Rough Leg	Hazel	14	Pigeon	Orange	7
Red Shoulder	Hazel	14	Plover	Brown	5
Sharp Shinned	Yellow	10	Prairie Chicken	Hazel	9
Sparrow	Brown	8	Quail	Hazel	7
Swainsons	Hazel	14	Rail-Clapper	Hazel	8
Shoveler	Yellow	10	Carolina	Red	8
Kingfisher-Belted	Brown	8	Little Black	Brown	5
Killdeer	Brown	6	King	Brown	9
Lark-Skylark	Brown	5	Virginia	Hazel	9
Mockingbird	Brown	5	Yellow	Brown	6
Mudhen	Red	8	Robin	Brown	5
Nighthawk	Black	7	Sandpiper	Brown	6
Owl-Arctic	Straw	18	Snipe	Brown	6
Barn	Brown	14	Sparrow	Brown	3
Burrowing	Yellow	10	Starling	Brown	5
Elf	Yellow	10	Swallow	Brown	4
Great Horned	Yellow	18	Swan	Brown	14
Long Eared	Yellow	14	Tern	Brown	6
Pigmy	Yellow	12	Thrush	Brown	6
Richardson	Yellow	14	Turkey-Wild	Brown	12
Screech	Straw	14	Woodpecker-Downy	Brown	5
Sawwhet	Straw	12	Flicker	Brown	7
Snowy	Straw	18	Ivory Billed	Yellow	10
Short Eared	Yellow	14	Red Bellied	Red	6
Partridge	Hazel	10	Red Headed	Brown	6
Pelican	Straw	16	White Headed	Red	6

Chapter 6
More Painting Techniques

The painting skills you learned in Project One form the foundation for all your other carving projects. To paint the Canada goose in this project you will learn some additional basic skills--how to blend the paint colors so they come together more smoothly and another way to edge feathers.

UNDERSTANDING COLOR

As you progress as a carver, you should study the colors of the actual species. The more you really look at the species, the more you will refine the paint colors you'll use. You'll see that their colors aren't plain, but have subtle variations. Some carvers think that it would be easy to paint an Old Squaw because it's "just black and white". However, if they'd really study an Old Squaw they would see it's not plain black and plain white but black and white with subtle variations. Actually, it's probably harder to paint such a bird than a more colorful bird.

The Canada goose in Project Two is a good example. The black on it is actually a blue-black. Black can also be a brown-black on some birds. And as you study the black on other species in a really good light you see traces of other colors--green, red, violet, and so on.

Painting with black can cause another problem. When 8 to 10 base washes of black are applied, they don't develop a soft sheen. They remain flat. This wasn't a problem in Project One and is not in this project because these are such small birds that the oils in your hands produce a sheen as you handle the birds. But on a larger carving the black probably won't build up a soft sheen. In this case, when the depth of color is right, rub your hands over the dry black paint to take away the flatness of the paint. If that doesn't work, use a matte clear acrylic spray, preferably by Blair.

Hold it 12 to 14 inches from the carving and lightly spray it over the black paint.

Some other paint colors also give a few problems. Greens and thalo colors get very shiny very quickly. When applying them, be especially careful to use very thin wash coats. Whites tend to be shiny unless some color is added to them. If you want a soft white, add a tiny bit of burnt umber or raw sienna to white paint. If you want a crisp white, add a very little ultramarine blue.

WET BLENDING

Looking at a live bird or a good mount, you'll see that there's always a smooth transition from one color to another. Wet-blending techniques duplicate this transition on a carving.

Basically what you're doing is painting two colors right up to each other and while they're still wet, blending them together. To do this you need semi-stiff bristle or acrylic fiber brushes. Several sizes will eventually be needed--a ¼, ½, ¾ and a 1-inch. For miniatures, the ½-inch brush suffices.

There are several ways to blend the two colors. You can stipple down the line with a dry brush. (Figure 135) In the photo a 1-inch brush is used, but a narrower one should be used in a smaller area. A short-bristle sable brush would also work. You can also drag a dry brush down the line (Figure 136) or go back and forth across the line. A fourth method is to drag a wet brush down the line. (Figure 137)

After you've blended the line of colors, you may find that the blended color is too thick on one side. Drag a clean brush across it. (Figure 138) If you wipe a clean, dry brush lightly over one color on one side of the line, and wipe a second clean brush over the other color, you will remove excess water and create a sheen, especially on textured surfaces.

Whenever paint is to be wet-blended, be prepared. Lay out the brushes you'll use and prepare several palettes with the different paint colors. You have to work quickly. Apply one color, then the other, right up to each other, and then blend them. If you don't work quickly the paints will dry before you can blend them. Don't just wet-blend the final washes of paint colors because a ridge will be left from the preceding washes.

Sometimes you'll be instructed to apply several base washes of a color, and then add a touch of a second color in one area and wet-blend it in. Using this method, you can lighten a cheek, say, or darken a crown and make it look very realistic and natural.

OTHER FEATHER EDGING

Some feathers have a touch of color just on their edges. This is a second type of feather edging and is much simpler to learn than making cupped feathers. It is used when the feathers are already outlined on the bird by texturing. Flatten the edge of a brush to a knife edge. Hold it perpendicular to the edge of the feather. Pull the brush into the feather, following the line of texturing, and lift it out quickly, leaving jagged edges on the interior of the feather. Steady your hand by resting your little finger somewhere on the bird. (Figure 139)

Fig. 136. Drag a dry brush down the junction of two paint colors to blend them.

Fig. 137. Drag a wet brush down the line to let the colors bleed together.

Fig. 135. With a dry brush, stipple down the junction of two paint colors to wet-blend them.

Fig. 138. After blending, if there is too much color on one side of the line, drag a clean brush over it.

58

Fig. 139. Edge a feather with a flat-edged brush
in a pull and lift motion.

Chapter 7
Carving Another Miniature Canada Goose

The Canada goose in this project is half the size of the goose in Project One. The size of miniature carvings is often determined by the availability of stock. Thus, the miniature goose in Project One was made out of 2-inch stock; in this project it is made out of standard 1-inch stock.

Because this miniature is so small, you should be able to carve it quickly, so you may as well make two. On the other hand, because it is so small, the work is more difficult and there's less margin for error.

ROUGHING OUT

I recommend basswood for this project because it is easier to detail than pine. You could use pine, but you would need to be extra careful with your burning pen.

It is easy to cut out two bird bodies and four wings at the same time. For the bodies, you need a block 3-inches wide x 4 3/8-inches long and 1½-inch think; for their wings, the block is the same width and thickness but 3¼-inches long.

Fig. 142. Plan view of wing

Fig. 140. Profile of miniature Canada goose

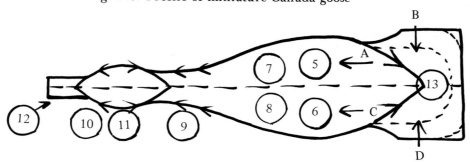

Fig. 141. Plan view (underside of bird)

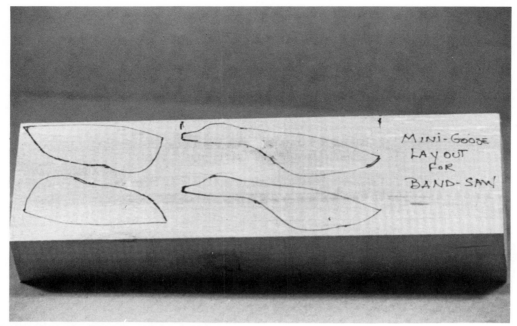

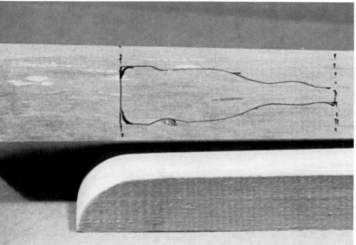

Fig. 144. Turn block on its side and draw one plan view of the body.

Fig. 145. After cutting the plan view, hold pieces back on block and cut out each profile.

Fig. 143. Draw the profiles of two bodies and plan views of two wings on a block of basswood.

On one side of the wood for the bodies draw the plan view (Figure 141) one time. Lay the bill in line with the grain of the wood. On the width, draw two profile views. (Figure 140) Be sure they are aligned with the plan view; in other words, the tails on all three drawings must start at the same point on the length of the block.

Draw two wing plan views (Figure 142) on the width of the block for the wings.

On the bandsaw, cut out the body plan view first. Holding the cut-off pieces on the block, turn the block so the profile drawings are upright and cut out each one. (Figure 145) Trim the excess wood from the body blocks with a knife because it's a little tricky to do on the bandsaw.

Cut out the plan views of the wings on the bandsaw. Turn one wing block on its side so that the leading edge faces you. Draw a straight line across this side of the block, ½-inch down from the top. Draw an arc (Figure 147) that extends from the ends of the line up to the center of the top of the block. Cut along this arced line on the bandsaw, thus preparing the curved surface. Scribe a new arc 1/8-3/16-inch down from the first arc and cut it out on the bandsaw. This is one wing. Turn the block over, and repeat this procedure to get the other wing for the bird. Then, make the wings for the second mini-goose out of the other block.

Fig. 146. Cut plan views of both wings on bandsaw.

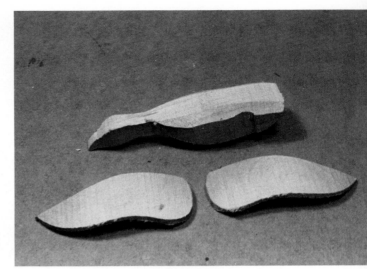

Fig. 149. Trimmed body block and wings are ready to be shaped with X-acto knife.

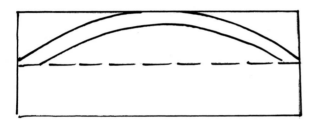

Fig. 147. Arced profile of wing

Fig. 148. Draw arc on leading edge of wing block and cut out the wing.

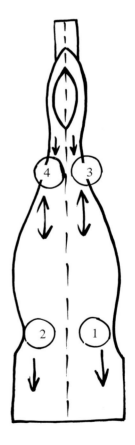

Fig. 150. Back of bird

CARVING

Follow the carving and shaping techniques in Project One to carve this goose.

The main difference in the carving procedure is illustrated by point 10 in figure 141, which is also shown in figure 152. The goose has a more realistic bill than the goose in Project One, so you do not make the straight cut across the bill as you did in point 10 in Project One.

After you make the cut between the cheeks and the sides of the bill, just as you did in Project One, make another cut to create a culmen. The culmen is a flattish area on the upper bill where it joins the forehead.

Draw the V-shaped line in figure 152 onto your carving to delineate the culmen. Back-cut along one side of the V into the edge of the forehead and repeat on the second side of the V. (Figure 154) Now make cuts at a 90° angle to the first cuts on the V. (Figure 155) This makes a sharp ledge. Shave the wood in the forehead so that it flows more smoothly into the culmen. You'll notice that the eye channel now flows right into the edge of the culmen.

Sand the head, bill and body completely smooth.

Draw the eyes, nostrils and the bill markings on your carving as illustrated in figures 152 and 153. Each of these marks will be burned with the sharp edge of the Hot Tool or sometimes just the tip. Use very light pressure because of the size of the carving. On the side of the bill, burn an indentation in the shape of a narrow V, simulating the separation of the upper and lower mandibles. (Figure 159) Burn the bill cut-in--an arced line just above this V to distinguish between the head and bill. On the upper mandible, burn a narrow line, which is a marking found on all upper mandibles. (Figure 160) Also burn the V on the underside of the bill where the point of the chin extends into the lower mandible. Burn small indentations for the nostrils with the point of the Hot Tool.

Fig. 151. Lightly carve head following direction of arrows. Scoop from crown to dotted line to create eye channel.

Fig. 152. Bill will be more realistic on this bird with a culmen, nostrils and other bill markings.

Fig. 153. Make a V on underside of bill where point of chin extends into lower mandible.

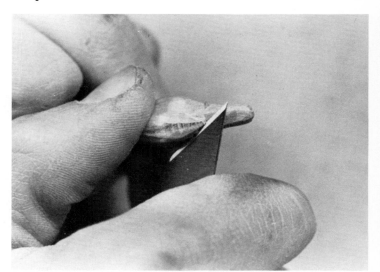

Fig. 154. To form culmen, back cut from bill into edge of forehead.

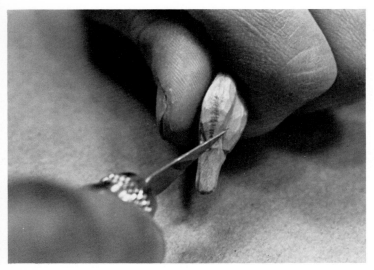

Fig. 155. Cut at a 90° angle to the first cuts to make a ledge.

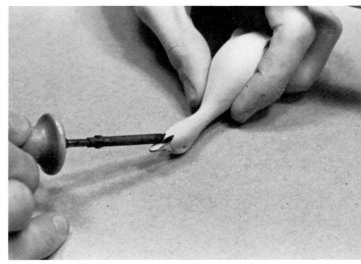

Fig. 158. With sharp edge of Hot Tool, burn in this V.

Fig. 156. Draw eyes on sanded head of miniature.

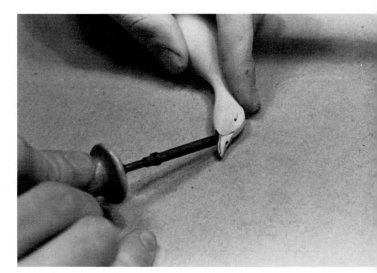

Fig. 159. Burn bill cut-ins with sharp edge of Hot Tool.

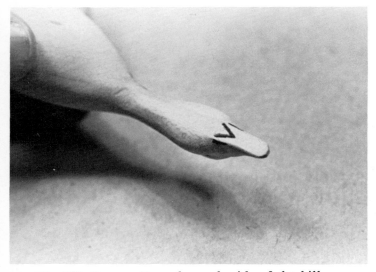

Fig. 157. Draw a V on the underside of the bill where the point of chin extends into lower mandible.

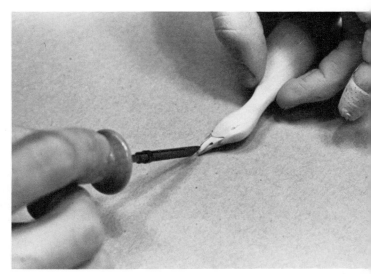

Fig. 160. Burn a thin line on upper mandible, which is a marking found on all mandibles.

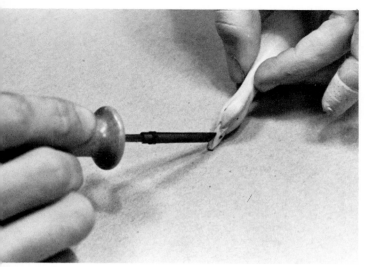

Fig. 161. With point of Hot Tool burn indentations for nostrils.

Fig. 162. Burning on bill is now completed.

Fig. 163. Miniature is ready for the burning of the eye cavities.

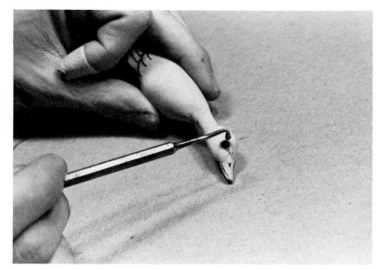

Fig. 164. Heat a tool that is diameter of eye and burn hole for eye.

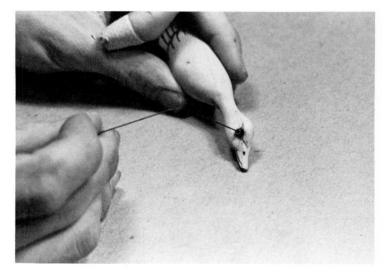

Fig. 165. Hold eye in burned hole to check size.

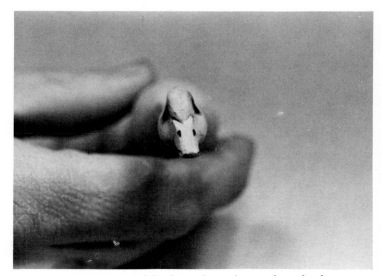

Fig. 166. Eye cavities have been burned on both sides of head.

The mini-Goose's eyes are 2mm. in diameter and colored brown. With a propane torch, heat a 2mm. round piece of metal until it is red hot. Briefly hold it on the dots drawn for the eyes to burn eye cavities.

Draw the outlines of the tail feathers on the top and undersides of the bird as shown in figures 167 — 169. Trace these lines with the point of the Hot Tool to burn them; then run the flat edge of the pen down the outside of these lines. Raise a quill in the center tail feather and center tail covert feather. These feathers lie on top of the other feathers, so the quills are visible in them.

Burn texture in the bodies with straight lines, working from the tail up curve the burning lines on the sides of the bird to simulate the side pocket feathers. The tail feathers on both sides of the center feather are burned on an angle to simulate the barbs flowing from the quill.

Carve the wings as you did before. The difference is that these are half as thick. After rounding and tapering the wing edges and sanding both sides of the wing, draw the feather layout on the top and underside, referring to figure 174.

Burn in the feather outlines and raise the quill on the tertials. Burn the wings on both sides with the Hot Tool, following the direction of the burn lines given in figures 179 and 180.

Cut notches in the bodies for the wings (Figure 184), but because they are so thin, don't tack the wings in place. Attach them with 5-minute epoxy and hold them in position until the glue dries. Fill the gaps around the wings with Wood Dough. Let it dry, then sand and burn to blend with the rest of the carving.

Put the eyes in the eye cavities as described in Chapter 5. Because they are so small, don't worry about eyelids. You may not even need to smooth the epoxy putty into the wood.

Clean the carving thoroughly with a fine suede brush to get rid of any charred wood left from burning. Run it lightly over the carving in line with the burned grooves. If the char is not fully removed, it will show up once the bird is painted and will have to be removed then.

Apply the mixture of white shellac and denatured alcohol on the Wood Dough to seal it. When it has dried, lightly spray the bird with Krylon 1301.

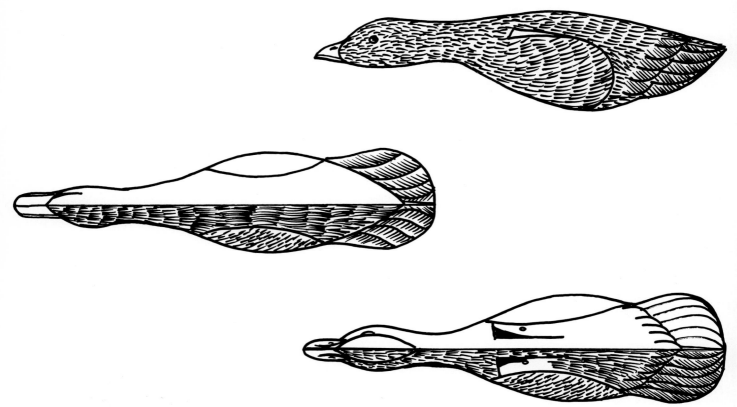

Figs. 167 — 169. Lines indicate tail feather layout and texturing.

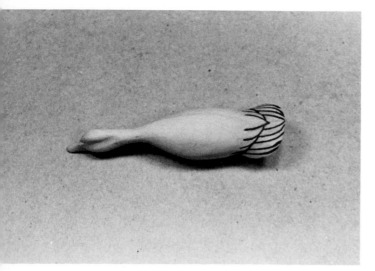

Fig. 170. Draw the outlines for tail feathers and tail covert feathers.

Fig. 172. Burn in texture, referring to Figs. 167-169.

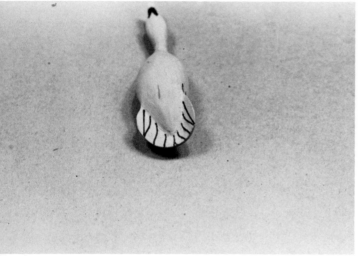

Fig. 171. Draw outlines for the underside of the tail feathers.

Fig. 173. Only the bill is not textured by burning.

Fig. 174. Burn layout of primaries, secondaries and tertials into wings.

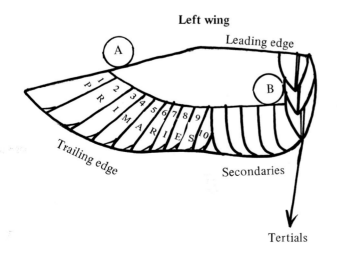

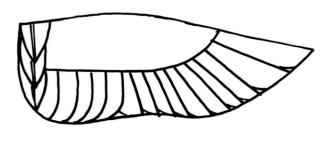

Left wing

Right wing

A

Leading edge

B

PRIMARIES

1 2 3 4 5 6 7 8 9 10

Trailing edge

Secondaries

Tertials

67

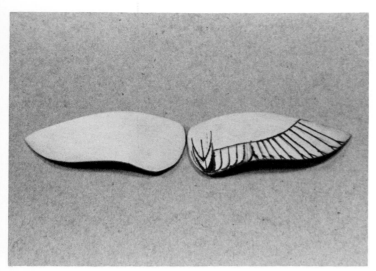

Fig. 175. Wings have been sanded smooth, edges tapered and rounded and feathers drawn.

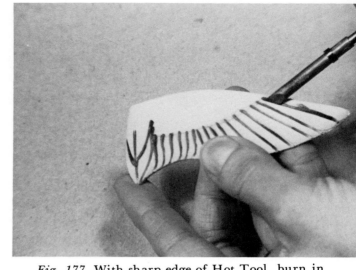

Fig. 177. With sharp edge of Hot Tool, burn in feather edges.

Fig. 176. Feathers on undersides of wings also must be laid out.

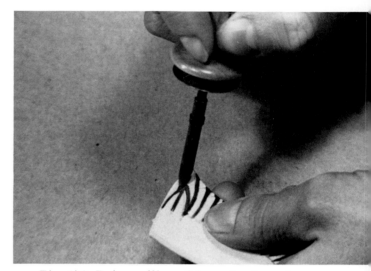

Fig. 178. Raise quills and burn feather edges on underside of wings, too.

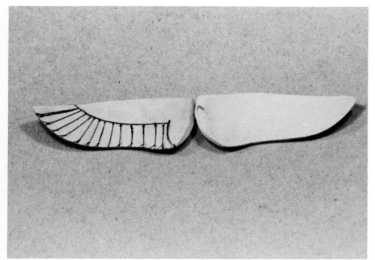

Fig. 179 & 180. Burn texture into uppersides of wings (top drawing) and undersides of wings (bottom).

Fig. 181. With Hot Tool, texture the wings.

Fig. 183. Burn texture into the undersides of wings, too.

Fig. 182. Top sides of wings are burned. Here, one wing is not completed.

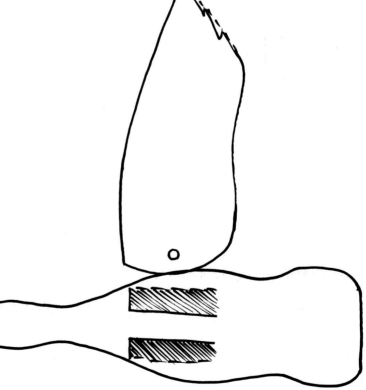

Fig. 184. Cut notches into back of bird for wings.

Fig. 185. Attach wings and fill gaps with Wood Dough.

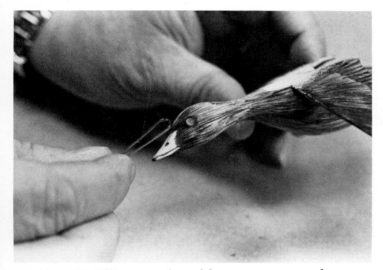

Fig. 186. Fill eye cavity with epoxy putty and insert eye.

Fig. 187. Epoxy putty around eye may be so minimal that no smoothing is necessary.

Fig. 188. Sand epoxy putty on wings and burn in texture.

PAINTING

Apply two wash coats of white paint to the bird.

Paint the rump, tail, head and neck on the top and underside with a mixture of black and a little ultramarine blue. Remember, use 8 to 10 washes of this color and all other base colors.

Paint the top sides of the wings and the back burnt umber. (You could just as easily paint the burnt umber base wash first and then do the black, as you did in Project One. The order for painting these two washes is not crucial.) While the wings are wet, edge the tips of the primaries, using the flat edge of the brush, with some of the black paint.

Prepare two palettes. One is for the belly paint. Make a whitish color by mixing a little burnt umber into white paint. Prepare another palette for the chest and sides of the bird, with a brownish-gray paint, made by mixing black, white and burnt umber. Now paint the belly, then immediately paint the chest and sides, so you can wet-blend these colors together. Repeat until you're satisfied with the depth and sheen of the paint.

Paint the undersides of the wings a medium dusky gray, made from a mixture of black, white and burnt umber. After 8 to 10 thin washes of this mixture, wet-blend some burnt umber into the leading edge and the trailing edge of the undersides of the wings. (Figure 193)

Paint the underside of the tail black.

Edge the feathers next, using a mixture of white with a little raw sienna in

Fig. 189. Apply two thin washes of white acrylic paint to cleaned and sealed carving.

Fig. 190. Paint rump, tail, head and bill with a mixture of black and ultramarine blue.

Fig. 191. Paint the underside of head and neck with the same black.

Fig. 192. Paint the wings and back burnt umber.

a heavy-cream consistency. Use the cupped brush, but since this bird is so small, make the feather edgings with just part of the cup. Do these feather edgings on the arm of the wing, the tertials and secondaries and the back.

Apply a toning wash of ultra-thin burnt umber all over the bird. Redo any area if necessary and apply the toning wash again.

Paint the white patches with white paint, using the straight edge of the brush to create jagged edges.

Paint the bill with a thicker mixture of the black paint, and finish with a coat of gloss medium.

Mount the bird in any way you wish, referring to Chapter 3 for suggestions.

Fig. 193. Paint belly whitish and chest and sides brownish-gray. Paint undersides of wings medium dusky gray and wet-blend some burnt umber into the edges.

Fig. 194. Edge feathers on arm of wing, tertials and secondaries and the back.

Project Three

Project Three gives you the opportunity to refine and reinforce all the skills you have already learned. The miniature Pintail in this project is very similar to the miniature Canada goose, with one exception. In life, the Pintail has vermiculations on its feathers, so you will learn how to paint these on your carving.

Chapter 8
Vermiculations

Many male ducks and some female ducks have vermiculations on some of their feathers. Vermiculations are striations of color--thin lines that appear to be random because of the way feathers lie but actually are fairly regular. They are generally on the sides and back of a bird, and sometimes extend through the tertials or down the rump or into the hindmost part of the chest.

Vermiculations are usually black, white, brown or brownish-gray on a white base, but they differ with every bird. Study the species to find the exact color of the vermiculations and the feathers they are on, as well as the area of vermiculations.

If you are going to carve a species that has vermiculations in life, you should include them in your carving. Find a method you can do well. I've seen a tremendous number of really fine, well-carved birds that have poorly done vermiculations. It's always better to do simple vermiculations well than to attempt a complicated version and do it badly.

Here are seven methods of producing vermiculations. The first four are simple ones that give the broad illusion of vermiculations rather than a totally accurate version. But if you're doing a fairly simple carving these simple vermiculations look just fine. All the methods are possible to do, even for the novice carver, if time is taken to practice. Experiment with the following methods on a board until you find vermiculations that you are able to do well. Then work on the carving.

METHOD 1

On a smooth surface, undercoat the area to be vermiculated with very thick gesso or a mixture of gesso and modeling paste. If the base color on the bird isn't white, tint the gesso to the correct color.

With an ordinary pocket comb put

swirls through the gesso and allow it to air dry. Do not dry with a hairdryer because if modeling paste dries too fast it cracks; if you hold the hairdryer too close to gesso, the ridges blow out.

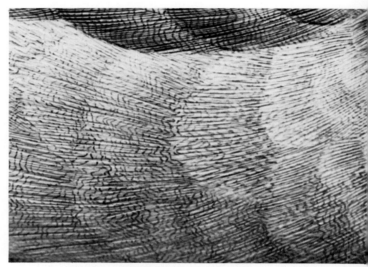

Fig. 196. This Mallard was vermiculated with the Pilot Pen.

Fig. 197. This carving of a Gadwall includes vermiculations done by method 7.

Mix the color for the vermiculations to a heavy-cream consistency and paint it over the combed area. (Figure 199) Let the paint dry, then lightly sand with 120-grit sandpaper to knock off the high spots you made with the comb. Apply a toning wash of ultra-thin burnt umber to tone down the starkness of the base color.

A variation of this method is to make swirls in the gesso with a stiff-bristle brush. (Figure 200)

METHOD 2

On a smooth surface, undercoat areas to be vermiculated with gesso, just as you did in Method 1. After it is dry, brush on a thick color of the base color in acrylic artist's paint. While this is still wet, stipple it with a stiff brush so it looks stuccoed. (Figure 201) Allow it to dry, then paint on the vermiculation color in a heavy-cream consistency. Let the paint dry, lightly sand, and apply the toning wash of ultra-thin burnt umber.

METHOD 3

On a smooth or textured surface (but it's not as good on a textured surface) paint the base color on the area to be vermiculated. Use a thicker consistency than your usual base wash. Mix matte medium (a varnish that is flat) with a tiny bit of color for the vermiculations and brush it on the base color. With a wash brush or a round red sable brush, depending on the look you want, pat and push the medium to create ripples and

Fig. 199. Paint over the combed area with the color of the vermiculations.

Fig. 200. In Method 1, you can also swirl the brush through the gesso.

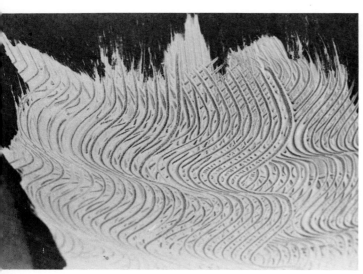

Fig. 198. Method 1. Swirl a comb through gesso and modeling paste.

Fig. 201. Method 2. With a stiff brush, stipple the gesso until it looks like stucco.

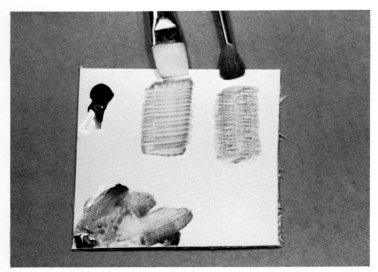

Fig. 202. Method 3. Create ripples and streaks in matte medium and paint using the brush of your choice.

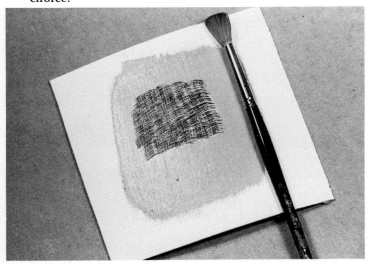

Fig. 203. In Method 4, paint lengthwise rows of colors until they meld together.

Fig. 204. Method 4 was used to create vermiculations on this bird.

streaks. (Figure 202) Let it air-dry. (A hairdryer will blow away the little waves you've created.) Finish with the ultra-thin burnt umber toning wash.

METHOD 4

Now the methods are becoming more realistic. On a smooth or textured surface, paint the base color.

Decide what color the vermiculations are. Let's just say they'll be white and black. Put some thinned white paint on your palette and build up the paint in a trimmed #8 round red sable brush. Very lightly apply the paint, holding the slightly cupped brush at a 90° angle to the surface. Leave little flecks of color in a lengthwise row across the area. Turn the bird around in your hand, and paint another row next to the first one; turn again and paint a third row; and so on. This creates a waviness rather than rows of arced feathers. Let the white paint dry. Then build up some black paint in the cleaned brush and paint on rows of black in the same way, overlapping the two colors slightly. Go back to white, then the black, and so on. The more times you do this, the more the flecks of color will meld together to simulate vermiculations. Take your time; the job looks better if you don't rush. Finish with the ultra-thin burnt umber toning wash. (Figures 203 & 204)

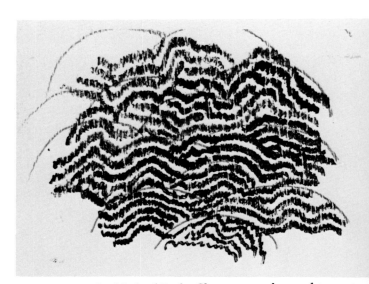

Fig. 205. In Method 5, the Sharpee can be used to draw vermiculations.

METHOD 5

On a smooth or textured surface (but textured is best) use a *permanent* felt-tip pen. The Fineliner Pilot Pen by Sc-uf or Sharpee Pen that has a broader point work well. Both come in black; only the Sharpee comes also in brown. Therefore you can use this method only if your vermiculations are these colors.

Undercoat the area to be vermiculated with the base paint. Draw the layout of the feathers that will be vermiculated. With the pen, draw squiggly lines starting at the innermost point of a feather and working outward until that feather is done. Then go on to the next. Do not try to do each feather exactly the same, because the effect will be too stiff. This is going to take a lot of time to do right. (Figures 205 and 206)

A problem with this method is if the bird's vermiculations appear to be gray all over. If so, wash over your black vermiculations with a white wash to soften them. This makes the surface look chalky,

METHOD 6

This method is done in the same way as Method 5, but here the vermiculations are done with a quill pen, using your choice of points by Speedball. The advantage of this method is that you can use any color of acrylic paint you need. Use a very thin paint consistency, like ink. (Figure 208)

Fig. 206. The Pilot Pen has a finer point than the Sharpee and is only available in black.

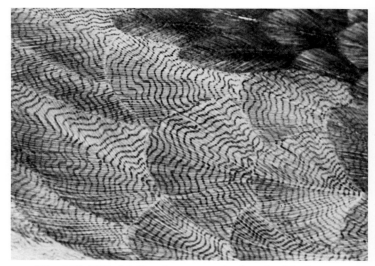

Fig. 207. This Mallard was vermiculated with the Pilot Pen.

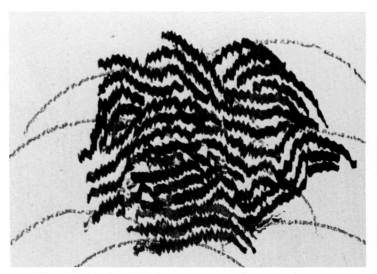

Fig. 208. Method 6. If you use a quill pen to draw vermiculations, you can use any color of paint.

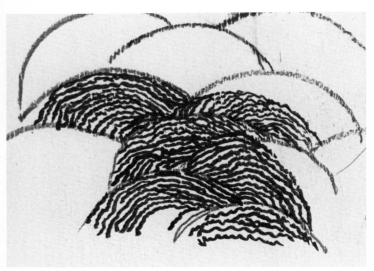

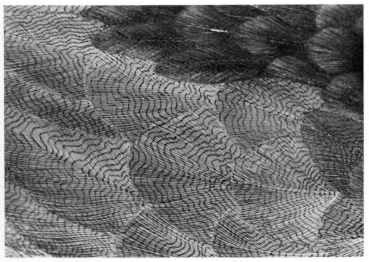

Fig. 209. Method 7 uses a brush and different paint colors in different areas.

Fig. 210. This carving of a Gadwall includes vermiculations done by method 7.

METHOD 7

Method 7 can be done on a smooth or textured surface, but it looks the best on the latter. This method is the most sophisticated because it enables you to highlight one area and darken another; you can't do this with any of the previous methods.

Undercoat different areas in different colors, or different hues of the same color, according to the color of the actual bird. Perhaps you will undercoat one area with gray and another area with white. Draw the outlines of the feathers. Paint thin squiggly lines for the vermiculations with a 0 round red sable brush or a #2 or #4 script brush, using any color acrylic paint you need in a fairly thin consistency. (Figure 209) Let's say that on the gray undercoat you will vermiculate with black, then on the white undercoat you'll vermiculate with gray. This method won't look very good in the beginning, but keep doing it until the colors meld and really look like the actual bird colors. Finish with the toning wash of ultra-thin burnt umber.

After all the vermiculations are done (by whatever method), highlight the edges of the feathers with white paint in a heavy-cream consistency. Don't apply it heavily. Pull the flat edge of the brush into a feather, following the lines you drew, and then lift the brush out, leaving a slightly jagged edge on the interior of the feather. In methods 1-4, if you choose to highlight the feathers, draw these lines with chalk and then edge the feathers.

When you are vermiculating your bird, do the vermiculations at about the same time you do the feather edgings. Do not try to precisely copy the vermiculations on one side of the bird on the other side, because the effect will be too stiff. If you happen to mess up the vermiculations, cover them with a couple of base washes of paint and start again. But if this happens too often, you'll fill in all the texturing and will have to sand down the bird and start again.

Chapter 9
Carving a Miniature Pintail

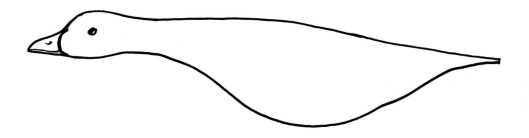

Fig. 211. Profile of miniature Pintail.

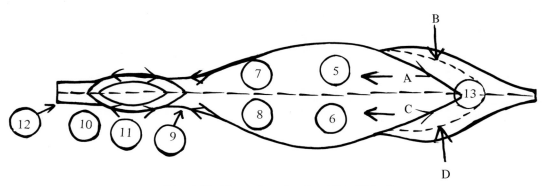

Fig. 212. Plan view (underside of bird).

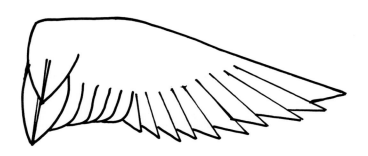

Fig. 213. Plan view of wing.

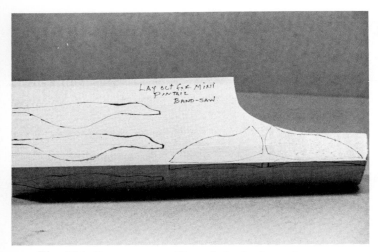

Fig. 214. Draw two profiles of the body and two plan views of the wings on the block.

Fig. 217. On bandsaw, cut profile view of body.

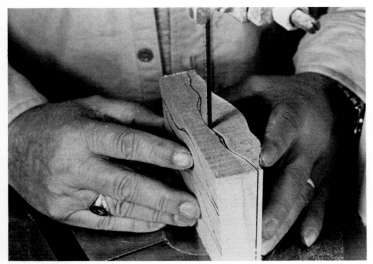

Fig. 215. Cut the plan view of the body first.

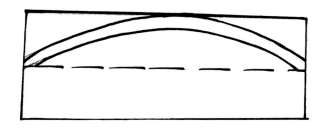

Fig. 218. Arced profile of wing.

Fig. 216. Holding the cut pieces on the block, turn it on its side to cut both profile views.

Fig. 219. Body has been trimmed and is ready to be shaped. Wings are roughed out as goose wings were.

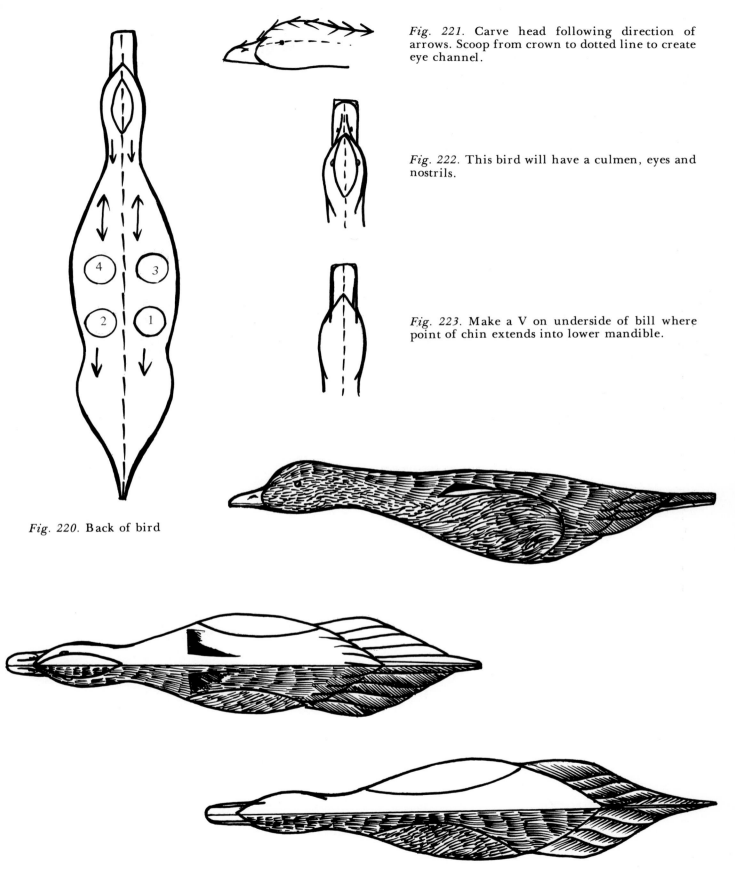

Fig. 221. Carve head following direction of arrows. Scoop from crown to dotted line to create eye channel.

Fig. 222. This bird will have a culmen, eyes and nostrils.

Fig. 223. Make a V on underside of bill where point of chin extends into lower mandible.

Fig. 220. Back of bird

Figs. 224 — 226. Lines indicate tail feather layout and texturing.

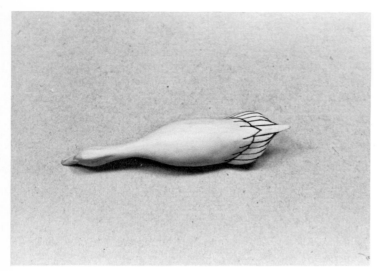

Fig. 227. After body is shaped and sanded, draw outlines of tail feathers and tail covert feathers.

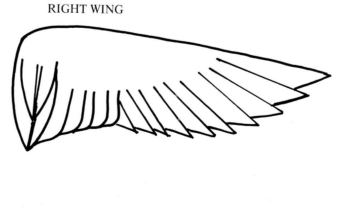

Fig. 229. Tail feathers on the underside are also burned.

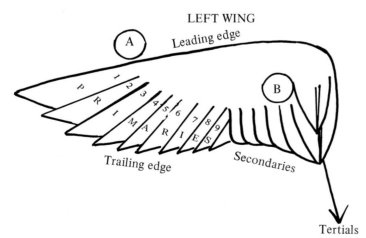

Fig. 228. Burn tail feather outlines with Hot Tool.

Fig. 230. Burn texture into the body referring to Figures 224-226.

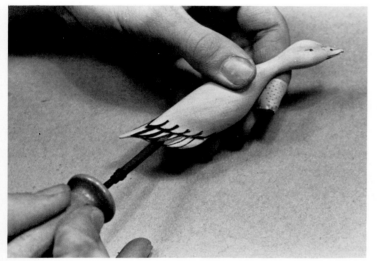

LEFT WING

Leading edge

A

P R I M A R I E S

1 2 3 4 5 6 7 8 9

Trailing edge

B

Secondaries

RIGHT WING

Tertials

Fig. 231. Burn layout of primaries, secondaries and tertials into wings.

Figs. 232 & 233. Burn texture into uppersides of wings (top drawing) and undersides of wings (bottom).

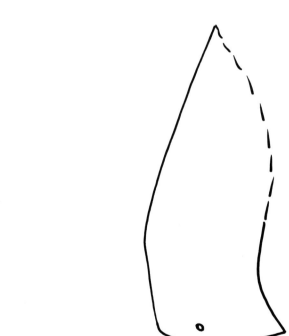

Fig. 234. Cut notches into back of bird for wings.

Fig. 235. Both sides of wings are textured by burning. Here, one wing is not completed.

Fig. 236. With wings attached and Wood Dough sanded and burned, the Pintail is ready to be undercoated with white washes.

Fig. 237. Paint Pintail back, arm of wings and tertials a medium dusky gray.

I chose the Pintail for this project because it is a very popular and graceful bird. Although it is vermiculated, it is still a rather simple bird to paint in this size. It will seem very easy to carve because you have done all the same steps on the miniature goose.

CARVING

For two Pintail bodies you need a block of basswood 3-inches wide by 5¼-inches long by 1½-inches thick. For their wings the block should be the same width and thickness but 3½-inches long.

Rough out the bodies and wings exactly as you did the miniature goose. Use the illustrations and photographs given in this chapter as reference and follow the techniques described in the earlier projects to carve the Pintail.

PAINTING

Apply two thin wash coats of white paint to the Pintail. Prepare palettes with paint mixtures for the body, because you should wet-blend the belly paint into the under-rump paint and the paint on the sides.

Paint the tail, top and underside, the back, the arm of the wings and the tertials a medium dusky gray, consisting of black, white and a little burnt umber. It is essentially the same color you used on the Canada goose. Remember, all the base paints are supposed to be a thin consistency and applied from 8 to 10 times.

Paint the sides the same color.

Paint the rump, under-rump and the pin feather of the tail, top and underside, black, mixing some ultramarine blue with the black.

For the belly, mix white with a touch of burnt umber to make a whitish color, so the white is not so stark. Blend this color into the black of the under-rump and the dusky gray sides. The belly color extends all the way up into the head. Paint the undersides of the wings medium dusky gray.

84

Fig. 238. Paint the sides of the Pintail medium dusky gray.

Fig. 241. Paint belly and chest whitish, and wet-blend it into paint on under-rump and sides. Paint under-wings medium dusky gray.

Fig. 239. Paint the rump and the center tail feather black with a little ultramarine blue added.

Fig. 242. Paint the head, top and underside, with burnt umber containing a touch of white.

Fig. 240. Paint the under-rump with the same black paint.

Fig. 243. Note how the whitish belly paint extends into the sides of the head.

Fig. 244. Paint the primaries a brownish-gray, by adding a little extra burnt umber to the dusky gray mixture.

Fig. 245. Paint cupped feathers on arms of wings. Edge tertials and tail feathers. Begin vermiculations, using Method 4.

Fig. 246. After you paint rows of white flecks, paint rows of black flecks.

Clean the white wash paint off the eyes, then paint the head, top and underside, with a mixture of burnt umber containing a touch of white. The crown and back of the neck should be a little darker; use a little less white in the mixture to paint it. Wet-blend the crown paint into the head color. Paint the bill black.

The primaries are a little more brownish than the arm of the wing. Add a little extra burnt umber to the dusky gray mixture to make this brownish-gray color.

With a cupped brush and white paint, paint cupped feathers on the arms of the wings. Edge the tertials and the tail feathers except the center one in white with the flat edge of the brush. Pull it slightly into the feathers in line with the texturing. (Figure 245)

Next, do the vermiculations. I used Method 4 on the Pintail, but any method will suffice. Chalk on the outline of the area to be vermiculated--the sides and across the back. Just slightly cup the round red sable brush #8 and lay on very fine flecks of white paint in lengthwise rows across the area. Remember to turn the bird each time you finish a row and your rows will seem wavy. When you finish with the white and let it dry, repeat the same procedure with black. (Figure 246) The finer you make the flecks of paint, the better. Take your time. You might even need to do the rows six times or so.

Paint the secondaries with a mixture of burnt umber and a little thalo bronze. (Figure 249) Thalo bronze, made by Hyplar, adds a little iridescence. If you can't find it, a green iridescent powder and burnt umber will approximate the color. When you use the thalo bronze, be extra careful that your paint mixture is very thin, because it can get shiny too quickly.

Paint the trailing edge of the secondaries with plain white, and the leading edge with a mixture of raw sienna with a touch of white. (Figure 250)

Paint the patch on the bill with a heavy cream type consistency of Payne's gray and white, referring to figure 252. Apply gloss medium on top of the entire bill.

Apply an ultra-thin toning wash of burnt umber all over the bird with the exception of the secondaries and the bill. If you think you should repeat the feather edgings, do so now, then apply the toning wash again.

Mount the bird as you wish.

86

Fig. 247. Go back to the white paint and do more rows of flecks.

Fig. 250. Paint the trailing edge of secondaries white, and the leading edge with a mixture of raw sienna with a touch of white.

Fig. 248. Vermiculations are also done on the sides of the bird.

Fig. 251. In this close-up view of back and arm of wings, note vermiculations and feather edging details.

Fig. 249. Paint the secondaries with a mixture of burnt umber and a little thalo bronze.

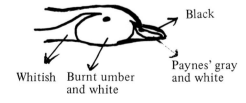

Black

Whitish   Burnt umber
and white

Paynes' gray
and white

Fig. 252. Painting of Pintail head and bill

Stocking the Workshop

As your interest in carving increases, you're sure to want and need more tools. Tools widen your potential as a carver, allowing you to try more involved carving projects and to work more rapidly. This is not to say that you must buy every imaginable tool made for woodworking. There are some that are very necessary and some you can manage without, at least until carving becomes a major occupation.

The following tools are the ones you will eventually want to own. Perhaps you've been using some that aren't on my list. If these work for you--fine, use them. It is more important that you find something you can use successfully than that you take all my suggestions.

Note: You get what you pay for. If you spend the extra dollars to buy a high-quality tool, you're making a once-in-a-lifetime investment that will last forever with reasonable care.

HAND TOOLS

Knives and chisels. As you work on larger carvings you'll find the X-acto knife is simply too short to use. If you try to reach across a broad surface with it, its handle drags on the wood and leaves an indentation. I therefore recommend that you also buy a knife with a 2½-inch blade.

Chisels can be more effective than knives when you have to cut against or across the grain. You have more control and reach with a chisel than with a knife. Fishtail chisels, which come in small and large sizes, help to remove excess wood quickly from a carving. Since a large fishtail chisel is wider than a small one, it can remove more wood in one stroke.

Offset chisels have a raised handle that does not touch or drag on the wood. They may be used to carve feather patterns in areas hard to reach with a knife. They come as straight-ahead, right and left

Fig. 253. From left to right, large fishtail chisel, small fishtail chisel, offset chisel, long-bladed knife, X-acto knife and Warren knife.

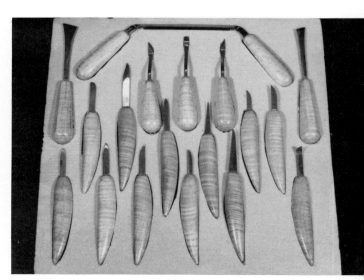

Fig. 254. Cheston Knotts' knives and chisels are excellent and worth collecting.

chisels. The straight-ahead chisel is the first one you should buy because you will need it more frequently. But there will be some occasions when you specifically need the right or left chisel.

I like the knives and chisels made by the Warren Tool Company because they come with one heavy handle and interchangeable blades. They are medium in price and of good quality. The best knives and chisels are made by Cheston Knotts. (Figure 254) These are more expensive but worth collecting because of their beautiful craftsmanship and their excellent cutting blades. The Warren Tool Company is at Rt. 1, Box 12B, Rhinebeck, N.Y. 12572. Cheston Knotts' address is: 106 South Ford Avenue, Wilmington, Del. 19805.

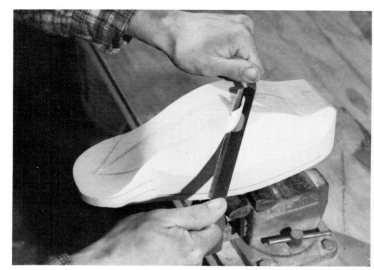

Fig. 257. A drawknife is used to remove excess wood from bandsawed block.

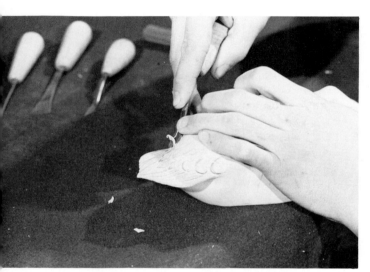

Fig. 255. The offset chisel has a raised handle so it does not drag on the wood.

Fig. 258. Curved surform rasp will remove wood as a drawknife does, but costs less to buy.

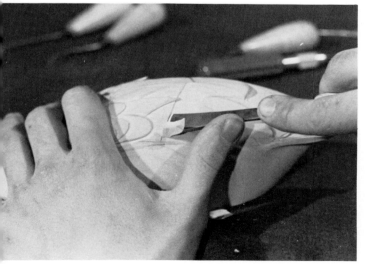

Fig. 256. A fishtail chisel helps remove excess wood quickly.

Fig. 259. Round surform rasp will remove wood in areas not reachable by the curved surform rasp.

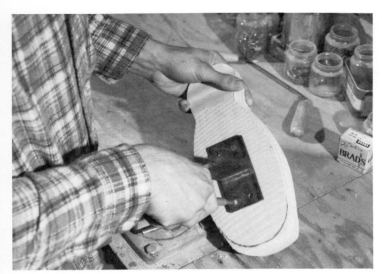

Fig. 260. Make a T-bar to hold block in vise for work with hand tools.

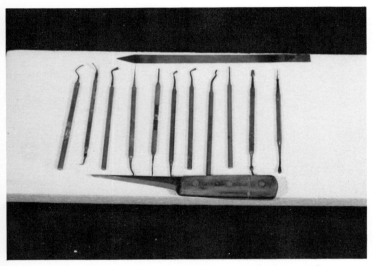

Fig. 261. Dental tools, and sharpened pieces of metal and knife are often heated with torch to burn holes in carving.

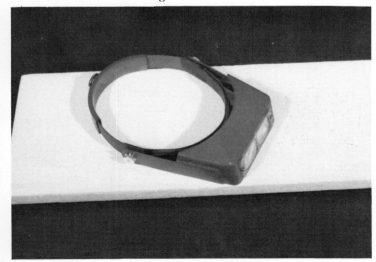

Fig. 262. If you wear a magnifier, you will be able to see your work much better.

Drawknife. A drawknife is a blade with two right-angle handles that you draw toward you across a block of wood to quickly remove excess wood. The average carver may prefer it for trimming a bandsawed block. Cheston Knotts' drawknife, which is 5¼-inches long by 5/8-inch wide by 3/16-inch deep, is outstanding. Good drawknives are also made in Germany and the Scandinavian countries.

Surform rasp. Use a surform rasp to remove excess wood if you don't want to pay the higher price for a drawknife. It also is used to remove wood in areas not reachable by a drawknife. You will eventually want a curved-blade and a round-blade surform rasp. All surform tools are made by the Stanley Works and sold in hardware stores.

T-bar. The T-bar is a device to hold a carving in a vise as you work on it with hand tools, such as a drawknife or surform rasp. You must make your own out of 3/16 or ¼-inch steel stock. Have it welded in a T-shape, 2 to 2½-inches wide. Drill holes in the top of the T for inserting screws into the bottom of the bird. The alternative is to use a 3-inch or longer flat angle iron. Screw one arm to the carving and hold the other in a vise.

Dental tools. There are many excellent carving tools used in the dental industry. Dentists throw them away when they are not sharp enough for dental use,

Fig. 263. The Foredom tool is the mainstay of the carving world today.

but they are still fine for wood carving. Ask your dentist for the tools he no longer can use. You'll find that his tiny knives, scrapers, brushes, etc. are perfect for carving.

Propane torch. A propane torch comes in handy whenever you need to heat a tool to use for burning.

Sharpened pieces of metal. To burn a channel in your carving you may sometimes need sharpened pieces of metal. Various sizes cut from round rods to flat bars are useful.

Magnifier. Whenever you are doing intricate work, wear some kind of magnifier so you can see clearly. Many people are embarassed to wear one, but once they do, they realize they've been missing a lot of detail. If you can see it, you can do it!

POWER TOOLS

If you want to do many carvings quickly, you should invest in some power tools. Some carvers like to use them as much as possible; some use both hand and power tools; and some resist them because they don't like the dust they make or because they prefer the feel of cutting wood by hand.

The following are the power tools you might want to own someday.

Foredom flexible shaft machine (or Dremel). This is the mainstay of the carving world today. It makes your work a great deal simpler and quicker to do. There is a vast assortment of accessories for shaping, sanding, detailing, cleaning--you name it. Actually, depending on the accessories you own, the use of this machine is as limitless as your imagination.

The accessories for the Foredom tool are held in handpieces. I own two handpieces, a 44A and a 30, because I have found this is the most convenient way to use the tool. The 44A comes with a full set of collets to accommodate the accessories. The ¼-inch collet accommodates all the heavy bits, such as the rasp and sanders, which have a ¼-inch shank. All the lighter bits, such as the channel cutter, need a different size collet in the 44A handpiece. Changing the collets, I've found, is a time-consuming nuisance. Therefore, I also own the 30 handpiece, which has a 1/8-inch geared chuck that

Fig. 264. For shaping a carving, you should have ½ and ¾-inch hollow Arco rasps for the Foredom tool.

Fig. 265. With the ¾-inch hollow rasp, the Foredom tool removes excess wood and shapes the piece at the same time.

Fig. 266. Flap sanders of varying dimensions and roll sanders are used with the 44A handpiece of Foredom tool.

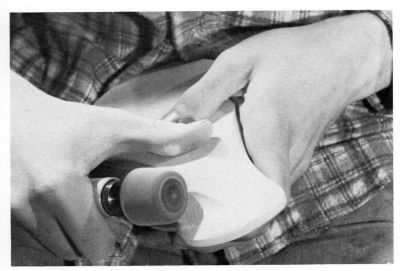

Fig. 267. Using the flap sander, you can quickly rough-sand a broad area.

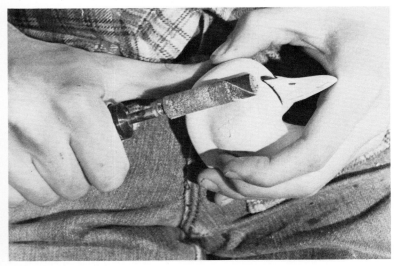

Fig. 268. Roll sander roughly sands an area that's too narrow for the flap sander.

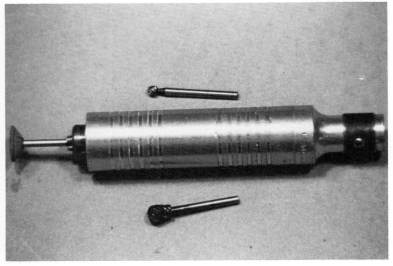

Fig. 269. The #30 handpiece holds a texturing stone, with burrs of different sizes beside it.

holds the smaller bits. It's much faster to change handpieces from the 44A to the 30 whenever I need to use a different bit than to change collets in the 44A handpiece. One drawback, however, is that the 30 handpiece costs about twice as much as the set of collets for the 44A handpiece. When you buy a Foredom tool, make a decision about the handpieces you want to own.

For shaping with the Foredom tool, use ½-inch and ¾-inch hollow rasps made by Arco. I use carbide rasps that cut fast, deep and sharp, but only experienced carvers should use these. Carbide rasps tend to jump or "walk" over the work if they're not held very securely. Hollow rasps are the safest and easiest to operate. As you gain experience, you might want to use a solid rasp with carbide chips embedded in it.

For sanding you should have a cartridge roll sander and a flap sander. The roll, which we affectionately call the "tootsie roll", is a ½ x 2½-inch roll of sandpaper on a ¼ x 1/8-inch reducing mandrel. It's just the right size for sanding tight areas--under the neck, for example. The flap sander, which comes in sizes from 1 to 3½-inch diameter and 1-inch wide, quickly sands a broad area. I recommend 80-grit sandpaper as the best for sanding with these accessories. Anything coarser tends to act like a rasp; anything finer tends to burn more than sand.

For drilling, cone-shaped and rounded Dremel bits are used. They have a shorter shank than ordinary drill bits so you can get your hand closer to your work to improve accuracy. Tapered bits are good in tight areas but must be used carefully because they may split the wood.

For texturing, use metal discs or Veri-thin dental separating discs. They are roughly 1-inch in diameter. When you use them, sandwich a third slightly smaller disc between two discs so they won't cut too deeply into the wood. The discs can't be used to texture a tight area, such as under the neck, so sharpen a screw or nail head, insert it into the handpiece and texture with it. But because it cuts only on one surface, it tends to cut more deeply into the wood than the discs do.

For coarser texturing, Foredom and Dremel make mounted abrasive points, also called stones. These are shanks, each one with a stone embedded at the end. The stones come in many different shapes to be used in different situations. If necessary,

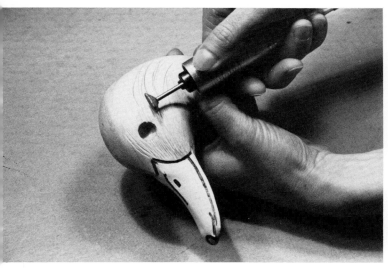

Fig. 270. Stones are used for coarsely texturing the wood.

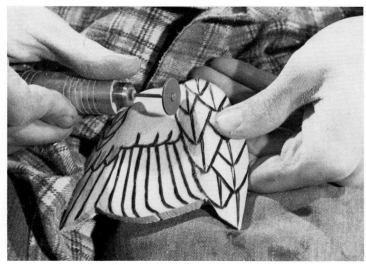

Fig. 273. With dental disc you can do fine texturing. Here, the barbs are being textured after the feather outlines have been burned.

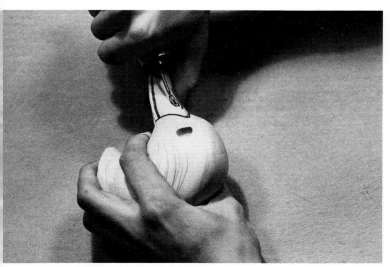

Fig. 271. Dental burrs will do fine detailing, such as around the nostrils.

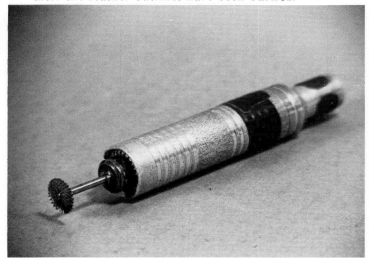

Fig. 274. A rotary metal saw blade is used in the #30 handpiece for cutting channels.

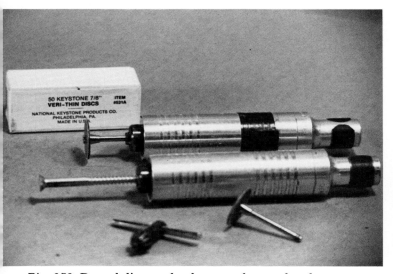

Fig. 272. Dental discs and a sharpened screw head can be used for fine texturing.

Fig. 275. Cut a channel for insertion of feathers in wing block.

Fig. 276. Denture brush is used on mandrel in 44A handpiece for cleaning carving.

Fig. 277. Carvings must be cleaned before they are painted. A denture brush is recommended.

Fig. 278. Use a wirebrush on Foredom tool to clean driftwood for mounting a carving.

sharpen the stone with a dressing stone, also sold by Foredom.

Fine burrs are used for detailing, as around the nostril and eye. There are literally thousands available. These are not as important to own as other accessories, because you probably can accomplish the detailing with something else, such as dental burrs.

A small rotary metal saw blade, made by Dremel, is used to cut a narrow channel for feather inserts or enlarging a seam. We refer to it as a channel cutter.

Clean the carving after it is textured or burned with a fine, round denture brush attached to a mandrel. This is faster than using a suede brush by hand. Also, small pieces of plastic scouring pads can be cut, attached to the mandrel and used for cleaning.

Use a wire brush on the Foredom tool to remove residue and rot from a piece of driftwood that will be used as a mount. The wire brush is too harsh to be used for any other purpose. Wear goggles when you use it.

Buy the Foredom tool from the Foredom Tool Company in Bethel, Conn. 06801. The accessories are available from Serabian, (P.O. Box 146, 195 Highway 36, W. Keansburg, N.J. 07734) and Craft Cove (2315 West Glen Ave., Peoria, Ill. 61614).

Bandsaw. A bandsaw makes the blank or rough cut of the carving. It is the carver's largest investment and is not an absolute necessity if you have access to one owned by someone else. If you do buy one, you can pay back your investment by roughing out blocks for nearby carvers. Be sure you buy one that will accommodate any size carving. A 12 inch bandsaw holds a bird 5 inches wide. (The average dabbling duck is 6 inches in width; the average diving duck is 7 inches wide.) A 14-inch bandsaw cuts out a bird 6 inches wide; most, however, have a split frame so you can build an extension or insert to be put in the frame to accommodate even thicker or wider birds. If you buy a bandsaw, be sure it has a split frame. Also buy a ½ x ¼-inch skip tooth blade with six or eight teeth to the inch.

Fig. 279. A drill press is used to hollow a carving that is supposed to float.

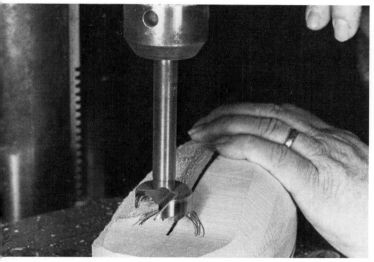

Fig. 280. A drill press may also be used to flatten area on body block for head.

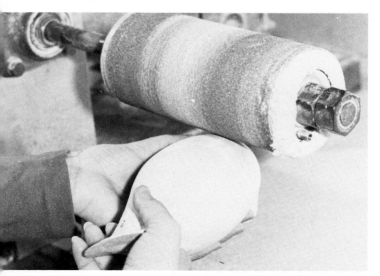

Fig. 281. Pneumatic drum sander roughly sands bandsawed blocks.

Fig. 282. Sand-o-flex by Merit is less expensive way to rough-sand body.

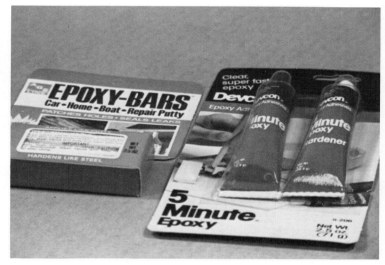

Fig. 283. Epoxy putty and 5-minute epoxy are supplies used in every carving project.

Fig. 284. You should have (from left to right) 2 wash brushes, 2 wet-blending brushes, a round red sable, a cat's paw and a script brush.

95

Drill press. It is not essential to own a drill press, but if you do, you'll find that hollowing out a bird carving is a very quick and easy job. The press is also used to flatten the area on the body where the head will be attached. You will need a multi-spur machine center bit or a Forstner bit. A spade bit is the least expensive to buy, but has a long lead point that may go right through the wood if you're not careful.

Sanders. Most people hate sanding wood. Power sanders will do all the rough sanding for you. Flap and roll sanders on the Foredom tool do rough sanding, but they're too small to be very effective on a large area.

I happen to own a pneumatic drum sander made by Sand Rite Manufacturers, (1611 No. Sheffield Ave., Chicago, Ill. 60614). It is a superior tool but is more expensive than other sanders. You can purchase the complete unit or just the drum and sleeves. If you do buy just the drum, get one 3 x 7-inches and build a mount for it.

You can also easily rig a belt sander with a motor and pulley using 2½ to 3-inch wide belts of 80-grit. Anything less than 2 inches wide tends to cut grooves in a block.

The least expensive power sander is a Sand-o-Flex, which is made by Merit and sold in hardware stores. It is about 8-inches in diameter and needs to be attached to a motor, such as an old washer or dryer motor or a small ¼ horsepower motor.

SUPPLIES

Your workshop should also include supplies. You've already stocked up on some but you will eventually need more. Whenever you buy a product, keep in mind its shelf life so that it does not deteriorate before you've used it up.

Superglue. I use superglue to set feather inserts in a carving. I can control it better than 5-minute epoxy in this application because if it runs it is absorbed in the wood. I prefer Bordens' simply because it has a stem. When using it, seal the wood first, because it won't adhere otherwise. If you find a superglue that will bond a porous surface, you will not need to seal the surface first.

Epoxy putty. Besides being used to hold eyes, epoxy putty (also called moldable epoxy or epoxy bond) can be used to make tufts on birds' legs, ridges around nostrils, or to fill seams. It can be textured with a knife when it is semi-hard and painted when it is still wet. These things can not be done with Wood Dough. Epoxy putty can not be burned because it breaks down under heat. It is found in automotive sections of discount stores.

Auto-body filler. Auto-body filler is also sold in automotive sections of discount stores. It is better to use than epoxy putty when you have to fill a big hole or quickly fill a seam. It hardens more quickly and can be textured as soon as it dries, but it can not be burned.

Duralay dental acrylic. This product must be purchased in a dental supply house. It is used to build up feet, coat cross-grained areas (like the hooked bill on birds of prey), and repair areas. It can even be used as a glue. It can be textured with the Foredom tool or burned under very low heat because it will curl under high heat.

Denatured alcohol. Besides being mixed with white shellac to seal Wood-Doughed areas of a carving, alcohol is used to prepare the wood for very fine sanding, such as on a bill.

Other paint brushes. Eventually you should own several wash brushes, such as Robert Simmons' Skyscraper #755 or #955, whichever you do not own yet. Also buy one about 1¼ or 1½-inches wide. Also buy a 0 round red sable or #4 script brush in sableine if you have not done so already.

Any other brushes you might ever buy would be only of psychological value. I'm as guilty as anyone of buying all new products that come down the pike, but I keep returning to my original brushes, which work more consistently. Of course, if you've been successfully using other brushes, I wouldn't suggest that you switch.

Iridescent powders. To simulate the colored patch on some bird species, you will need green, blue and rose iridescent powders. I use the Venus brand made by U.S. Bronze Powders, Inc., (Box 31, Flemington, N.J. 05822). Use them sparingly or they will look gaudy. Mix a little with water and apply on top of the paint, or mix a little into the paint. Another supplier is Craft Cove.

Matte medium. Besides being used for vermiculations, matte medium is used to tone down shiny paint. Mix it with a base wash mixture and apply a couple of times.

Finishing nails. Use finishing nails to hold wings on large birds.

Polyurethane. Seal the bottom of a floating bird with polyurethane or Zar (a clear acrylic coating).

Flux brushes. Buy a supply of inexpensive flux brushes to use for messy jobs and then discard.

Face mask. Hardware stores sell a variety of face masks (disposable particle masks) for you to wear when you're working with power tools.

Goggles or safety glasses. Anytime you operate motorized equipment, wear goggles or safety glasses to protect your eyes.

Aloe plant. I've found that an aloe plant in the workshop comes in handy whenever I cut or burn myself. Break off a leaf, open it up, and lay it on the cut or burn to make it heal more quickly.

WOOD SUPPLY

If you're going to do a great deal of carving, you may want to buy wood to have on hand. There are several types of wood generally used in bird carving as well as veneer for feather inserts. Keep your wood supply in a dry area.

Sugar pine. Sugar pine, used for the Canada goose, is widely available. It is a loosely-grained wood that will take minimum detail. Northern white pine is an alternative, but it has a harder grain.

Basswood. Basswood, which you used for the miniatures, comes from the linden tree. It is the most common wood used in carving because it is readily available through most shops catering to carvers. Though listed as a hardwood, it is quite soft, has a tight grain and takes detail well, so it is relatively easy to carve, even across the grain. But it's not a pretty wood, and because the grain is so tight, it does not lend itself well to staining.

Water tupelo or tupelo gum. This wood is grown in swampy areas of the South and is used by Southern carvers. It is not readily available. It is a tightly-grained wood, therefore easy to carve, even across or against the grain. Being semi-hard, it is desirable for carving. (The harder the wood, the more durable the carving.)

White cedar. This is good for hunting decoys because it doesn't rot. However, it is so soft between the grain that you get a ripple effect if you try to detail it. It is no longer readily available.

Jelutong. This is readily available through specialty shops, but is fairly expensive. I do not recommend it to beginners because it is so soft that they tend to dig into it. It also burns very quickly. But it is quick and easy for advanced carvers to use.

Veneer. Inserts are made out of veneer. I buy sanded basswood veneer 1/32-inch thick at hobby shops. It is a little more expensive than unsanded basswood and not as readily available. Specialty shops carry all types of veneer in wide, long and unsanded sheets. Maple is a hard veneer so it is slower to burn or texture than basswood. Holly is good for inserts because it is very resilient and can almost be tied in a knot. Some people like to use an insert even harder than holly, but I think they are too brittle.

Veneer and wood supplies are available from Craftwoods (8 Beaver Run Lane, Cockeysville, MD 21030) and Felix V. Bass (611 Delsea Drive, Westville, N.J. 08093).

Fig. 285. This is what you should not do--but you probably will, just as I did!

Fig. 286. Sharpen your knife when it is dull.

Fig. 287. After sharpening, strop knife on piece of leather.

USE AND CARE OF TOOLS

Tools are expensive. If you maintain them, you won't need to replace them. If they are in good condition, they will do a good job quickly and with less chance of an accident. Always work in a well-lighted, well-ventilated area. Rig up some sort of vacuum system to remove the dust from your workshop when you're using power tools. Keep your mind on what you're doing whenever you work with a power tool or you may have a serious accident. Protect your eyes with goggles or safety glasses and wear a face mask.

Occasionally a knife blade seems dull. Blades get dull from use, but dullness comes particularly quickly from cutting a sanded area that has not been cleaned. To sharpen the blade, use a piece of marble or an Arkansas stone. Run each side of the blade over the stone about ten times. Then go back to the first side and stroke again, say, five times, and repeat on the other side. Finish by stroking once on one side and once on the other side. This makes the knife blade perfectly even. (Figure 286)

Now you'll notice that a small burr is created on the sharpened edge. Stropping knocks that burr off and smooths out the edge. Use 600-grit aluminum oxide and a drop of oil on a piece of leather, or just plain leather or even cardboard. Run your knife over the strop just as you did on the stone. (Figure 287)

Burning tools also need to be sharpened occasionally to keep them sharp and clean of charred wood. Sharpen a Hot Tool with a fine flat file, or, to get a really fine edge, use two 7/32-inch chain saw files taped together at the ends. Draw the blade down these files to hollow-grind the tip. Between filings lightly touch the edge with fine sandpaper.

The wire tips of the Feather Etcher, Detailer and Detail Master are so fine that if they are sharpened with a file they will wear out. They will last much longer if they are sharpened on an Arkansas stone just enough to clean off the charred wood.

Project Four

The Green-winged Teal hen carving project introduces several new techniques. This flat-bottomed bird is carved in two pieces, so you must learn how to make a seam that will really hold. It is textured with a Foredom tool, though you could also use a burning pen, and has two inserted feathers made of basswood veneer. The bill is more intricately carved than those in prior projects. If you wish, it can be turned into a floating decorative carving for competition purposes; but in that case it must be hollowed out.

Chapter 10
Texturing with the Foredom Tool

You have already learned how to texture a carving with a burning pen. The other way to texture is with a Foredom tool.

Foredom tool texturing goes much faster than burning. If you're carving birds to sell, chances are you will want to texture them with the Foredom tool as a matter of economics. The Foredom tool, however, can not produce such fine and tight texturing as the burning pen. On the other hand, sometimes burning may seem too tight and perfect and the somewhat coarser and broader Foredom tool texturing seems just right. It's also a possibility that you'll become more skilled with the Foredom tool than with the burning pen.

Actually, if you had to make a choice, you can conceivably do without the Foredom tool as far as texturing is concerned, while you really wouldn't want to do without a burning pen. There will be some areas on your carving that are inaccessible to the Foredom tool. It is difficult, for instance, to texture around the bill with the Foredom tool, but it's no problem with the burning pen.

Many carvers discover that a combination of texturing systems provides the look they want. Take a feather, for instance. You can carve the feather outline with a knife, making a flat cut which gives a clean and crisp edge. You can also use the burning pen, as you've already learned. The third alternative is to use a small, untapered bit on the Foredom tool, but it's probably the most difficult method to master. Now decide how you will finish texturing the feather. You can burn in the texture or use the Foredom tool. I often burn the feather outlines, raise the quill with the burning pen and then create the barbs with the Foredom tool. (Figure 291) You might even burn the barbs in the feathers you want to emphasize and do

straight texturing of the rest of the body. (Figure 292) This is a way to simplify the feather layout.

If time is a factor, I generally burn all the areas on a carving that are particularly prominent or important and use the Foredom tool for everything else. But if I'm entering the carving in a competition, I burn the texture on the entire carving.

Experiment with different texturing accessories on the Foredom tool. Discover what you can accomplish with each one. Learn how to make the short strokes to duplicate the pin feathers on a bird's head and the longer strokes needed on a bird's under-rump. There's an infinite variety of things you can do to create subtle variation in texture. Please yourself by developing systems you like.

When texturing with the Foredom tool, remember:

1) After shaping and sanding the carving, spray it all over with Krylon 1301 before you texture. The texturing instrument is abrasive and tends to burr up the wood and make it fuzzy. Krylon 1301 makes the surface a little harder so that it won't become fuzzy.

2) Wear a face mask and safety glasses. Abrasive discs may shatter as you use them. It is imperative that you protect your eyes.

3) Whenever possible, do not texture a surface where you've used 5-minute epoxy or superglue because the friction from the texturing causes fumes to be released that are very irritating to the mucous membranes.

4) You can Foredom tool texture an area where you've used auto-body filler or epoxy putty.

5) Before painting, clean a textured surface to get rid of the residue left in the grooves by the Foredom tool. The denture brush on the Foredom tool will do this very

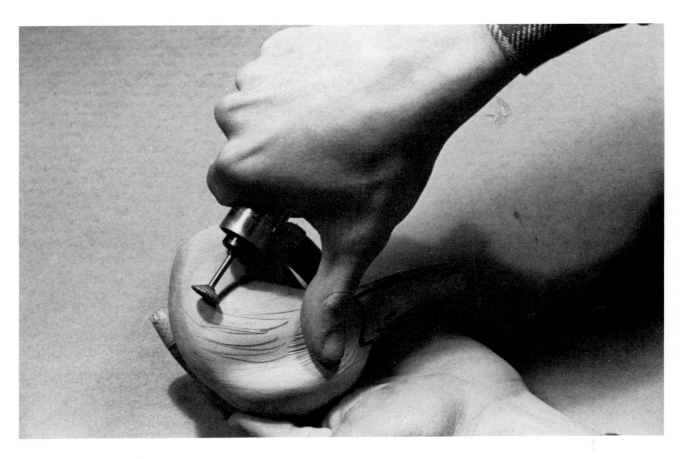

Fig. 289. The correct way to texture with the Foredom tool is to utilize the natural arc of your hand.
Fig. 290. Shows the incorrect method.

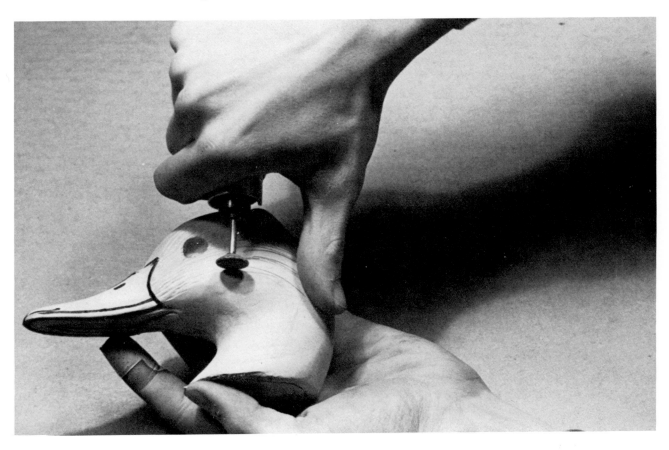

Fig. 291. Combine texturing techniques, if you wish, by burning feather outlines and quills and Foredom tool texturing the rest.

Fig. 292. Another texturing combination is to burn some of the feathers entirely and Foredom tool texture the rest.

well; run it in line with the texturing very lightly and at low speed so it does not cut into the wood.

6) After cleaning, spray the carving with Krylon 1301 again so that the wood will not burr up under the washes of paint.

7) Give a Foredom tool textured surface two thin washes of burnt umber followed by two thin white washes to provide a base for the paint colors. The burnt umber washes cover the wood more quickly than white washes. If you try to cover the surface with many coats of white, you will end up with a slick, shiny surface. (A burned surface is given just the two white washes because it is already darkened from the burning.)

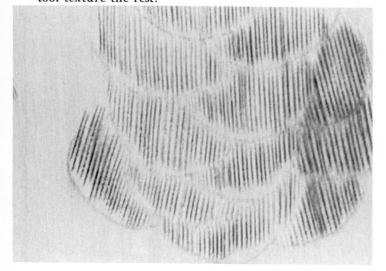

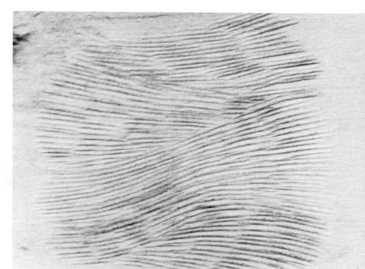

Fig. 293 & 294. Experiment with different texturing accessories on Foredom tool.

102

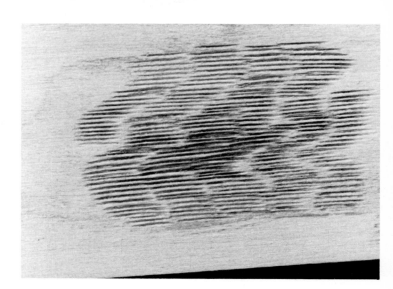

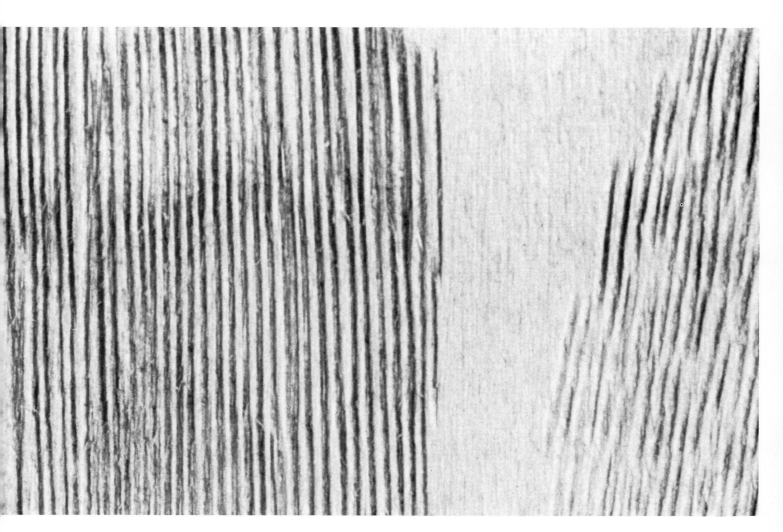

Figs. 295, 296, & 297. Practice different texturing
techniques with the Foredom tool.

Chapter 11
Making Seams That Really Hold

The Green-winged Teal hen will be made in two pieces, one for the head and one for the body. There are two reasons for this. (1) You would need a very large block of wood to make the carving in one piece. Wood is expensive; you would waste a lot of wood if you made it in one piece. (2) I like to turn the head on a bird carving just slightly to one side. If the bill is dead-straight, it looks too stiff. If you used one block of wood to carve this duck with its head slightly turned, something in the carving would have to be cut across the grain. It would probably be the bill or tail, the two weakest parts of the bird. This might work if you were using very hard wood, but for a waterfowl carving we don't.

Therefore, there will be a seam in this carving between the head and the body. One of the most important procedures in a carving that I've never seen sufficiently explained in any carving book is how to make seams. There is hardly any carving done without a seam somewhere. If the seam is not done right, all the work that has gone into making the carving will be for nothing.

Wood expands and contracts in direct proportion to atmospheric pressure. On a humid day, wood will expand. On a dry day, it will dry out and contract. Different types of wood expand and contract differently. They may not be the same age or from the same tree or location. There are all kinds of factors that will affect how much a piece of wood will expand and contract.

This fact has to be taken into consideration when two pieces of wood are joined. Visualize how a bird carving would look if the wood in it started to move. The paint would crack at the seam line and the carving would be a mess. Always use the same kind of wood; always have the grain flowing in the same direction on both pieces; and even then, don't expect glue to keep the two pieces from moving.

I've devised the following method of filling seams. The pieces of wood are glued together and a channel is cut along the seam to give "purchase area" for the fill. Wood plastic, preferably Wood Dough, is used as the fill. It is a bit elastic so it has enough resiliency to move with the wood. It is applied in a ¾ to 1-inch wide band across the seam. When the band is this wide, it will move with the wood. If it is narrower it won't keep the seam from showing.

Here's the way to make the seam. Sand the joining edges of the two pieces so they're flat and smooth. Glue them together with 5-minute epoxy and let it dry. With the channel cutter, cut a channel 1/8-inch wide and 1/8-inch deep along the seam line. (Figure 298) Sand the channel edges to get rid of any wood fuzz so it does not get into the Wood Dough.

Put about a ½-inch thick roll of Wood Dough along the channel. (Figure 299) Wet a soft brush with acetone and smear the Wood Dough into the channel as well as into a ¾ to 1-inch wide band that overlaps the channel. (Figure 300) Smooth it into the wood, making a featheredge. The smoother you get it with the acetone, the less sanding you'll have to do. Let it dry about 24 hours and then sand.

You could use moldable epoxy or auto-body filler if you need the seam to dry very quickly, but they are brittle, so they will probably crack over a period of time.

A note of caution here: If you sand all the way back to the channel, your seam will show. You must maintain a broad band of fill. (Figure 301) If you are able to see the line of fill inside the channel, chip out all the Wood Dough and refill.

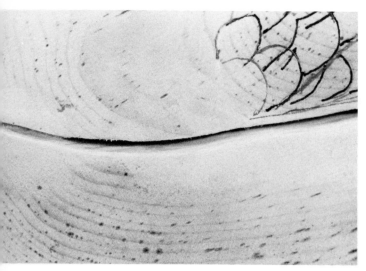

Fig. 298. Cut a channel 1/8-inch wide and 1/8-inch deep along the seam line.

Fig. 300. Wet a brush with acetone and smear Wood Dough into channel.

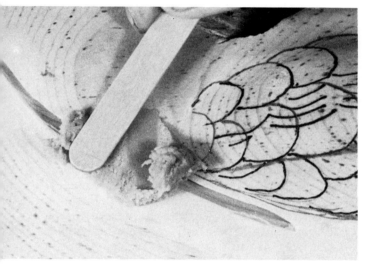

Fig. 299. Apply a large amount of Wood Dough onto channel.

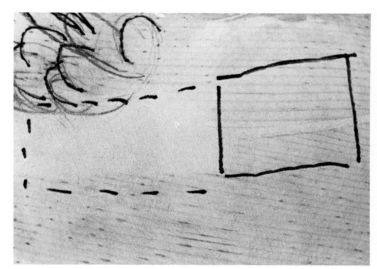

Fig. 301. Square indicates area where Wood Dough has been sanded too much. Broad band of fill (area outlined with dots) should overlap seam.

Chapter 12
Making Feather Inserts

Feather inserts, if used judiciously, add realism to a bird carving. When a bird sits on the water the tips of its primaries are raised. Using primary feather inserts on a flat-bottomed carving will duplicate this pose. When a bird extends its wings preparatory to taking flight, its primary and secondary feathers often are separated slightly. This position can only be duplicated by inserting feathers in the arms of the wings. The Ruddy duck has stiff, upright tail feathers. Tail feather inserts are often used when carving this duck.

There are all types of inserts, as you will discover in the forthcoming projects. You can even use a variety of inserts in the same carving. Many carvers, however, believe in using no inserts at all and call inserting feathers model-building. I believe that the use of inserts should be judicious, that they should be kept simple and well done. A good rule of thumb is: if in a given area five inserted feathers would fit, use four, with the exception of definite feather groupings such as primaries where there are always ten.

Inserts are generally inserted in a channel cut into the carving. If the channel-cutter disc can not be used, heat a flat piece of steel red hot with a propane torch and burn a channel. (Figure 302)

FLAT INSERTS

The simplest insert is flat and made from a piece of 1/32-inch or thinner piece of basswood or holly veneer. In Project Four there are two inserts, shaped and textured to resemble primaries lying one on top of another, simulating the raised tips of primaries on a floating duck. Inserts may also be individual primary, secondary, tertial or tail feathers cut out of veneer. Some people go so far as to insert every

feather on a duck, which makes a ridiculous looking carving because it's so overdone.

It is necessary to make a paper pattern for each individual insert to be used. The projects in this book that utilize inserts supply patterns for them. Insert the pattern into the channel to check that it looks the right size. If you're making a number of inserts, also check their patterns in the channel. Trace the pattern onto the veneer, following the grain line for extra strength, and cut it out with a knife. Fine-sand the edges of the veneer with 120-grit sandpaper to bevel them. (Sand the whole insert if it's unsanded veneer.) Draw on the feather pattern and burn or texture it in. Burn or texture the quills and barbs as well. You only need to show the feathers on the top side of an insert if it is the only side that is visible; otherwise, do both sides.

Check that the feather inserts fit inside the channel. If they don't, the channel isn't wide enough or deep enough and will need to be enlarged. On the other hand, if the inserts slide out, the channel is undoubtedly too large. In this case, put a wedge of wood inside the channel under the feathers to hold them against the top of the channel while you glue them.

Note: There must always be a smooth, flowing line from the body or arm of the wing to the inserts. The inserts must not bend upwards or look as if they're just glued on top of the wood, because they would not look realistic. Really study the inserts from all angles. If there's not a smooth transition, figure out why and what you can do to fix it. In many cases it's possible to build up the transition area between the body and the inserts with Wood Dough. If you had to use a wedge in the channel, fill the gaps under it with Wood Dough so there's a smooth, flowing line into the rump.

OTHER TYPES OF INSERTS

Sometimes an insert is not flat because a bird may have a curled feather, or you might want to give the feeling of motion with a bent feather.

You can curve an insert by boiling it for 10 to 15 minutes. Build a jig by driving parallel rows of nails into a board in the shape you want the feather to bend. Put the wet feather in the jig until it is dry. (Figure 304)

Twist an insert by boiling it 10 to 15 minutes, then putting a small C-clamp on each end. Anchor one clamp to a table edge and twist the other end until it is the shape you want and then anchor that clamp. Keep the feather in this position until it is dry.

An insert can also be slightly bent, and in this case, it is not made out of veneer. Draw the insert pattern on a block over one-inch thick and cut it out on a bandsaw. (Figure 305) Sand the top of the block and raise the quill and burn the barbs. (Figure 306) Cut this drawing off the block in a slice about 3/32-inch thick. (Figure 307) The feather is now slightly arced. Sand the underside of the feather and burn the texture into it. Now it has even more of an arc shape. (Figure 308) This method works because when you apply heat to a thin piece of wood, it bends on the side on which the heat is applied. The thinner the wood, the more it will arc.

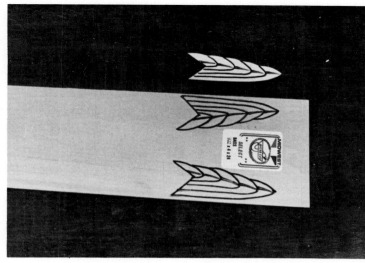

Fig. 303. A simple insert, made out of basswood veneer, resembles the primaries lying one on top of the other.

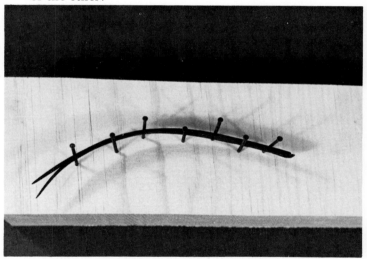

Fig. 304. Curve a flat feather by boiling it, then holding it in a jig in desired curvature.

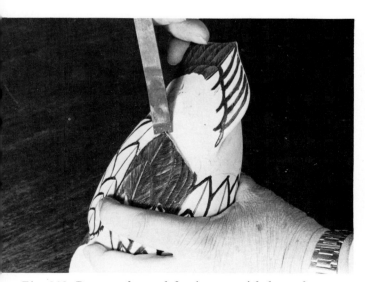

Fig. 302. Burn a channel for inserts with heated piece of steel.

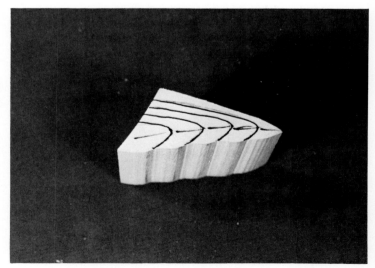

Fig. 305. To bend an insert, cut out plan view of insert on bandsaw.

Fig. 306. Burn the texture onto the block.

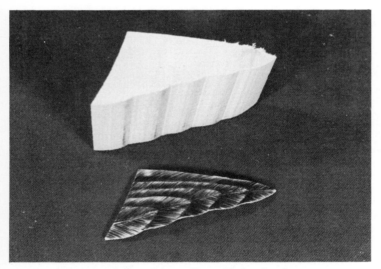

Fig. 307. With bandsaw, slice off the feather.

Fig. 308. When texture is burned into underside of insert, it bends in an arc shape.

The curling tail feather of the Mallard drake may be made from light gauge sheet lead or carved out of wood. Cut it to size from a pattern and texture it with a knife. Curve the end into the necessary curl.

INSERTING INSERTS

I glue inserts inside their channel with superglue. Superglue works best here because you don't have the bulk you get from other glues. You don't need much. It flows very readily, has good strength and dries quickly. Also, it's easier to break the line of dried superglue than dried epoxy if an insert ever needs to be replaced.

First seal the channel with Krylon 1301 so the superglue will adhere. (If you burned the channel, the burning seals the wood.)

An alternative method to using a channel is to glue the insert on top of the wood with epoxy and fill around it with Wood Dough to create a smooth transition. This is not an ideal method, but if you've made an unalterable error with the channel, this is a viable alternative to throwing away the carving.

Sometimes the inserts aren't put into their channel until everything is painted. This is true in Project Four. The reason is that it would be too difficult to paint the rump of the bird if the inserts were already attached. In most other applications, the inserts are glued in and painted as part of the carving.

↑ *Fig. 309.* Simple inserts may also be individual feathers cut out of veneer.

Fig. 310. This carving has inserted primaries and secondaries. ↓

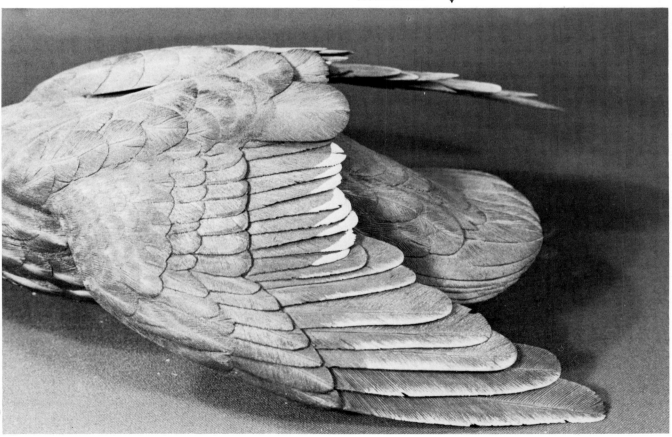

Chapter 13
Bills

At this point you should be able to progress to carving more realistic bills than you've made before. It is particularly important that you duplicate a live bird's bill exactly if you are planning to enter your carving in a show, for likeness to species is a criteria of judging. The novice carver, however, can get away with carving a satisfactory bill without including every single detail found in the actual bill. The bill of the Green-winged Teal hen in this project is a good example.

Do not fall into the trap of worrying that you can't carve a realistic bill and putting a cast bill, which you buy, on your carving. The principal advantage of cast bills is that they are an excellent reference for making bills. But if you use a cast bill on a carving, the carving will probably be disqualified in competition, and definitely will be if you're competing in the professional class.

Cast pewter bills are made in two pieces by Richard Delise (920 Springwood Drive, West Chester, PA. 19380). Plastic cast bills are made by Bob Bolle (26421 Compson, Roseville, Mich. 48066). Consider ordering some of these bills for study purposes.

CARVING A BILL

Remember that when you draw a head pattern on the block preparatory to bandsaw cutting, the bill must lie in line with the grain to have maximum strength.

Refer to the drawing of a bill (Figure 311) and keep the following points in mind when you carve a bill.

1) The forehead at the centerline extends into the bill in a V-shape.

2) The culmen is basically flat.

3) The distance between the points of the culmen where they meet the head should be about half the width of the bill.

4) The bill is made up of the lower mandible and upper mandible. Care must be taken to define the edges of the two mandibles.

5) The bill joins the head at the juncture of the lower mandible at three levels that can be seen from the bird's profile: (a) at the upper mandible; (b) at part of the edge of the lower mandible where it joins the head (everywhere else the edges of the upper mandible conceal the lower mandible when the bill is closed); (c) at a V of the chin where it joins the center of the lower mandible.

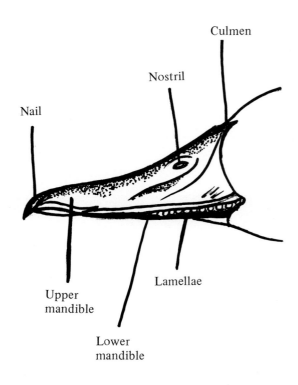

Fig. 311. Learn how to duplicate a live bird's bill.

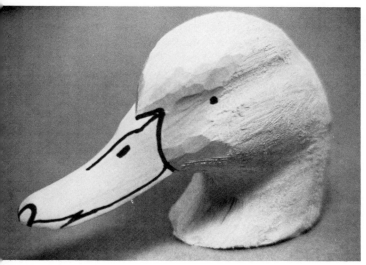

Fig. 312. A Mallard's head is carved and bill laid out for detailing.

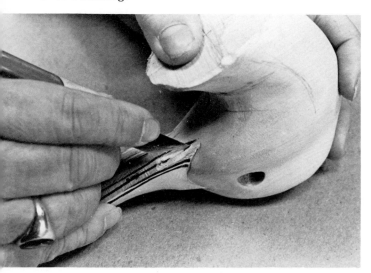

Fig. 313. Trace the lower mandible with knife, preparatory to separating it from upper mandible.

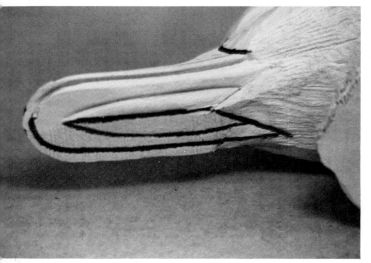

Fig. 314. On the underside of lower mandible, one side is completed and the other side is laid out.

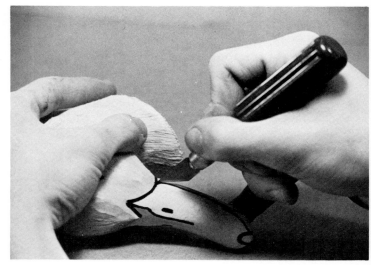

Fig. 315. Trace the line on the upper mandible with knife.

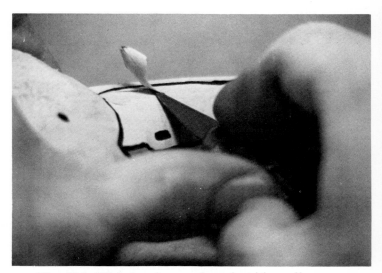

Fig. 316. With head turned on its side, relieve tiny sliver from edge of upper mandible.

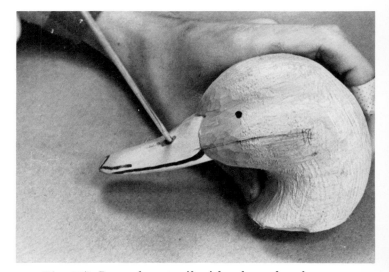

Fig. 317. Burn the nostril with a heated tool.

111

6) Looking at the underside of the lower mandible you can see a long V-shape depression in it. This is the skin-like membrane that serves as a pump. You can also see the separation between the mandibles.

7) The upper mandible of all birds is marked with thin lines.

The bill of the Green-winged Teal hen in this project will give you experience in bill carving.

SANDING THE BILL

In life, waterfowl bills are smooth and waxy. In carvings, bills should be sanded smooth and be slightly glossy. Many carvers sand bills super-smooth; in effect, making them look better than life. In my opinion, a super-smooth bill looks terrific but a little unnatural, so I don't sand it to that extreme. How much you sand the bill is entirely a matter of personal preference.

After the carving is done, sand the bill with a strip of 120-grit sandpaper. Wipe alcohol over the bill and sand again, this time using 180 or 220-grit. Wipe it again with alcohol and progress to an even finer sandpaper, and so on. The alcohol raises the fine nap of the wood, so it helps to make it very hard and smooth. Some people continue sanding until they finish with 600-grit sandpaper or 0000 steel wool. (This sanding technique may be used anywhere you want a carving to be super-smooth.)

Another method uses sanding sealer or shellac between sandings with 000 steel wool or buffers on the Foredom tool. Finish with 220-grit sandpaper.

NOSTRILS

Nostrils can always be formed by burning small indentations as you did in Projects Two and Three. In life, however, nostrils are elongated holes which lie at such an angle that they touch each other. You should actually be able to see light when you look through one nostril. Burn them with a piece of metal of the proper size and shape. (Figure 317)

There are always ridges around the nostrils. These can be duplicated by carving the bill to leave ridges in the wood or by forming them with epoxy putty. Make a long, thin roll of the epoxy, just as you do for eyelids, and align it around the nostril. (Figure 318) Crimp the edges into the wood and smooth it in with a wet brush. (Figure 319)

Some birds have indentations around the nostrils which are carved into the wood, using bill photos or drawings as reference.

NAIL

The nail of the bill is the small bump at the tip of both the upper and lower mandibles. I do not always make the nail on the underside because it is not very noticeable, but I always do it on a carving that I'm entering in a show.

There are three ways to create a nail. The first is to leave a small bump in the wood as you carve the bill. The second is to fashion the nail with moldable epoxy, let it dry and sand. The third method is to make it out of 5-minute epoxy after the bill is carved and sanded. One drop of epoxy from a popsicle stick onto the tip of the bill should be just enough to give the rounded appearance of the nail. (Figure 321) Do not touch the stick to the epoxy once it's on the bill because you may destroy the rounded shape. When it has dried, turn the head upside down and make the nail on the underside, if desired.

If you are not satisfied with the shape of a nail, chip it off or sand and try again.

OPEN BILL

Whenever you wish, you may carve the bill open instead of closed, but naturally, it takes more time to do.

Begin with a standard head pattern and shape the head and upper bill as usual. Then, at the point where the bill joins the head, cut to the upper mandible line with a knife, removing the lines delineating the lower mandible. Turn the head over and hollow the upper mandible with a small burr on the Foredom tool. (Figure 322) Sand the inside of the upper mandible smooth, beginning with the roll sander and finishing by hand.

Cut the lower mandible and tongue out of 1/8-inch basswood. The lower mandible is the same shape as the upper mandible, but smaller. Carve the details into the underside of the lower mandible as usual. The tongue is the same shape but smaller still. With a heated steel rod burn two channels 1/4-inch deep into the head at the juncture of the upper mandible, one for the tongue and a slightly wider one for the lower mandible. Check that they fit in these channels.

Burn in the nostrils and finish detailing the upper mandible. Paint the

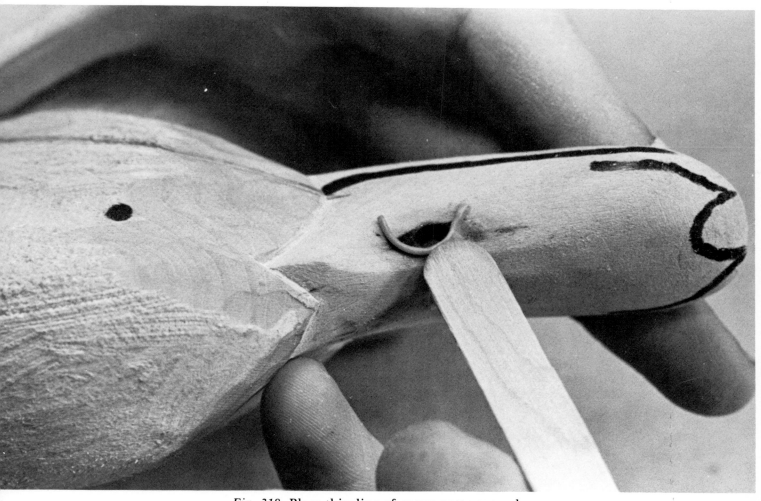

Fig. 318. Place thin line of epoxy putty around nostril and crimp it into wood.

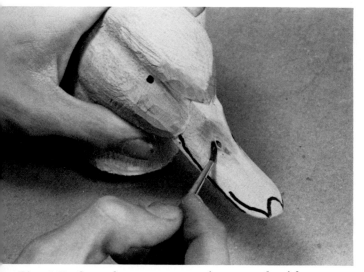

Fig. 319. Smooth epoxy putty into wood with damp brush.

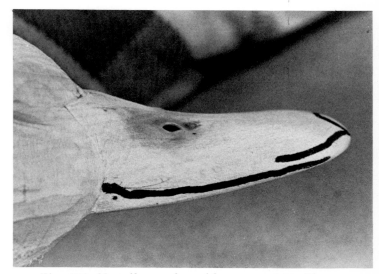

Fig. 320. Nostril now has ridge around it, like that of live birds.

Fig. 321. Create a nail on upper mandible with a drop of 5-minute epoxy on its tip.

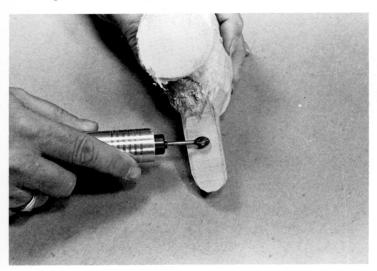

Fig. 322. The first step in making an open bill is to shape and then hollow out the upper mandible.

Fig. 323. Burn channels for the lower mandible and tongue with heated steel rod.

tongue and the inside of the bill while they're still separate, using birds for your reference. When they're dry, set the tongue and lower mandible in place, using superglue or 5-minute epoxy. With Wood Dough, fill the joint under the lower mandible where it joins the head. Form the V that's always found at this spot and texture it to resemble the feathers on the chin.

PAINTING BILL

Bills are normally painted with just a few coats of slightly thicker paint than the base washes used on the rest of the carving. Refer to the list of bill colors when painting. Finish by giving the bill a soft sheen with gloss medium. This sheen can also be obtained by painting the bill six or seven times and hand-rubbing it between coats.

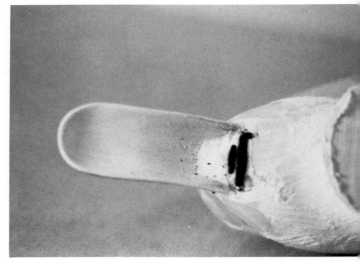

Fig. 324. The channels are the width of the tongue and the lower mandible.

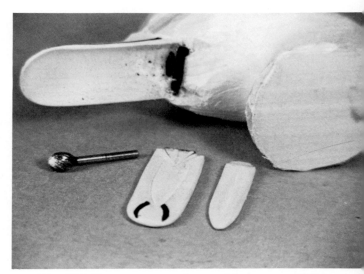

Fig. 325. Note tongue and carved lower mandible and the marks drawn on lower mandible for nail.

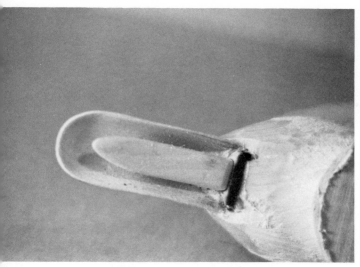

Fig. 326. Insert tongue in channel to check the fit.

Fig. 327. Check fit of lower mandible. Note area under it that needs to be filled with Wood Dough.

BILL COLORS OF SOME COMMON WATERFOWL

	MALE	FEMALE
Blue-winged Teal	black	dark gray at head, blended into black at tip, series of black dots in gray area
Cinnamon Teal	same as above	same as above
Green- winged Teal	same as above	same as above
Wood duck	red, white and black, banded with yellow along head	medium gray
Baldpate	blue-gray tipped with black	darker
Gadwall	black, orange along edge of upper mandible	orange mottled with brown
Pintail	black, blue-gray patch	medium gray
Shoveler	black	orange, mottled with brown
Mallard	yellow (use yellow ochre) black nail	orange, mottled down ridge with brown
Black duck	yellow to dark olive, may be mottled with black	same
Ruddy duck	bright blue in eclipse plumage, gray in winter plumage	gray, black nail
Canada goose	black	same
White fronted goose	pink	same
Lesser Snow & Blue goose	pink	same
Brant	black	same
Harlequin	blue-gray	same
Old Squaw	black, flesh color tip, black nail	same
Canvasback	black	brown-black
Bufflehead	blue-gray, black nail	a little darker
American Golden-eye	black	dark gray, orange near tip, black nail
Barrow's Golden-eye	black	dark gray, orange near tip, black nail
Greater & Lesser Scaup	blue, black nail	same
Redhead	blue, white band near tip, black tip	same
Ring-necked duck	blue gray, white band near tip. Tip black band, white border where bill joins head extending along lower edge of upper mandible	same
American Merganser	red, black ridge	black, orange on edges
Hooded Merganser	black	same
Red-breasted Merganser	black ridge, red sides	same

115

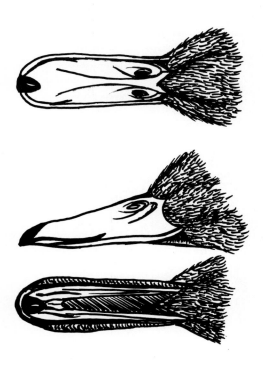

Fig. 328. Blue-winged Teal—F

Fig. 329. Blue-winged Teal—M

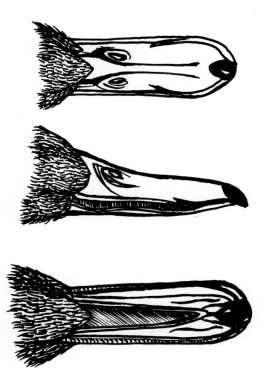

Fig. 330. Cinnamon Teal—F

Fig. 331. Cinnamon Teal—M

Fig. 332. Green-winged Teal—F

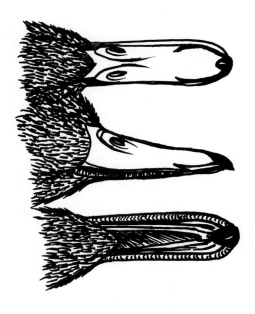

Fig. 333. Green-winged Teal—M

Fig. 334. Wood duck—F

Fig. 335. Wood duck—M

117

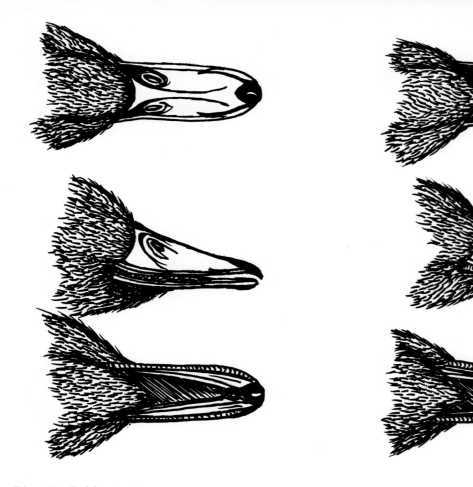

Fig. 336. Baldpate—F

Fig. 337. Baldpate—M

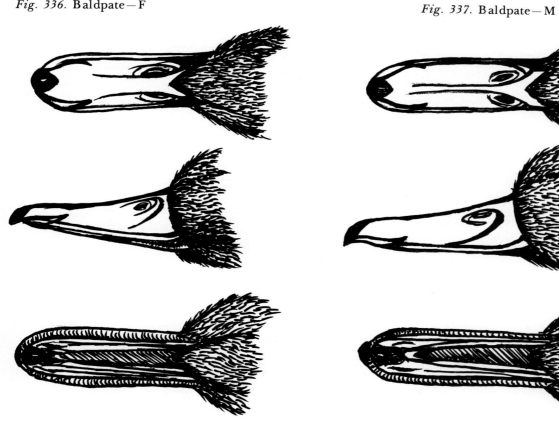

Fig. 338. Gadwall—F

Fig. 339. Gadwall—M

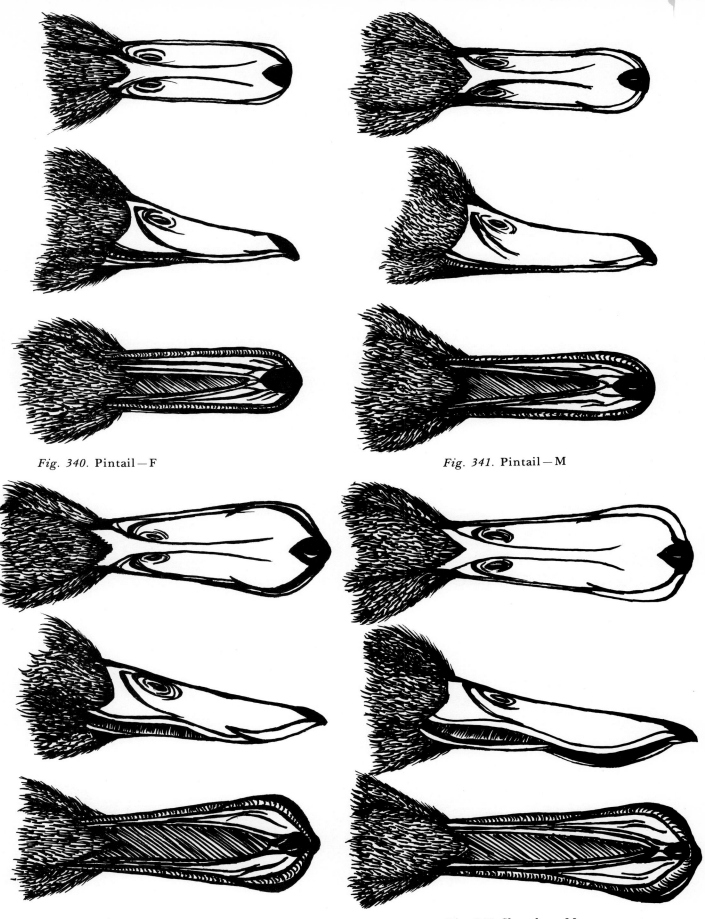

Fig. 340. Pintail — F

Fig. 341. Pintail — M

Fig. 342. Shoveler — F

Fig. 343. Shoveler — M

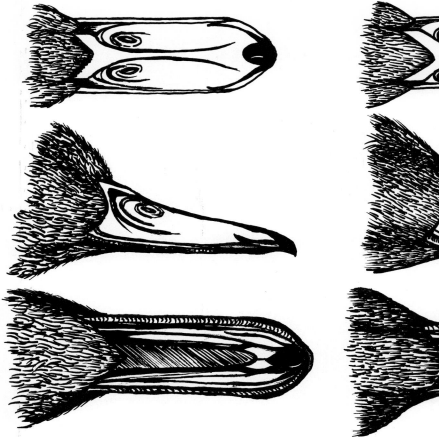

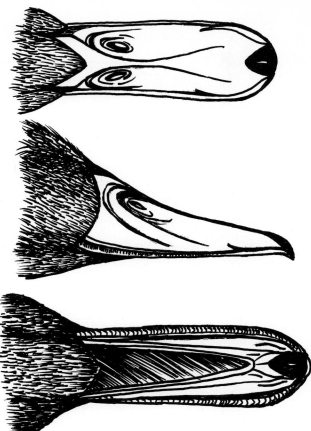

Fig. 344. Mallard—F

Fig. 345. Mallard—M

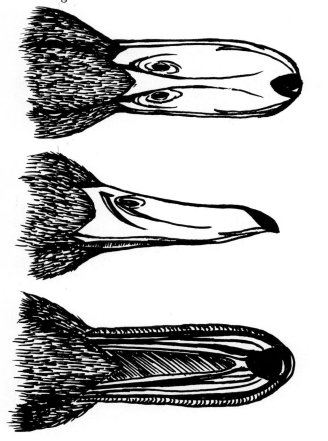

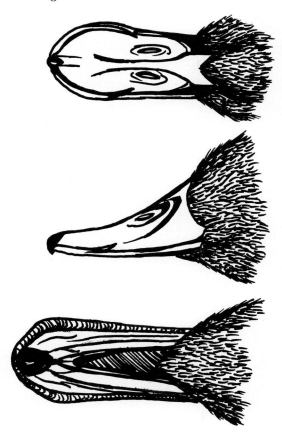

Fig. 346. Black duck—M

Fig. 347. Ruddy duck—M

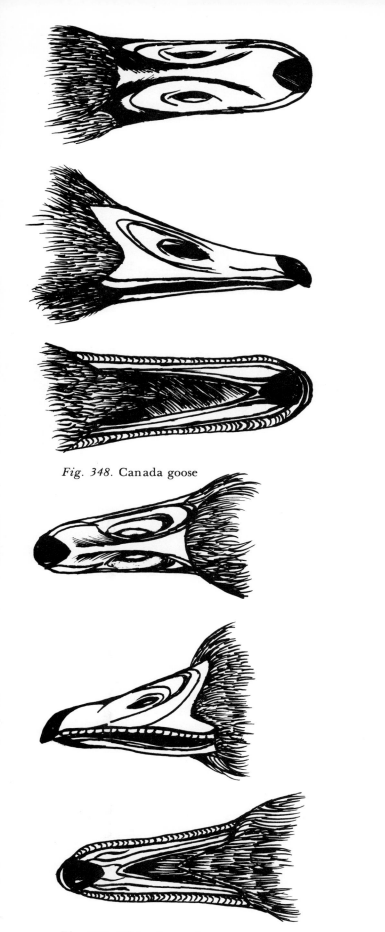

Fig. 348. Canada goose

Fig. 349. Brant (American or Black)

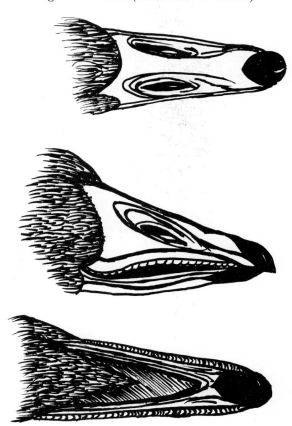

Fig. 350. White fronted goose

Fig. 351. Snow or Blue goose

Fig. 352. Harlequin—F

Fig. 353. Harlequin—M

Fig. 354. Old Squaw—F

Fig. 355. Old Squaw—M

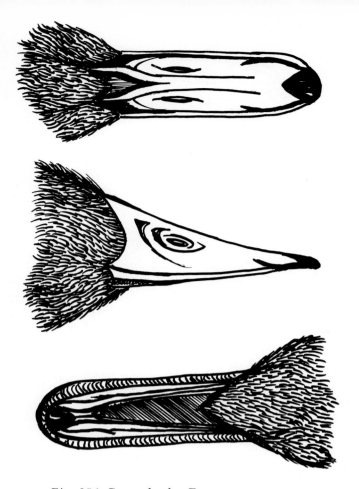

Fig. 356. Canvasback — F

Fig. 357. Canvasback — M

Fig. 358. Bufflehead — F

Fig. 359. Bufflehead — M

Fig. 360. American Golden-eye—F

Fig. 361. American Golden-eye—M

Fig. 362. Barrow's Golden-eye—F

Fig. 363. Barrow's Golden-eye—M

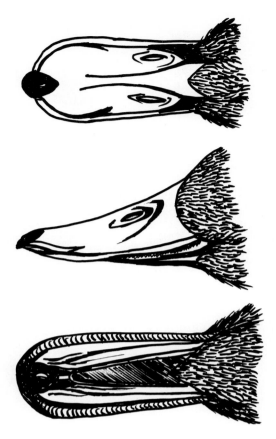

Fig. 364. Greater Scaup—F

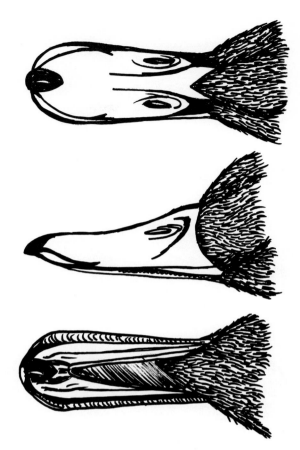

Fig. 365. Greater Scaup—M

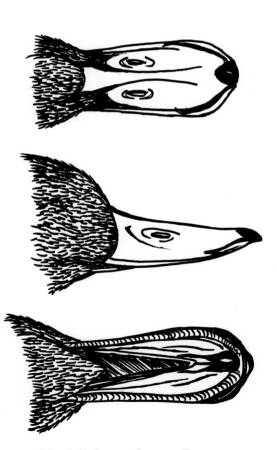

Fig. 366. Lesser Scaup—F

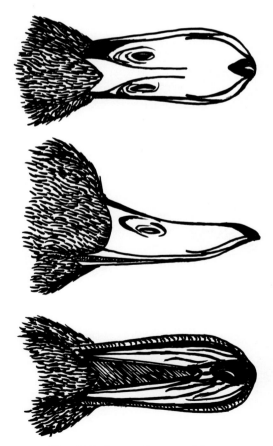

Fig. 367. Lesser Scaup—M

125

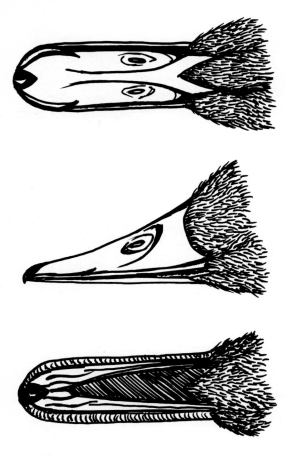

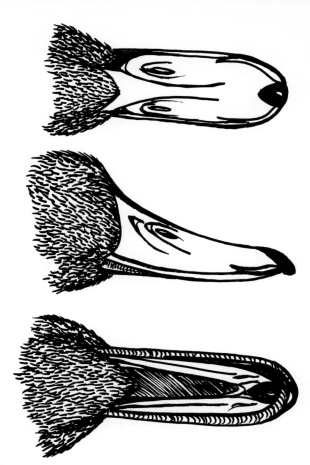

Fig. 368. Redhead—F

Fig. 369. Redhead—M

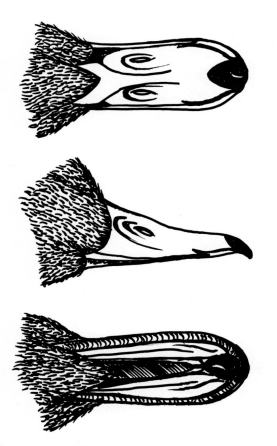

Fig. 370. Ring-necked duck—F

Fig. 371. Ring-necked duck—M

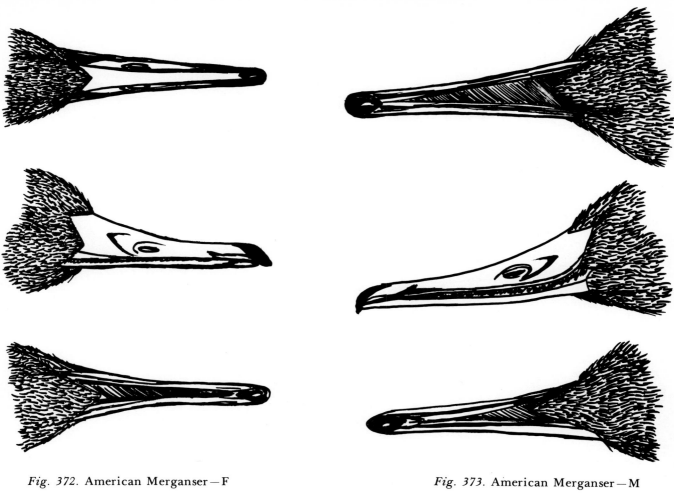

Fig. 372. American Merganser—F

Fig. 373. American Merganser—M

Fig. 374. Hooded Merganser—F

Fig. 375. Hooded Merganser—M

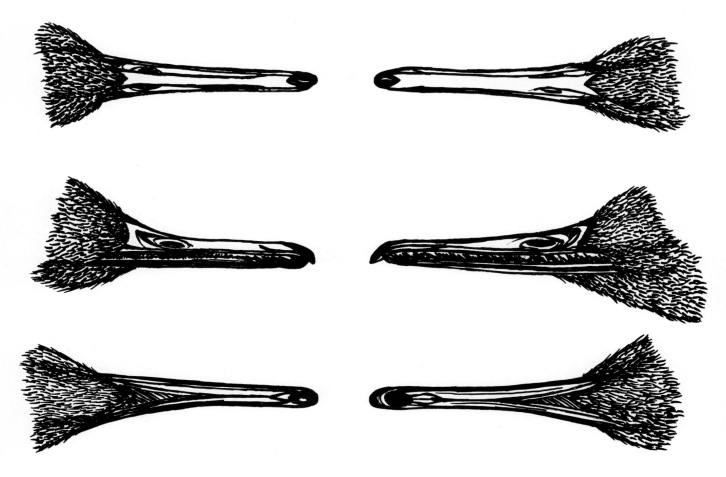

Fig. 376. Red-breasted Merganser — F

Fig. 377. Red-breasted Merganser — M

Chapter 14
Floating Decorative Carvings

If you are interested in competition with a flat-bottomed bird such as the Green-winged Teal hen, you'll have more chance of winning a ribbon if you turn it into a floating decorative. A flat-bottomed bird rarely wins a ribbon in the decorative category because it's competing against carvings that are more elaborate and intricate with feet and a display built around them. The only other division in which a flat-bottomed bird has a chance of winning is in the floating decorative decoy division, but to compete, it must be able to float.

A floating decorative carving differs from a hunting decoy because of that one word--decorative. A hunting decoy is very plain and made just for working purposes while a floating decorative carving can be as decorative as you wish, with texturing, inserts, etc.

Floating decoratives evolved from hunting decoys. In fact, at one time there was a competition division called decorative decoys in which the entries had to be rigged and keeled like hunting decoys. These rules changed in time so that floating decoratives no longer have to resemble hunting decoys. They have become so popular that their division at carving shows generally has had to be broken down into different waterfowl species.

Whether they are to float or not, all flat-bottomed birds are shaped and carved in the same way, with one important exception. A carving that is supposed to float must be hollow inside to be buoyant. It must also balance from front to back and side to side. To accomplish this, you often have to weight the carving.

HOLLOWING

Carve and shape your flat-bottomed bird. Get a piece of ¼-inch marine plywood or basswood. Trace the bottom of the bird on the board. (Figure 378) Remove the bird, and draw a new line 3/8 inch in from your traced line (Figure 379) on the board. With a bandsaw, cut the board on this second line. This is the insert plate.

Place the insert plate on the bottom of the bird and trace around it. (Figure 380) Draw a new line 3/8 inch from that traced line. (Figure 381)

The bird is hollowed out inside that second line with a drill press. If you don't own a press, use a Foredom tool with a round ball bit, a hand drill with a spade bit, or a chisel. Start from the second line and work toward the center, keeping in mind that you want to leave a wall on all sides about ½-inch thick. (Figure 382) The body block must be hollowed evenly to balance. (Figure 383)

The two lines you drew on the block become the ledge on which the insert plate rests. Trace around the outer line with a

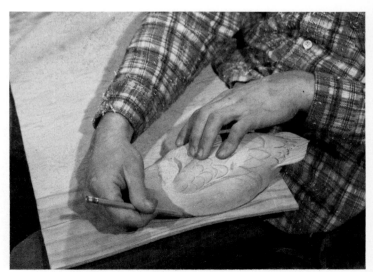

Fig. 378. Trace the bottom of bird on piece of ¼-inch marine plywood.

129

Fig. 379. Draw a new line 3/8-inch in from the traced line.

Fig. 382. Hollow the body block within the second line.

Fig. 380. Cut board on bandsaw and trace around it onto the bottom of bird.

Fig. 383. Be sure the body is hollowed evenly, leaving a wall all around about ½-inch thick.

Fig. 381. Draw a new line 3/8-inch in from that traced line.

Fig. 384. Trace the outer line with a knife.

knife. (Figure 384) Then, with a square bit on the Foredom tool, cut a ledge that stops at the outer line and is the depth of the insert plate. (Figure 385) The ledge is the correct depth when the insert plate fits into it and the bottom of the bird is level.

WEIGHTING

Weighting is done after the head is set and the shaping is completed.

Put the plate in the bird. Select a flat lead weight of any size. Attach it to the bird bottom with a rubber band. Put the bird inside a plastic bag, close it tightly and float it in a tank of water.

Note: To float the bird, find a place big enough so you can see it from all angles. I once floated a large carved goose in the bathtub and it seemed well-balanced. But when it floated in the tank in a competition, it listed horribly to one side. My error was that I never had a good view of the goose in the tub. Now, if I do such a large carving, I put a torpedo level on its back to check if it's balanced side to side.

Keep moving the lead around and add more or take away some as necessary until the bird is perfectly balanced from front to back and side to side.

When it is balanced, remove the bird from the bag and trace around the lead with a pencil. You could glue the lead in this spot and not lose any points for it, but you'll be prouder of your work if you conceal the lead inside. This isn't difficult to do, but it's important to do it accurately.

With a ruler or any straight-edge, extend the lines made around the lead to the outside edges of the plate. (Figure 388) Remove the piece of lead and write "outside" where it had been, so you will not confuse this side with the inside of the plate. (Figure 389)

Fig. 385. With square bit, cut a ledge the depth of the insert plate.

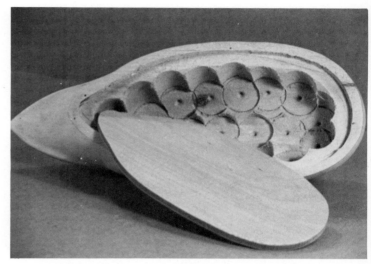

Fig. 386. Block is hollowed and insert plate can be set in place.

Fig. 387. Insert plate should be level with the bottom edges.

131

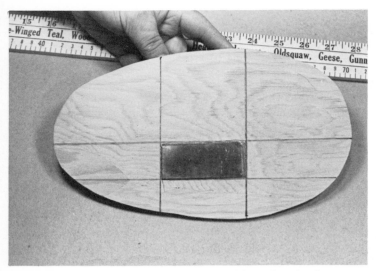

Fig. 388. After determining position for lead weight, trace around it and extend lines to edges.

Hold the ruler under the plate and align it on both ends with one penciled line. Scribe a line along the ruler edge. Move the ruler so it's aligned with a second penciled line and scribe another line along the ruler edge. Repeat until all four lines are scribed. Turn the board over and you'll find that you've outlined the exact spot where the lead must be glued on the inside of the board. (Figure 390) Glue the lead there with a liberal amount of 5-minute epoxy.

Put the bird in the plastic bag again to confirm that it is well-balanced. If it isn't, keep trying. Once it is balanced, glue the plate in place with 5-minute epoxy, make a channel and fill the seam with Wood Dough and acetone. Sand the bottom smooth. Apply several coats of polyurethane or Zar to the bottom so it is totally sealed and protected against water.

Warning! Do not ever put polyurethane or any other sealer inside a hollow bird because you'll seal the natural moisture of the wood inside the bird, and that will eventually crack the wood and paint. The wood needs to breathe.

Fig. 389. Mark that spot "outside" so you do not confuse the sides of insert plate.

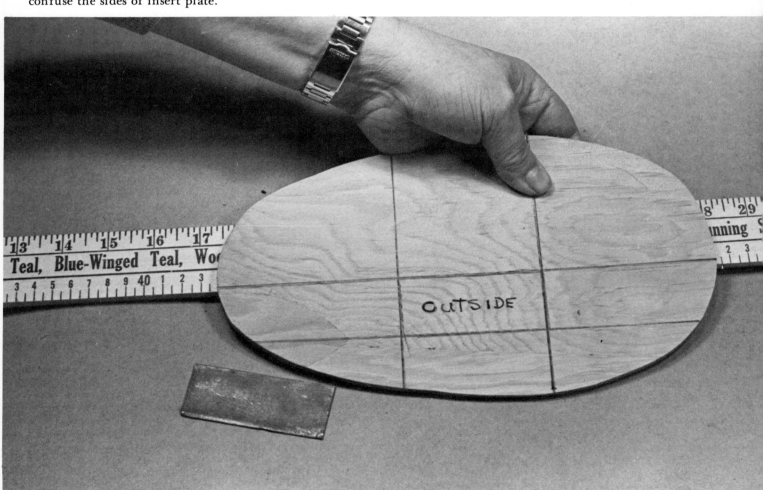

Before entering the carving in a show, float it once again to check its balance. If it is unbalanced, hold a piece of lead on the bottom of the carving with a wide rubber band (Figure 391) to find the amount and position needed for the additional piece of lead. Finally, glue the lead onto the bird bottom.

There is no rule that says a floating decorative has to be flat-bottomed. It can be a full bird with carved wood feet if you wish. In this case, you'd still have to hollow the bird, starting with two pieces of wood instead of one solid body block. Finish making the bird before experimenting with it in water. Attach the lead to the bottom of the inside of the bird, using the same method as you used on the flat-bottomed bird. Finally, glue the two pieces together, cut a channel to widen the seam, and fill it.

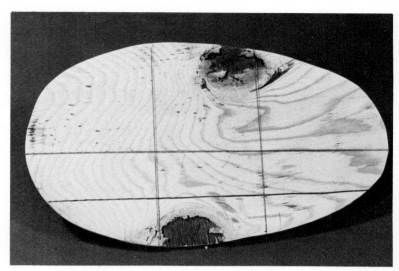

Fig. 390. Scribe those lines on other side of insert plate to find exact placement for lead weight in inside of bird.

Fig. 391. If carving is still unbalanced attach lead with a rubber band and float once again.

Chapter 15
Carving a Green-winged Teal Hen

The Green-winged Teal is the smallest of the ducks, so you can do a lifesize carving of it relatively easily and quickly. My philosophy in teaching is that you will develop more rapidly if you carve something small and move right on to the next project than if you do a large carving.

Another reason why I chose this project is that carvers generally consider hens difficult to paint. Early in my carving career I found them so impossible to paint that I spent a great deal of time studying and working on hen carvings. Now I believe that the techniques I use to paint hens make them easier to paint than drakes.

To make the Green-winged Teal hen you will need two blocks of basswood. You can also use pine, but you must be very careful when you work on it. The block for the body should be 4½ x 10 x 3-inches. The block for the head should be 3 x 4 x 1 5/8-inches. I shape the head and body with hollow rasps on the Foredom tool but you can use a 2½-inch bladed knife and surform rasps instead.

CARVING THE HEAD

Draw the profile of the head on the basswood, laying the bill in line with the grain of the wood. (Some carvers make the Green-winged Teal hen head out of a 1½-inch block, but I prefer to use a slightly larger block so the bird looks cheeky instead of skinny and gaunt.)

Looking at figure 393, note: Point 1, where the point of the forehead extends into the bill and Point 2, where the point of the chin extends into the lower mandible.

Bandsaw the profile of the head, cutting it exactly on the line. Measuring carefully, draw the plan view (Figure 394) on the head and cut it out. Follow the dotted lines and directional arrows so you do not cut away the chin and cheek areas.

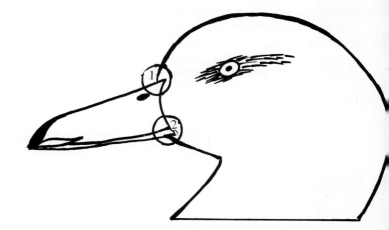

Fig. 393. Profile of Green-winged Teal hen's head

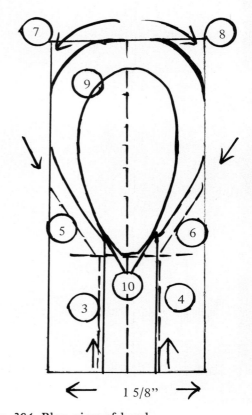

Fig. 394. Plan view of head

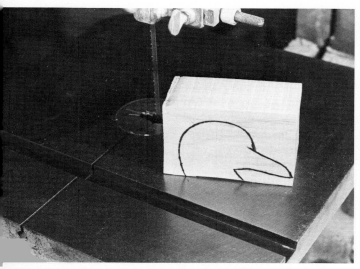

Fig. 395. Draw the profile view of head on block of wood.

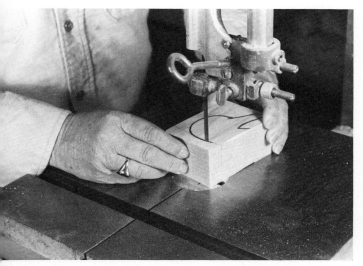

Fig. 396. Use bandsaw to cut out profile, cutting exactly on the lines.

Fig. 397. Draw the plan view on the head block and cut it out.

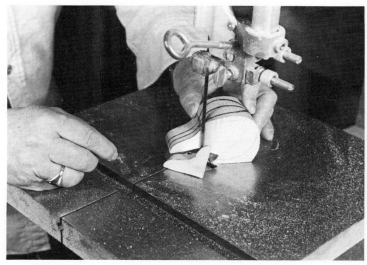

Fig. 398. Trim the excess wood from the head block.

Fig. 399. The head is now ready to be shaped.

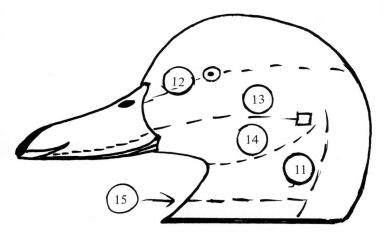

Fig. 400. Draw guidelines on both sides of head.

135

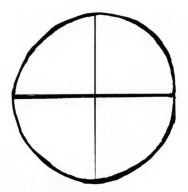

Fig. 401. Draw circle on bottom of head.

Trim the excess wood off the corners. (Figure 398)

If you have not already done so, draw the centerline down the back of the head and under the bill. It is a finite point of reference and the head's exact profile, and should remain the same throughout the carving procedure. Another finite point of reference is the bill width.

Referring to figure 400, draw the numbered points on one side of the head block and repeat on the other side. Trace the circle in figure 401 on the bottom of the head. This circle is another point of reference. Occasionally hold the head in such a way that you can "eyeball" whether everything is balanced along the centerline down the back of the head and the centerline on the bottom of the head. The circle will also be your guideline for shaping the sides of the head.

From line 11 on both sides of the head round the back of the block to the centerline that runs down the back of the head. (Figure 402) When you're done, the back of the head will have a nice arc shape. (Figure 403) Use a ½-inch hollow rasp on the Foredom tool or your knife.

The eye channel (#12) is formed between line 13 on the cheek and line 9 on the crown. It runs from the bill to the end of the crown at the back of the head. If you're using a knife, create the eye channel by scooping out the wood. If you're using a ½-inch hollow rasp, slide it along the line to remove the wood. (Figure 404) Keep checking that the eye channels are symmetrical by eye-balling the head from the front and the back. (Figure 405)

Round the area under the chin and shape the neck. This is done by working around the front of the head from line 11 on one side to line 11 on the other side. If you're using a rasp, slide it along this area

as shown in figure 406. If you're using a knife, scoop upwards or downwards according to the grain line from the centerline under the bill to line 11. Smooth out any ridges remaining on the neck.

Mark the high point of the cheek (indicated by the small square in figure 400). Shave the cheek to round it from front to back and from top to bottom. (Figure 408) You will just barely shave off the mark for the high point. Do not go beyond line 11 because there must be a roundness left in the back of the neck to flow into the body.

After both cheeks are rounded, smooth out any ridge left around line 11.

Now the crown has very sharp edges. First shave off those edges (Figure 410) and then round the crown to the centerline. (Figure 411)

The bill is still very square. Using a rasp or knife, cut into the area at the edge of the culmen so the eye channels appear to flow into the bill. (Figure 412) Then round the bill from the edges of the lower mandible to the centerline of the upper mandible, (Figure 413) leaving the underside of the bill squared off and flat. Do not cut into the culmen. It is now the only flat area on the top of the bill.

Draw a short line following the slope of the bill back into the head on both sides of the head. Place your knife blade flat on the bill and cut into the head along one of these lines. (Figure 414) Repeat on the other line. Cut down to the first cut with the knife at a 45° angle to the centerline, relieving a small piece of wood. (Figure 415) When this cut is taken on the other side of the culmen, the forehead at the centerline extends into the bill in a V. (Figure 416)

Turn the head over so you can work on the underside of the bill. Looking at figure 418, trace lines A and B with your knife, the lines C and D, and finally, lines E and F.

Lay your knife flat where line X meets the intersection of lines A and B. Make a back cut toward the head along line A, starting with no depth and going to about 1/16-inch depth where line A meets the head. Repeat on line B. This raises a little V on the chin where it joins the lower mandible. Round the sharp edges of the V working toward the bill, leaving the centerline as the high point.

Lay the knife flat at line Y on the outer edge of the bill beyond line C. Make

Fig. 402. With rasp or knife, round the back of the head.

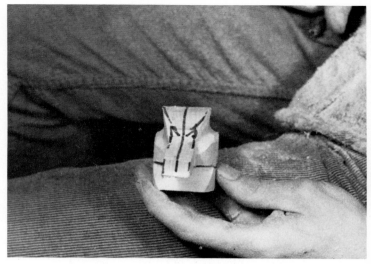

Fig. 405. The eye channels should be symmetrical.

Fig. 403. You're finished when the back of the head has a nice arc shape.

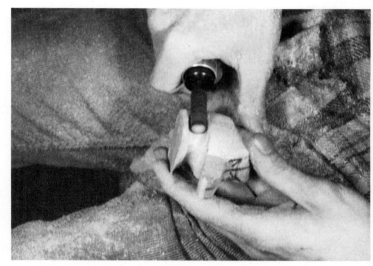

Fig. 406. Round the area under the chin and shape the neck.

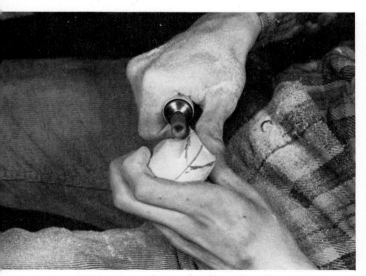

Fig. 404. Slide rasp along the line for the eye channel.

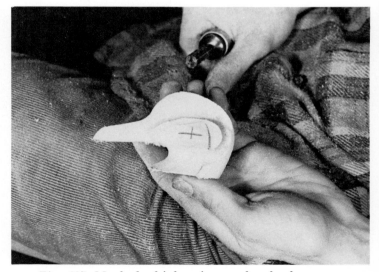

Fig. 407. Mark the high point on the cheek.

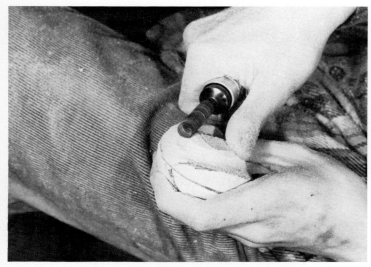

Fig. 408. Shave the cheek to round it from front to back and top to bottom.

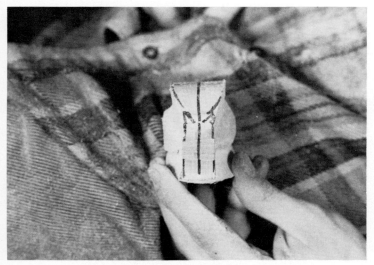

Fig. 409. One cheek is rounded while the other is still flat.

Fig. 410. Shave the squared edges of crown.

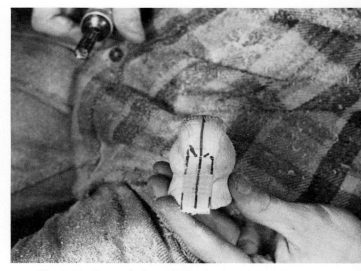

Fig. 411. Round the crown to the centerline on both sides.

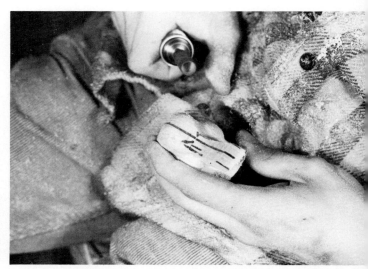

Fig. 412. Cut into area at edge of culmen so eye channels appear to flow into bill.

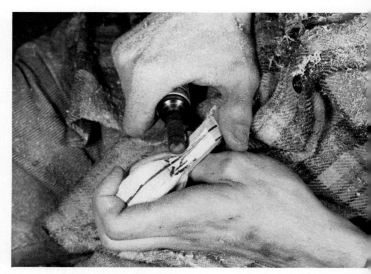

Fig. 413. Round bill from edges of lower mandible to centerline of upper mandible.

a back cut toward the head along the edge of the bill into line C, making a 90° cut to line C. Then, at point A, cut the piece you've just relieved to make it pop out. This cut defines the upper mandible and allows a slight bit of the edge of the lower mandible to show as in point 20 in figure 417. Repeat on the other side. Now the three levels where the bill joins the head are visible on the head profile.

Run your knife along the outside edge of line C working toward the tip of the bill at about a 45° angle to relieve a small sliver between it and the outer edge. Repeat on line D. This cut delineates the separation of the upper and lower mandibles.

Relieve a small sliver from inside lines E and F, creating the V-shaped depression in the lower mandible. This is the skin-like membrane that serves as a pump.

Sand the head smooth with a strip of 120-grit coated abrasive.

Mark the position of the eye cavities. Drill holes for 7 mm. hazel eyes. Check that the holes are big enough for the eyes; do not set them until after the head is textured.

Cut in line 17 in figure 417 by tracing it with a knife. Relieve a small sliver from the bill side of the cut.

Draw lines 18 and 18A, trace them with a knife and relieve from above the cut. You can trace them with a burning pen instead, but this isn't as neat a method.

Draw the nostrils. Heat a narrow dental spatula or knife blade red hot and

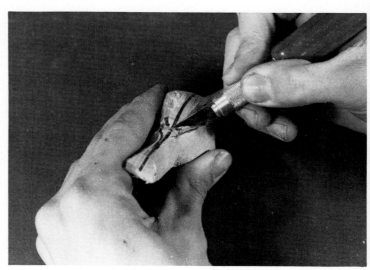

Fig. 415. Cut down to first cuts to relieve a small sliver of wood.

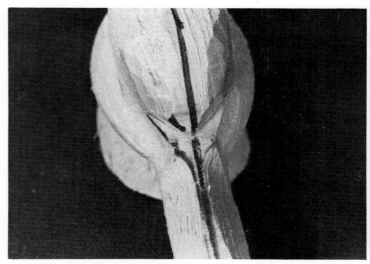

Fig. 416. Head is now ready to be sanded.

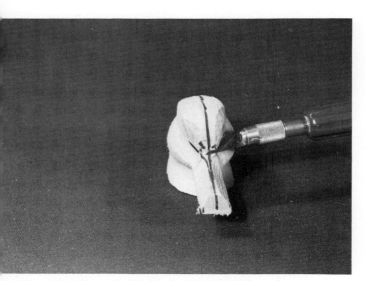

Fig. 414. Place knife blade flat on bill and cut back into head along drawn lines.

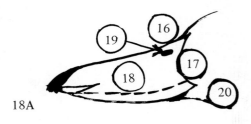

Fig. 417. Note position of nostrils and other bill markings on bill profile.

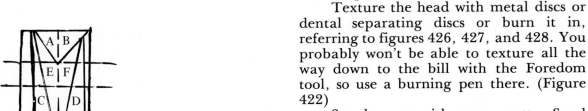

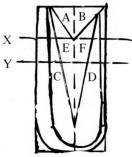

Fig. 418. Carve underside of bill along the marked lines.

burn small indentations to simulate nostrils. (Figure 420) (If you wish, you can make more elaborate nostrils with ridges, following the instructions in Chapter 13.)

Texture the head with metal discs or dental separating discs or burn it in, referring to figures 426, 427, and 428. You probably won't be able to texture all the way down to the bill with the Foredom tool, so use a burning pen there. (Figure 422)

Set the eyes with epoxy putty. Sand the bill smooth and create a nail at the tip of the bill with 5-minute epoxy. (Figure 423)

Fig. 419. After head is fully sanded and carved, draw guidelines to aid in texturing.

Fig. 421. Head is finished. Note epoxy putty smoothed around eyes and burned lines of bill.

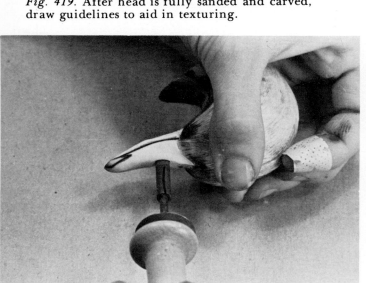

Fig. 420. With Hot Tool, burn indentations for nostrils. This can also be done after bill is carved.

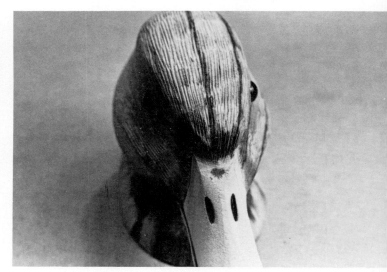

Fig. 422. Note flattish area of culmen and positioning of nostrils.

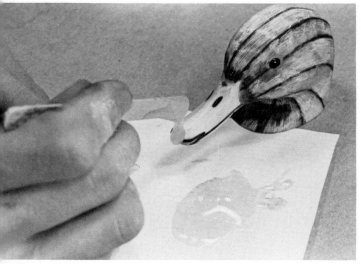

Fig. 423. With popsicle stick, drop 5-minute epoxy onto top of bill to form nail.

Fig. 424. Note carving of under-bill and burning of area around bill.

Fig. 425. When Foredom tool can't reach an area, texture it with burning pen.

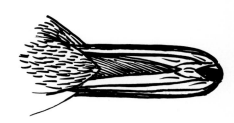

Figs. 426 — 428. Texture head with a burning pen or Foredom tool, referring to texturing patterns.

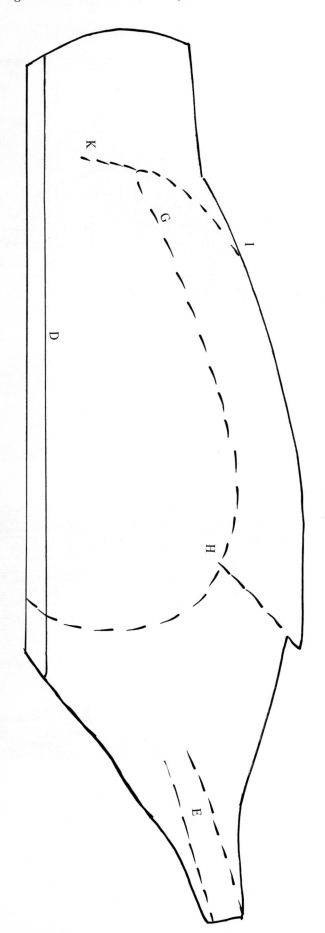

Fig. 429. Profile of hen's body

CARVING BODY

Draw the profile view of the body (Figure 429) on one side of the block and the plan view (Figure 433) on the top of the block, keeping them aligned. Since this is a flat-bottomed bird, the bottom of the profile is the bottom side of the block.

Cut out the plan view first. (Figure 431) Hold the cut-off pieces on the block and cut out the profile view. (Figure 432) Trim off the excess wood on the bandsaw, or use a drawknife or surform rasp. (Figure 434)

Draw guidelines on the block, following figures 429 and 433. (A) centerline down the back; (B) the circle for the head; (C) the body line above and under the tail; (D) the dotted line near the bottom of the block, on both sides of the block; (E) tail guidelines; (F) the oval on the bottom of the block (Figure 448). These guidelines will help you shape the body and keep it balanced.

With a ½ or ¾-inch hollow rasp on the Foredom tool, round the block from the centerline on the back to line D on both sides. This also can be done with a surform rasp, drawknife or 2½-inch bladed knife. Just round the block gradually, not sharply, so that when you look at it from the chest it will resemble the drawing on the left instead of the one on the right. (Figure 437) As you cut away the excess wood on the tail, the rump and under-rump begin to flow into the tail.

Draw more guidelines on the rounded body block, referring to the drawings, beginning with letter G. These guidelines simulate the way the wings are folded onto the body and should be drawn in the same way on both sides. (Figure 438)

With a ½ or ¾-inch hollow rasp on the Foredom tool, cut in the guidelines you made for the folded wings. Begin at point G, cutting it in at a depth of ¾-inch. Proceed to H, gradually reducing the depth so you cut ¼-inch deep at H, and continue around the ball to the end of the line. Repeat this procedure from G, cutting at ½-inch depth as you proceed to I, and then to J where you're cutting at no depth. Lay the rasp on G and cut at ½-inch depth down to no depth at all at K. Repeat these steps on the other side of the body. (Figure 440)

Now the body has hills and valleys that need to be smoothed out. The dotted line L represents the high point on the sides. Round the body by rolling a rasp

Fig. 430. Draw the plan view on one side of the
block and the profile view on the other side.

Fig. 431. Cut plan view on bandsaw first.

Fig. 432. Hold the cut pieces on the block as you
cut out the profile view.

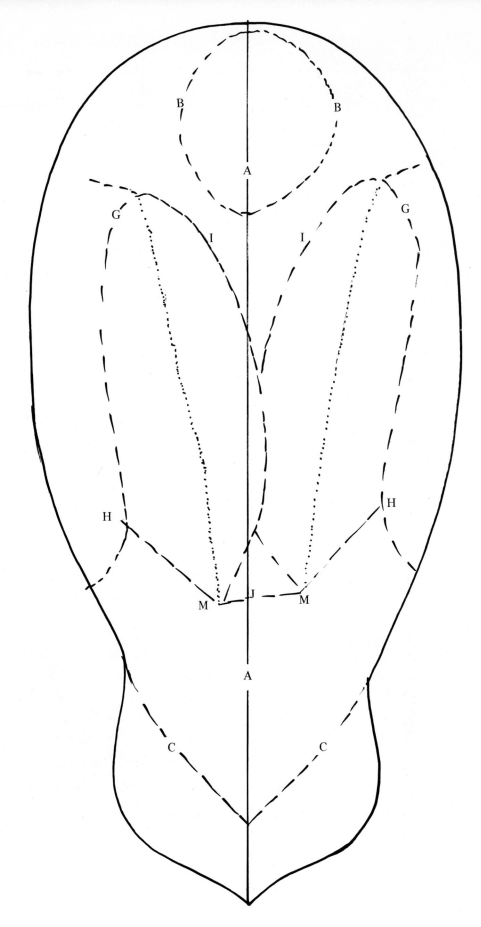

Fig. 433. Plan view of hen's body

Fig. 434. Tilt bandsaw table to trim excess wood from the block.

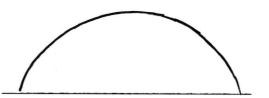

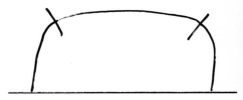

Fig. 437. Round the block so it has the shape of the drawing on left, not the one on the right.

Fig. 435. Draw tail guidelines "E" and body line "D" on block.

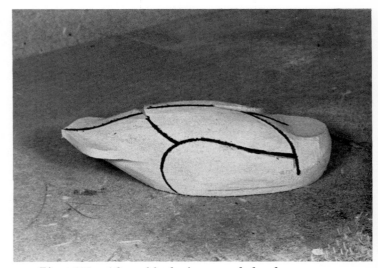

Fig. 438. After block is rounded, draw on guidelines beginning with "G".

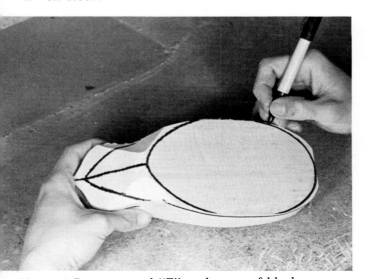

Fig. 436. Draw an oval "F" on bottom of block.

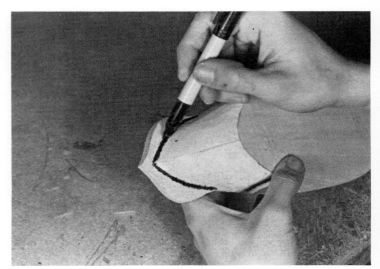

Fig. 439. Take tail down to 1/8-inch thickness, keeping a balance on each side of centerline so it is not crooked.

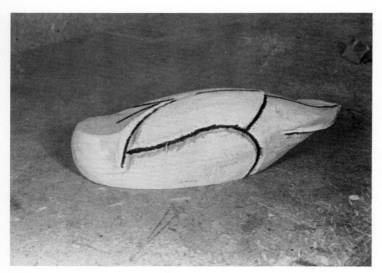

Fig. 440. With a rasp, cut in the guidelines to simulate the way the wings are folded onto the body.

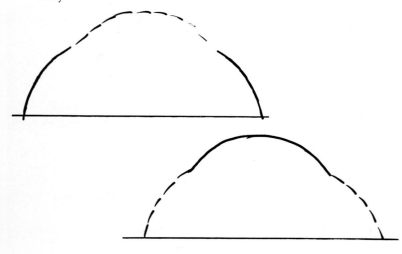

Fig. 441. Round the back of block so it has the shape of the drawing on left, not the one on right.

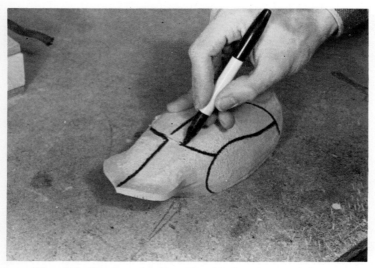

Fig. 442. Draw guideline H—M for the tertials and secondaries.

across it. Round the chest by rounding up from line D to the center of the chest. When you finish, the back should resemble the drawing on the left in figure 441, not the one on the right.

Draw the guideline, marked H-M, for the tertials and secondaries. (Figure 442) Working from the rump, cut along the edge of this line with the rasp and extend it to the centerline to create a ledge under which you will later make a channel for the primary inserts. (Figure 444)

Roughly sand the body with 80-grit sandpaper. Fine-sand with 120-grit until the body is smooth.

Lay out on the body block the feather pattern shown in figures 443 and 447. Note that some of the feathers do not have raised quills. On live birds, all feathers have quills, but they are often invisible to the naked eye. Therefore, it isn't necessary to put quills in these feathers on a carving. Burn or carve in the feather pattern. (Figure 446) Figure 448 shows the underside of the tail feathers if you wish to include them on the carving.

Spray the wood with Krylon 1301.

Using a texturing disc or burning pen, texture the block. Within all the feathers that have a quill, the barbs should flow from the quills toward the back of the feather. On the rump and chest, texture with flowing straight lines over the burned arcs. Texture the under-rump with straight lines.

ATTACHING HEAD AND BODY

Set the head on the body, turning the head just slightly in either direction so the bill is not dead-straight. Trace around the neck onto the body. Set the head aside and flatten the spot for the head on a drill press or with a rasp on the Foredom tool. (Figure 452) When you're satisfied with the fit, attach the head with 5-minute epoxy. Let it dry. Sand or rasp the head and body where they meet, if necessary, so the head appears to flow into the chest.

Cut a channel with the channel cutter all around the seam line. Fill the seam with Wood Dough. Wet a brush with acetone and saturate the Wood Dough as you smear it into the channel and feather it into the wood. Let it dry, then sand the neck joint smooth. Remember to maintain the broad band of fill. Burn in the outlined feathers that are covered by the Wood Dough. Retexture, using a sharpened

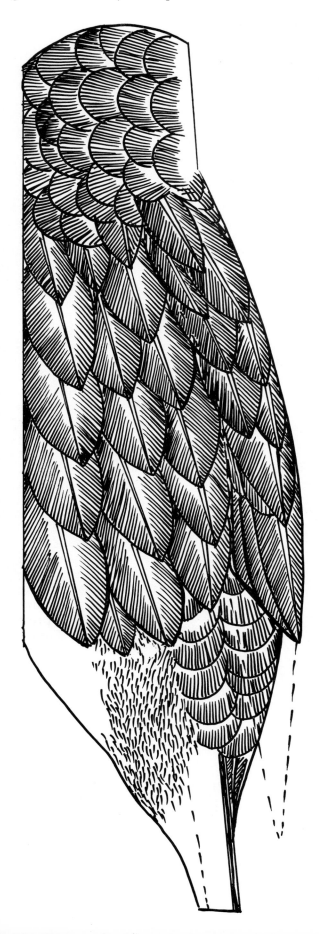

Fig. 443. Feather layout on profile of bird.

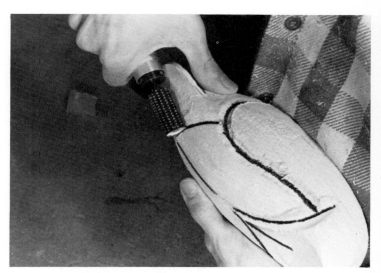

Fig. 444. Cut along this line with rasp to create a ledge.

Fig. 445. Draw feather pattern on sanded body.

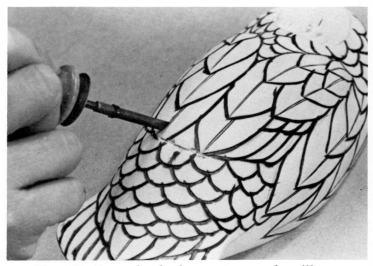

Fig. 446. Burn the feather pattern and quills with Hot Tool.

147

Fig. 447. Feather layout on back of bird.

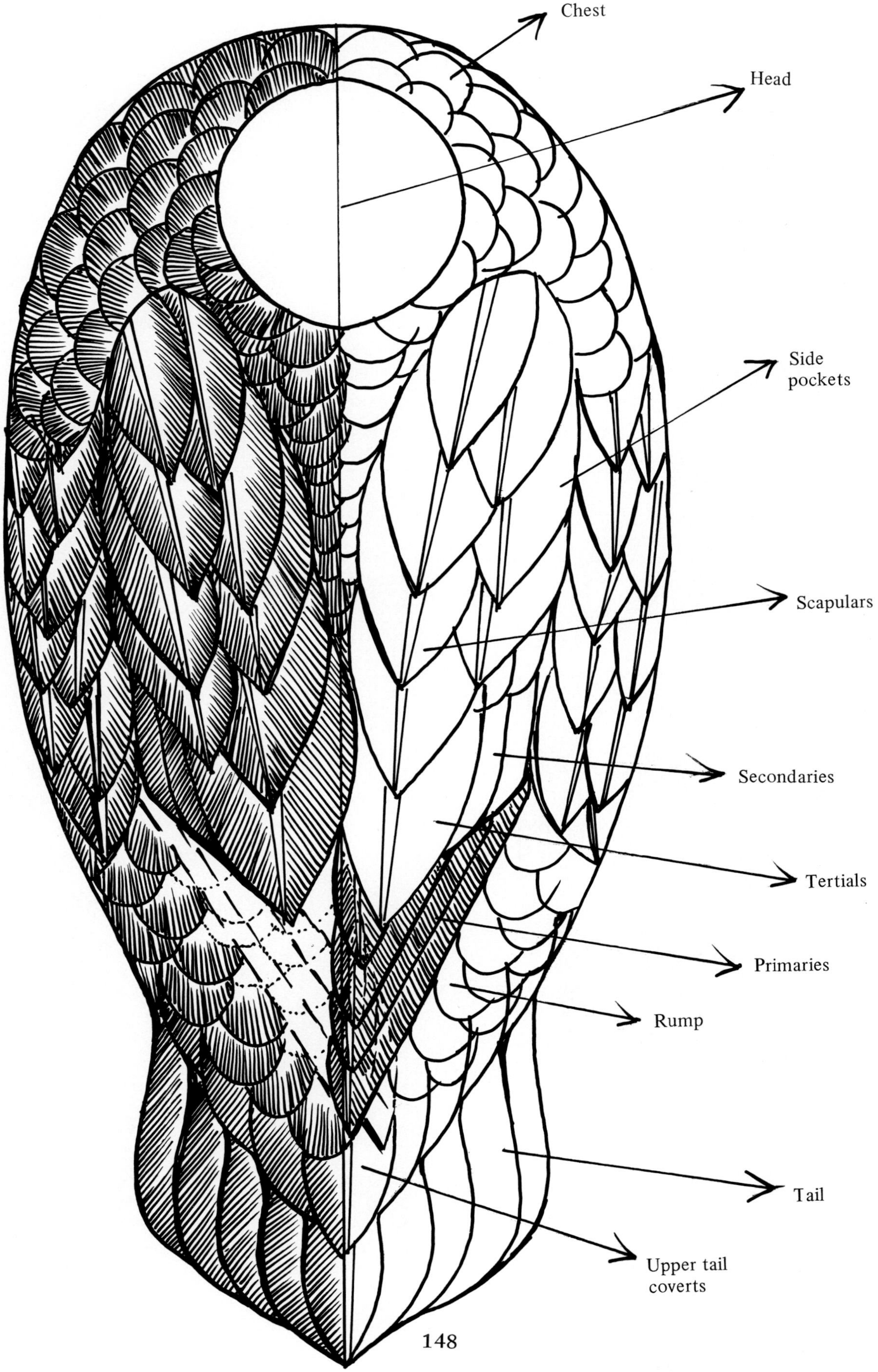

Chest

Head

Side pockets

Scapulars

Secondaries

Tertials

Primaries

Rump

Tail

Upper tail coverts

148

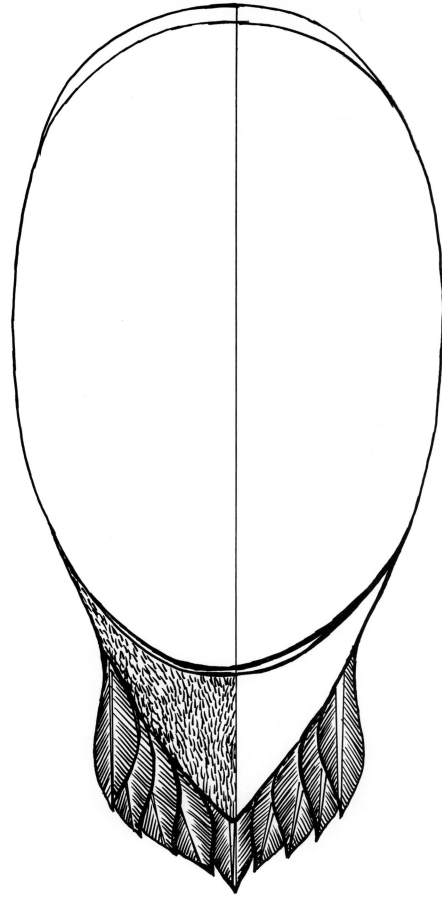

Fig. 448. You may include the underside of tail
feathers if you wish.

Fig. 449. Texture the body with the Foredom Tool.

Fig. 450. The barbs have been textured to flow from the quills. Channel has been cut for primary inserts.

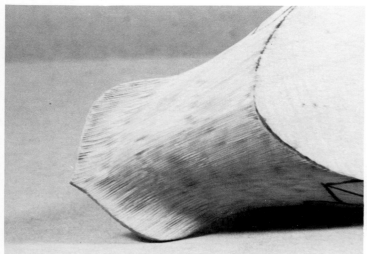

Fig. 451. Texture the under-rump with straight lines.

Fig. 452. Flatten area on body for the head with a drill press.

Fig. 453. Turn head at slight angle to body and glue with 5-minute epoxy.

Fig. 454. Cut a channel at seam line to give purchase area for the fill.

150

screw or nail head to do the more restricted area under the neck.

Clean the carving thoroughly and seal it with Krylon 1301.

PAINTING

Apply two thin washes of burnt umber and then two thin washes of white to prepare the surface for your base coats of paint.

Prepare two palettes of paint. One is for the body color. Mix a thin wash of burnt umber with a touch of white. On the other palette, mix the head color. This is a soft buffy color made by mixing white with raw sienna and a touch of burnt umber. On the same palette, mix the medium buffy color for the under-rump by adding

Fig. 457. Sand the epoxy putty on neck joint smooth.

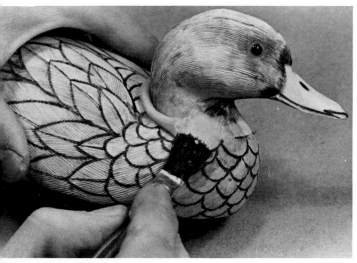

Fig. 455. Put epoxy putty around neck on the seam and saturate it with acetone.

Fig. 458. With dental separating discs texture the neck joint as close to the chin as you can reach.

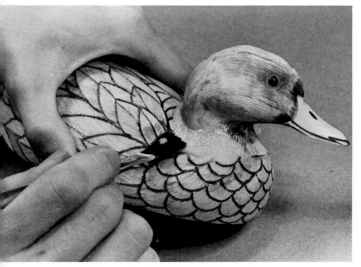

Fig. 456. With brush, smear putty into seam and feather it into wood on both sides of seam.

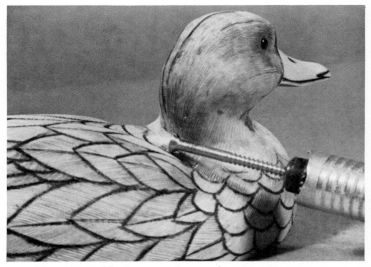

Fig. 459. With sharpened screw head on Foredom tool, texture the more restricted neck areas.

151

Fig. 460. After two thin washes of burnt umber, apply two thin white washes.

Fig. 461. Paint head and body simultaneously so colors can be wet-blended at the neck.

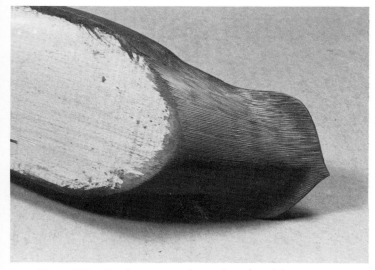

Fig. 462. Under-rump is painted with raw sienna, white and burnt umber and wet-blended into the sides.

Fig. 463. Edge the rump feathers with a cupped brush, following the arcs burned into the wood.

a little more burnt umber to the head mixture.

Paint the body, then immediately paint the under-rump and wet-blend the paints together where they meet on the sides of the bird. Go on to the head and wet-blend its color into the body color at the neck. Paint the eye channel with the body color and wet-blend it into the head color. Let all the paints dry, then start again. The order you paint in isn't crucial as long as you work quickly so the paints can be wet-blended. Apply 8 to 10 washes of the paints to achieve a depth of color and a soft sheen. The eye channel probably won't need so many washes. If you think the body is getting too dark, add a little more white to the mixture and apply it a few times.

The feathers are edged with a mixture of white and a touch of raw sienna. Have very little paint in your brush because it is better to edge and re-edge several times than to have a heavy edging.

Edge the chest and rump feathers with a cupped brush, following the arc lines burned into the wood. (Figures 463, 464, and color plate 39)

Edge the back, side and tail feathers with the brush flat with a knife edge. Set the brush perpendicular to the edge of the feather, pull it into the texturing and lift out, leaving jagged edges on the interior of the feather. (Figure 465) The secondaries are not edged because they are brightly colored and will be painted later.

Mix an ultra-thin toning wash of burnt umber and apply it all over the body. Edge all the feathers again. This time, add markings in the interior of the back and side feathers, using a brush with a straight edge and the pull and lift method. (Figure 467) Again, apply the toning wash all over the body and re-edge all the feathers. Each time you edge, pull your brush into the feather a little less so you eventually get a graduation of color from dark to light. You may need to do the edgings and toning washes three times or more. The more often you do it, the softer the feather edges will be in tone. (Color plate 40)

Paint the crown of the head with a mixture of burnt umber and a touch of black or ultramarine blue in a whole-milk consistency. With a cupped brush and using a stippling-type motion while maintaining a sharp edge on the brush, paint the crown and back of the neck. Just barely touch the wood with the brush. (Figure 469) Fill in empty spaces and overlap the stippling until only a few flecks of the base color show. (Color plate 42)

With the same paint mixture and a #2 round red sable brush or a white sable Windsor Newton #4 script brush, place little flecks, like tiny stripes, on the rest of the head, following the flow of the texturing. (Figure 471) Stagger these paint flecks so they are not in straight lines. (Color plate 43)

Fig. 465. Edge the back, side and tail feathers with the flat edge of the brush.

Fig. 466. Apply an ultra-thin toning wash all over the body.

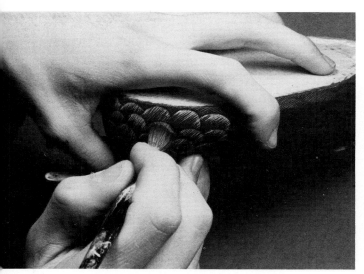

Fig. 464. Edge the chest feathers in the same way, with a mixture of white and raw sienna.

Fig. 467. Re-edge all the feathers, and paint markings in the interior of the back and side feathers.

153

Fig. 468. You may need to do the edgings and toning washes three or more times.

Fig. 471. Use a script brush to paint little flecks on the rest of the head.

Fig. 469. With sharp edge of brush paint crown and back of neck.

Fig. 472. Paint flecks should be staggered so they are not in straight lines.

Fig. 470. The crown is finished when only a few flecks of the base color show.

Fig. 473. The under-rump is painted with slightly longer stripes of color than head.

154

Wash the head with the ultra-thin toning wash of burnt umber. If your flecks of paint are dark enough, you don't need to repaint them. That's the purpose of the black in the paint mixture. (Color plate 44)

The under-rump is streaked the same way the head was, using slightly longer stripes of color. (Color plate 45) If you carved the underside of the tail feathers, paint them a medium dusky gray.

Paint the bill dark gray, using black and white. Wet-blend a little black near the end of the bill. When the bill is dry, paint 5 to 7 small black dots under the nostril and toward the head on each side of the bill. (Figure 475) Coat the entire bill with gloss medium.

Mix thalo green with a touch of thalo yellow green (or light cadmium yellow) to make a wash for the secondaries. Wash them three or four times. Paint a 1/8-inch stripe on the trailing edge in white. Finish with a light wash of green iridescence, using green iridescent powder mixed with white. Paint the secondary coverts with a mixture of raw sienna and a touch of white, and edge with a 1/8-inch white stripe. (Figure 476)

INSERTS

Make a pattern for the primary inserts, referring to the dotted lines in figures 443 and 447. Check that it is the right size. (Figure 477) Cut the insert out of 1/32-inch basswood veneer, sand, and texture. (See Chapter 12.) Spray the inserts with Krylon 1301, then paint them with a burnt umber wash. On the fourth wash or so, put a dot of white in the center of each feather and dry brush it out, going slightly lighter toward the center and darker toward both edges. Paint the underside of the inserts medium dusky gray, made out of black, white and burnt umber. It isn't necessary to use thin washes to paint them.

Set the primaries in place with superglue, so that the upper primary is on the same side that the head is turned. (Color plate 41)

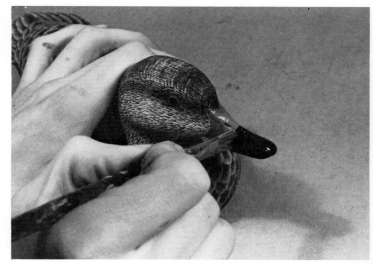

Fig. 474. Wet-blend some black with the dark gray bill paint.

Fig. 475. Paint a few small black dots on the bill.

Fig. 476. Paint the secondaries and secondary coverts and their edges.

155

Fig. 477. Check that the insert pattern looks the right size for the carving.

Fig. 478. Paint the primary inserts with a burnt umber wash and lighten the center with white.

Project Five

The extended-wing carving of the Green-Winged Teal drake and/or hen is your first truly decorative carving project that can be entered in the decorative division in a competition with a good chance of winning. It has feet, vermiculations and extended wings with ten inserted primaries in each wing. It should be mounted in an attractive display.

Chapter 16
Displaying a Decorative Carving

Making a decorative carving entails not only carving a bird, but also creating a display--a scene or setting--for the bird. It does not have to be elaborate, but it must, at the very least, complement the bird. I've seen some fine decorative carvings mounted very poorly. Do not make this mistake. If you're going to take the time to make a decorative carving, you certainly should put some time into designing a simple and attractive display for it.

Any carving can be mounted, even a flat-bottomed decoy. Some carvings must be mounted because they're supposed to be standing up or lying on a base. How elaborate or simple a mount you use is your decision. There are no absolutes about the way a carving is displayed as long as it is complemented and never overpowered by the mount. Experiment with an assortment of mounts. Try out your ideas. Look for a mounting idea that's not too big or too little, not unrealistic or unbalanced.

There are softwood and hardwood bases made specifically for display purposes in a variety of shapes and sizes. Shop around for some you like. Driftwood makes an interesting mount for waterfowl. It may need to be attached to a base for visual or physical balance. Look for pieces of driftwood whenever you're at a beach and save them for future use. Remember to spray the driftwood with an insect spray to get rid of any insects living in it. Driftwood can be burned with a propane torch; wirebrush away the char. It becomes darkened and attractive; wax or shellac it as you wish.

You can change a base by building a scene on it. Build up auto-body filler or epoxy putty to simulate something, such as marsh mud around some marsh birds. If a bird is standing on a base, build up a sandy area around its feet to appear like a beach. Drill holes for the feet into the base. Take metal rods the same size as the pins on the feet and stick them into the drilled holes so sand doesn't fill up the holes. Build up coats of sand and glue, as many as you want. Take the rods out of the holes and set the bird in place. Add more sand and glue and fill all around the bird's feet to cushion them in the sand.

Study other people's carvings and displays. Look at the photos in this chapter. To do justice to your carving, take the time to display it well.

Fig. 481. A book makes a nice display for the Blue-winged Teal decoy by Paul Suarez.

Fig. 482. You can buy a variety of sizes of unfinished display bases.

Fig. 485. Use wood stain of your choice on softwood bases.

Fig. 483. This unfinished round base is just another example of available bases.

Fig. 486. Coat a base with glue and sprinkle on sand.

Fig. 484. Torched bases have a nice rustic look. Burn a base with a torch, wirebrush away the char and seal with shellac.

Fig. 487. Build up a depth of sand with several applications of glue.

Fig. 488. Flying miniatures on a piece of driftwood can be displayed under this glass dome.

Fig. 489. Turn an attractive piece of wood into a display base.

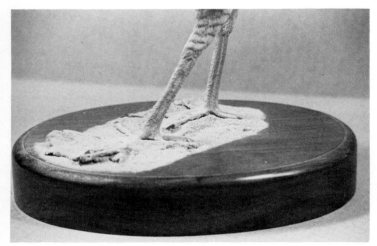

Fig. 490. Cushion feet of standing bird in sand on base.

Fig. 491. Canvasback hen by Sid Bozarth is mounted on a waxed piece of driftwood.

Fig. 492. Full-bodied floating decorative Canada goose by Fred Simmerman requires a custom-made stand for display purposes.

Fig. 493. American Merganser hen by Tom Fitzpatrick is displayed on a piece of cork.

Plate 1. Wood ducks--William Veasey (in collection of Donald Griffith)

Plate 2. Gadwall drake--James Dodd

Plate 3. American Merganser hen--Tom Fitzpatrick

Plate 4. Mallard drake--Sina Pat Kurman

Plate 5. Common Loon--Ken Blomquist

Plate 6. Wood duck drake--Jan Calzert

Plate 7. Mallard hen & ducklings--Peggy Jahn

Plate 8. Shoveler drake--Penny Mace

Plate 9. Golden-eye drake--Tom Herron

Plate 10. Canvasback drake--Hal Hopkins

Plate 11. Golden-eye hen--Rose Darlington

Plate 12. Pintail hen--Lyse St. Onge

Plate 13. Green-winged Teal drake--Tom Jacobs

Plate 14. Redhead drake--John Patton

Plate 15. Canvasback drake--Bill Maicaig

Plate 16. Ruddy duck drake--Harold Veasey

Plate 17. Mallard drake--John Hemphill

Plate 18. Red-breasted Merganser drake--Carolyn Thomas

Plate 19. Gadwall drake--Glenn Young

Plate 20. Canada goose--Fred Simmerman

Plate 21. Pintail drake--Lisa Schuler

Plate 22. Canvasback pair--Debra Norvell

Plate 23. Blue-winged Teal drake--Paul Suarez

Plate 24. Woodcocks--Rosalyn Daisey

Plate 25. Green-winged Teal drake--Sina Pat Kurman

Plate 26. Brant--Fred Simmerman

Plate 27. Swan--John Archer

Plate 28. Canvasback hen--James Warrington

Plate 29. Redhead drake--Sid Bozarth

Plate 30. Ring-necked Pheasant--Dave Pergrin

Plate 31. Mockingbirds--Don Vassallo

Plate 32. Wood duck drake--Nina Grannett

Plate 33. Bufflehead hen--Jack Hemphill

Plate 34. Project Two--Canada goose

Plate 35. Project Two--Canada goose

Plate 36. Project Three--Pintail

Plate 37. Project Three--Pintail

Plate 38. Project Four--Green-winged Teal hen

Plate 39. Painting cupped feathers

Plate 40. Feather edging

Plate 41. Close-up of secondaries

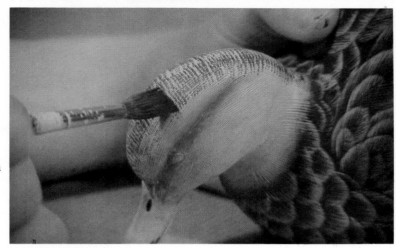

Plate 42. Painting crown

Plate 43. Painting cheek

Plate 44. Finished head

Plate 45. Finished under-rump

Plate 46. Extended-drake, wings down

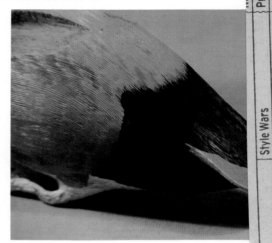

Plate 47. Rump and back painted

Plate 48. Undertail cove

Plate 49. Head and chest painted

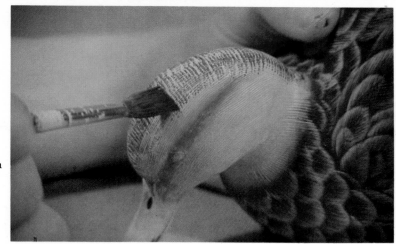

Plate 42. Painting crown

Plate 43. Painting cheek

Plate 44. Finished head

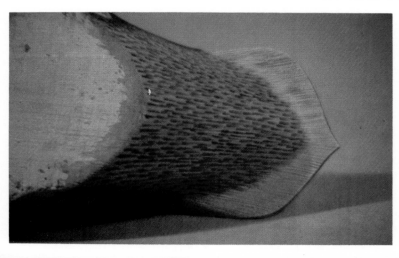

Plate 45. Finished under-rump

Plate 46. Extended-wing Green-winged Teal drake, wings down

Plate 47. Rump and back painted

Plate 48. Undertail coverts and belly

Plate 49. Head and chest painted

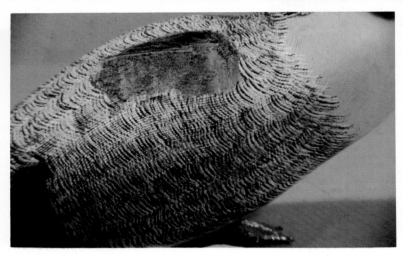

Plate 50. Beginning of vermiculations

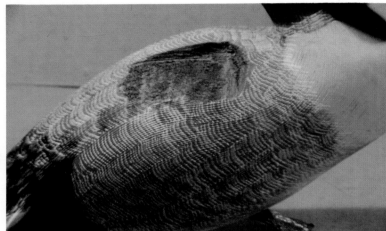

Plate 51. Vermiculations completed before toning wash

Plate 52. Rump and tail detail

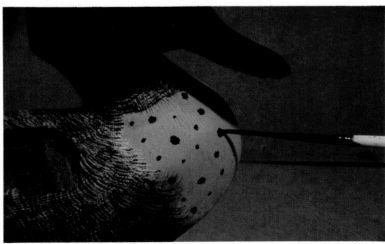

Plate 53. Chest detail

Plate 54. Finished chest detail

Plate 55. Head detail

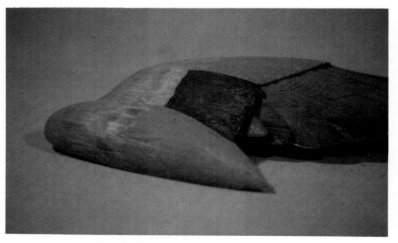

Plate 56. Wing undercoated

Plate 57. Wing detail

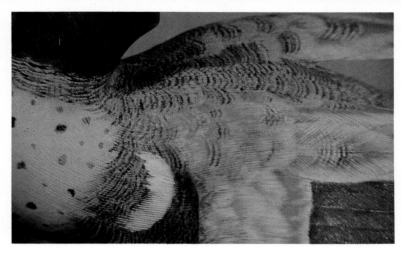

Plate 58. Shoulder joint detail of Green-winged Teal drake

Plate 59. Extended-wing drake, wings up, by Tricia Veasey

Plate 60. Project One--Canada goose

Plate 61. Antique Swan

Plate 62. Clapper Rail

Plate 63. Old Squaw

Plate 64. Preening Whistling Swan

Plate 65. Preening Canada goose

Chapter 17
Feet

Carving a flat-bottomed duck is much simpler than carving one with feet. Learning how to make a carving with feet, however, is a skill you should learn. The carvings that win in the decorative division of a carving show almost always have feet.

Choosing the feet you'll use depends on your expertise as a carver and the type of display chosen for the carving.

CAST FEET

It is really difficult to carve good feet. I recommend to the novice carver that he use cast feet. In competition, judges will not disqualify a carving with cast feet in the novice class, but will strongly discourage the use of cast feet in the professional class.

The best cast feet are made by Richard Delise (920 Springwood Drive, West Chester, PA. 19380). He makes pewter feet that are generally used when the bird stands on a solid base. They can also be bent slightly to fit the curves on driftwood. Cut into the underside of the leg in a few areas (Figure 494) and heat them in boiling water for a couple of minutes. While they are hot, bend them with your fingers. If they start to cool off, heat them in the water again.

Delise will also make to order feet that are harder than the pewter ones if you want them absolutely rigid, or lead feet if you want pliable ones.

Cast feet come in a variety of sizes and types but you won't be able to find everything. You may need to make do with feet close to the actual size and type recommended for the species.

After shaping and texturing the body, decide where to insert the feet. This is determined by the bird's anatomy and the position the bird will be in. Drill two holes at the correct angle, using a drill bit the size of the leg. (Figure 496) Drill deep

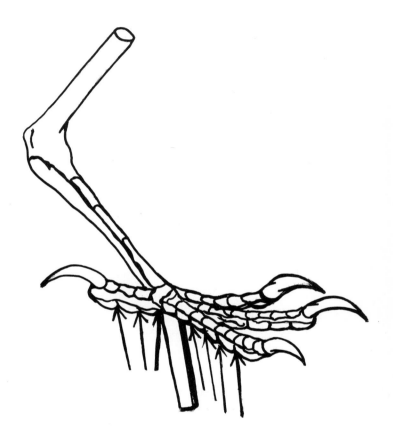

Fig. 494. Bend Richard Delise's cast pewter feet by cutting notches into the underside where arrows indicate and boiling them in water.

enough so the leg will go in as far as the knuckle (bend in the leg).

Set the feet in place with 5-minute epoxy. Around the legs, where they join the body, make tufts out of moldable epoxy or Wood Dough and texture it to simulate feathers. (Figure 497)

Spray the feet with Krylon 1301 or wipe them with alcohol before you paint them with the colors recommended in the chart.

177

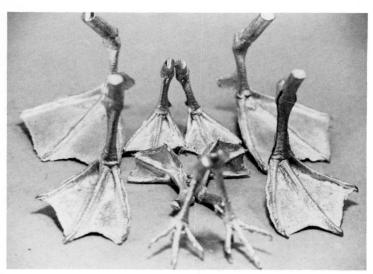

Fig. 495. Cast feet are made in a variety of shapes and sizes.

Fig. 498. Cast pewter feet are used for this bird.

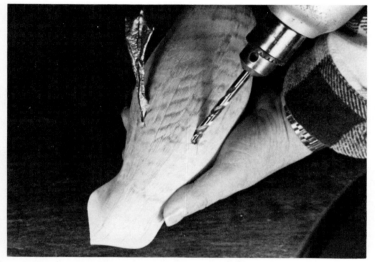

Fig. 496. Drill a hole for feet in the desired angle.

Fig. 499. Paint cast feet in the recommended colors.

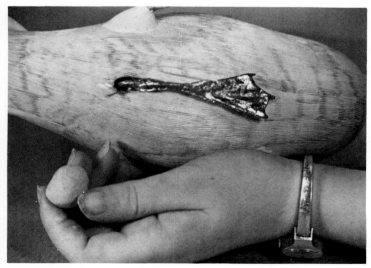

Fig. 497. Build a tuft around the leg and texture it to simulate feathers.

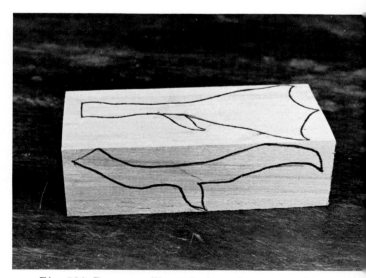

Fig. 500. Draw profile and plan views of foot on block of wood.

MAKING FEET

Eventually, as part of your development as a carver, or for competition purposes, you should make your own feet. Make a pattern for them, referring to the feet on mounts or cast feet.

A simple foot can be made out of moldable epoxy. It's fine for looks, not for support, but should be perfectly satisfactory if the bird is resting on the mount. Mold the epoxy to fit the pattern, smooth it onto what would be the thigh of the bird, and then mold it around the driftwood. This can be done within the 2 or 3 hours the putty takes to dry. Texture any of the putty that is visible, again using real feet or cast feet as your reference. Then apply paint.

If you want to use epoxy feet but need to support the weight of the bird on the display mount, use a metal rod. Drill a hole (or two if the bird is large) into the bird. Drill a corresponding hole into the mount. Cut a 1/8-inch steel or brass rod just long enough to fit both drilled holes, and put 5-minute epoxy on the ends of the rod. Insert it into the holes. The rod is concealed, but it supports the weight of the bird.

If the bird is standing on the base, one or both of its feet have to do the supporting. Find a narrow brass or steel rod long enough to be inserted in the body and mount. Mold epoxy putty around this to form a leg and foot, and texture it while it's still malleable. You can also use Duralay dental acrylic that dries very quickly. Burn the detail into it and scrape away all residue from the burning.

WOOD FEET

Wood feet are much more complicated to make. They are carved the same way whether they are supportive or not.

Draw the profile and plan views of the feet on blocks of any semi-hard wood, such as basswood or tupelo. (Figure 500) Rough-cut these on a bandsaw, being especially careful of the hind lobe, since it is cut on the cross-grain. (If that's a worry, you can carve the hind lobe out of harder wood and insert it later.)

Pencil in the toes, top and bottom. With a knife or the Foredom tool, relieve the web area of the foot on the top and bottom to make it thinner. (Figure 503) The leg is rounded front and back but is relatively flat on the sides. After the foot is basically shaped and sanded, draw on the

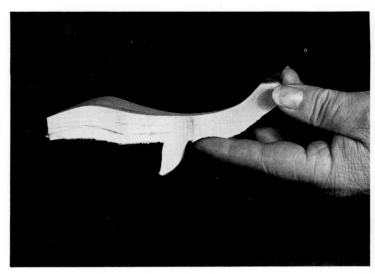

Fig. 501. Cut out foot on bandsaw.

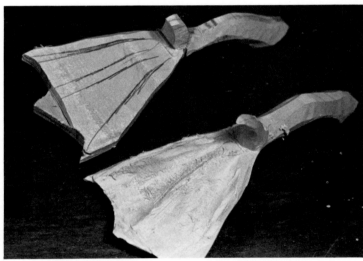

Fig. 502. One foot is laid out to be relieved, and the other is already done.

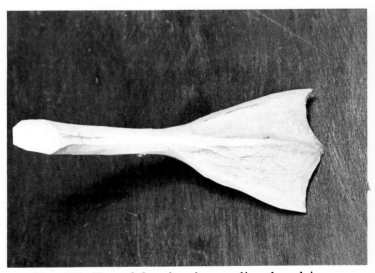

Fig. 503. Top of foot has been relieved and is ready to be sanded.

179

Fig. 504. Burn the detail into sanded foot.

texturing layout, using actual feet as your reference, and burn it in. (Figure 504)

Clean and seal the feet before painting them. Insert them into the body either before or after painting. Glue them into drilled holes with 5-minute epoxy.

If you need one or both of the wood feet to be supportive, have it cast in metal.

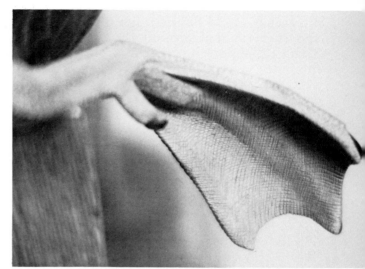

Fig. 506. If the underside of the foot will be visible, detail it, too.

Fig. 505. Note the detailing of this wood foot of a Black duck.

180

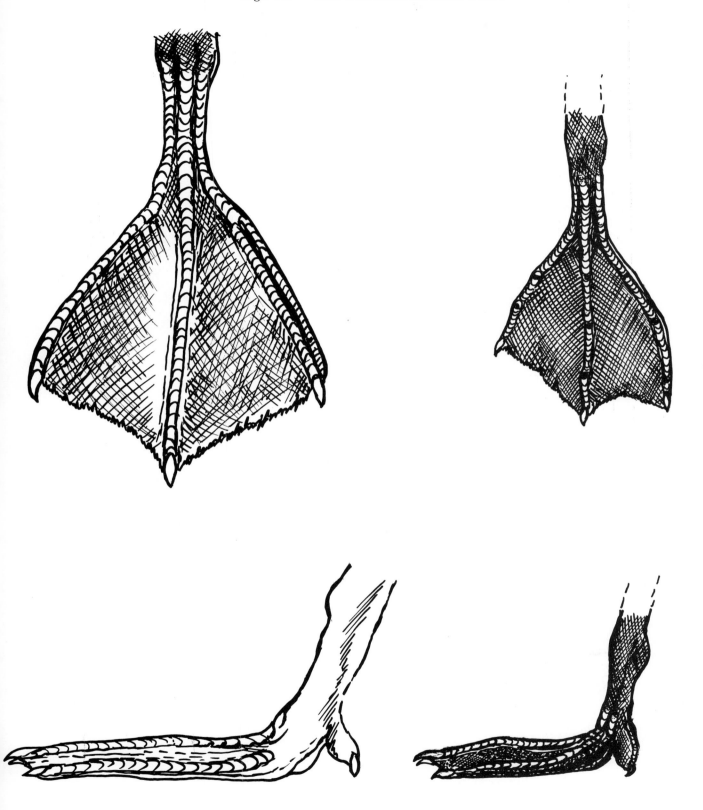

Figs. 507 & 508. Large diver's foot-Canvasback   *Figs. 509 & 510.* Small diver's foot-Bufflehead

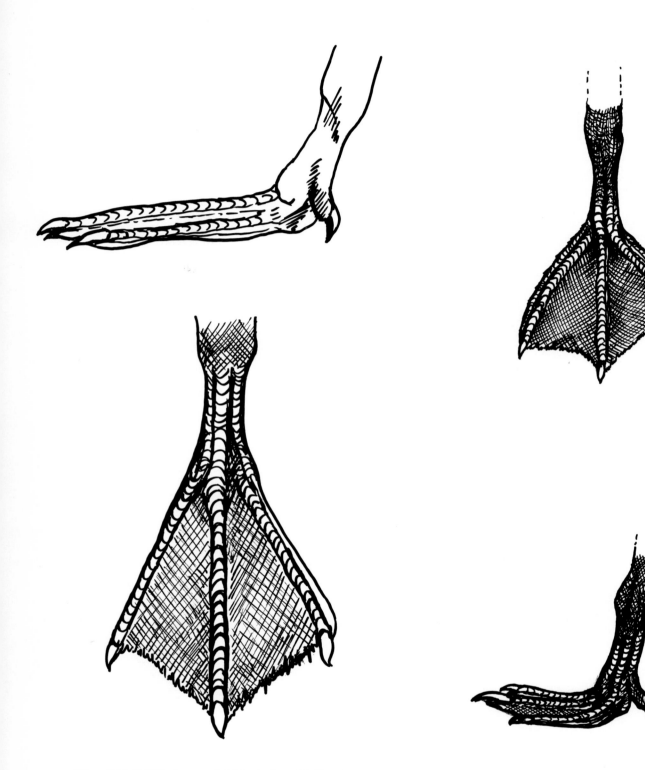

Figs. 511 & 512. Large dabbler's foot-Mallard

Figs. 513 & 514. Small dabbler's foot-Green-winged Teal

FEET COLORS OF SOME COMMON WATERFOWL

	MALE	FEMALE
Blue-winged Teal	dull yellow to yellow-orange, dusky webs	dull yellowish, dark webs
Cinnamon Teal	dull orange-yellow, dusky webs	same
Green-winged Teal	bluish-gray to olive-gray, dusky webs	bluish-gray, dusky webs
Wood duck	dull yellow to orange-yellow, blackish webs	dull yellow, dusky webs
Baldpate	grayish-blue, dusky webs	same
Gadwall	bright orange-yellow, blackish webs	dull yellow, dusky webs
Pintail	grayish-blue to olive-gray, dusky webs	dark grayish blue to greenish-gray, dusky webs
Shoveler	orange-red to vermillion	orange
Mallard	bright reddish-orange or yellowish (duller in the fall)	pale orange-red
Black duck	orange-red to coral-red	brown with some orange or salmon
Ruddy duck	bluish-gray, dusky webs and nails	same
Canada goose	black	same
White fronted goose	orange to yellow	same
Lesser Snow goose	dull reddish	same
Blue goose	light purplish to pinkish	same
Brant	black	same
Harlequin	grayish-blue to grayish-brown, dusky webs	duller
Old Squaw	bluish-gray, dusky webs	grayish-blue or greenish-gray
Canvasback	grayish-blue to yellowish-blue, dusky webs	same
Bufflehead	flesh, black nails	purplish-gray
American Golden-eye	bright orange or yellow, dusky webs and nails	paler
Barrow's Golden-eye	bright orange or yellow, dusky webs and nails	paler
Greater Scaup	light blue-gray to greenish-dusky, webs often blackish	dark blue-gray, blackish webs
Lesser Scaup	light gray-blue to greenish-dusky, dusky webs	dark blue-gray, blackish webs
Redhead	bluish-gray, dusky webs	duller
Ring-necked duck	grayish-blue to light buffy-gray, blackish webs	same
American Merganser	red, dusky nails	duller
Hooded Merganser	dull yellowish-olive to light brown, dusky webs	greenish to brownish, black webs
Red-breasted Merganser	red	same

Chapter 18
Carving an Extended-wing Green-winged Teal Drake and Hen

Many of the carving techniques you have learned are utilized in this carving project. I will not describe them in detail again, but will cover just the new techniques instead.

The head of the Green-winged Teal drake has a crest--a tuft of long feathers on the back of the head that are held erect most of the time. With the exception of the crest, the drake's head is carved and shaped as the hen's head is.

The bodies of the drake and hen are rounded in this project because they are standing and their wings are extended. If the birds were sitting, the bodies would show the indentations made by the wings folded into the bodies. The bodies also are slightly curved, with the head in an arc with the tail, to give the impression of motion.

This project includes a technique we have not used before. A shelf is included on the body where the head is to be set. I do this for two reasons. One, is that in basic shaping, the shelf makes it a bit easier to flow the neck into the chest; and 2) if you wish, the shelf can be cut at a slight angle instead of leaving it parallel to the body. Then, when the head is set to the side these angles create a slight tilt, giving a nice, pert look to the head. Such a shelf can be utilized in other projects whenever the neck is elongated and the head is set at an angle.

If you'd like to make tail feather inserts, instead of burning tail feathers in the block, cut a channel at the tail end of the bird and insert separate tail feathers.

The hen and drake can be displayed individually or together in a tableau. If they are to be together you might want to set their heads and wings differently.

Use basswood or pine. The body block should be 10 x 4 x 4-inches. The head block should be 1 5/8-inches thick.

WINGS

Two wing patterns for both the drake and the hen are included in this project. One pattern is for wings that are extended upward; the bird should then be fully standing to look more alert. The other pattern is for wings that are extended downward; in this case, the body would rest on the mounting base. Choose the position you want the bird to be in; that will determine the wings you use. The wings are attached to the body in slightly different ways, depending on the type you choose.

Use basswood for the wings because they need a lot of strength. Draw the wing plan view on a 1½-inch thick piece of basswood. When drawing the pattern on the wood lay the tertials and secondaries in line with the grain. Cut it out on the bandsaw, then split it in half to have a right and left wing.

Study figure 537. Draw a centerline from the shoulder through the tertials on the wing block. This is the high point of the wing. Rasp or shave the wood from the centerline to the squiggly line where there will be a slight groove. The horizontal arrow marks the high point of the rest of the wing. Roll the rasp from that line to the leading edge to round it. (Figure 540) Shave the trailing edge to the line shown in figure 538. Roll the tertial edge of the wing to the line shown in figure 539.

Now the wing is rounded and basically shaped, but it is still thick. Turn the wings over. Pencil an arced line where under-primary coverts would lie as shown on the wing on the right in figure 541. With a hollow rasp on the Foredom tool, remove the excess wood from under the secondaries and tertials, leaving wood intact in the area of the primary coverts. Taper from the forward area of the wing to the

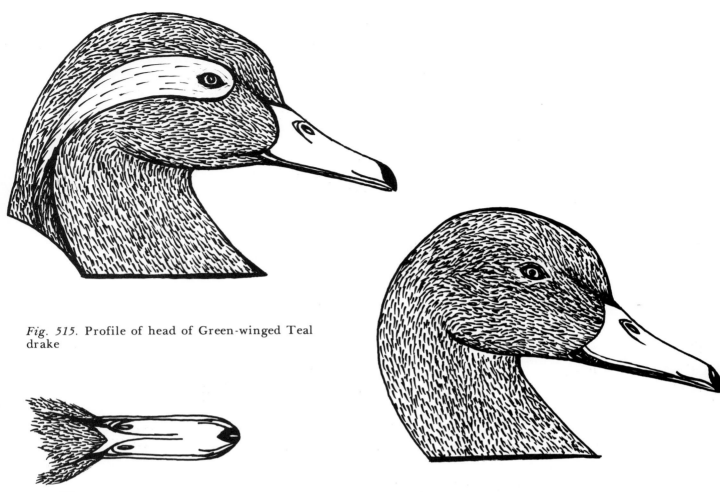

Fig. 515. Profile of head of Green-winged Teal drake

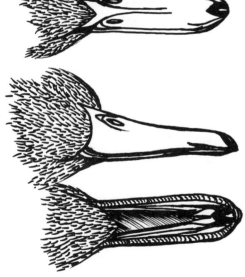

Fig. 516. Three views of drake's bill

Fig. 517. Profile of head of Green-winged Teal hen

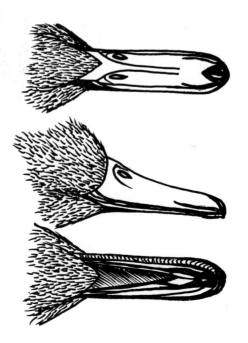

Fig. 518. Three views of hen's bill

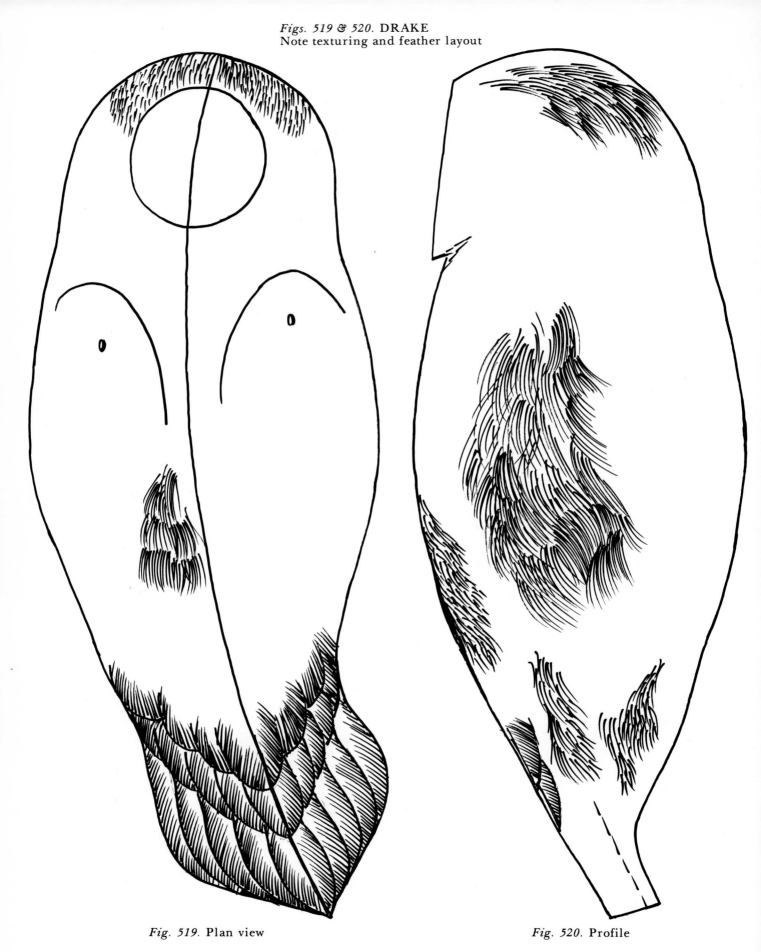

Fig. 519. Plan view   *Fig. 520.* Profile

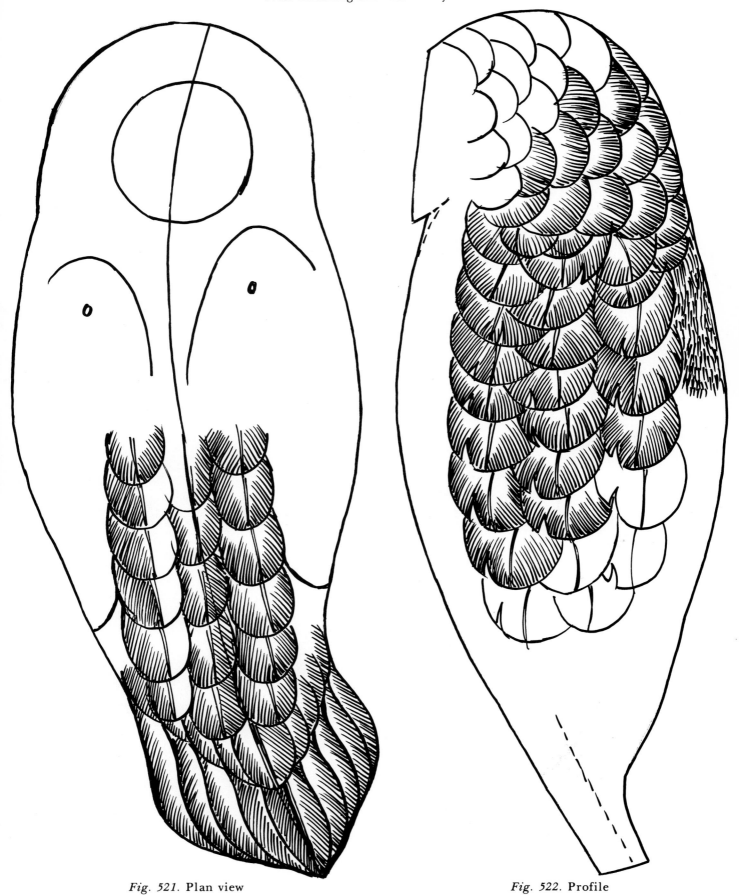

Fig. 521. Plan view

Fig. 522. Profile

187

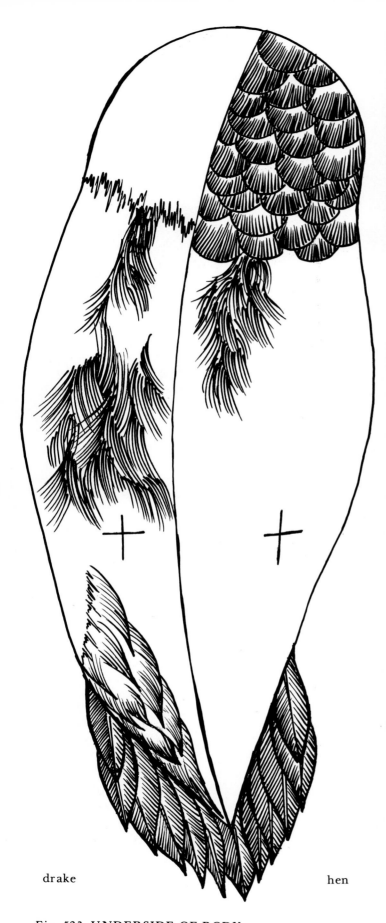

drake   hen

Fig. 523. UNDERSIDE OF BODY

Fig. 524. The body block includes a shelf where head is to be set.

Fig. 525. Turn head to side to give a nice, pert look to head.

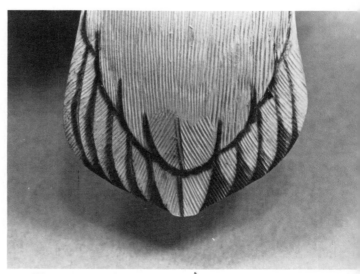

Fig. 526. Tail feathers are burned into the carving and textured.

Fig. 527. If you want to use tail feather inserts, cut a channel at the tail end.

Fig. 528. Cut tail feather inserts to fit inside channel.

Fig. 529. Note the underside of the tail feathers.

trailing edge of the secondaries to a thickness of about 1/16-inch. Cut up to the extended pencil line, creating a 90° angle there. Cut a channel along the primary covert line so your wing now looks like the one in figure 544. Repeat this process on the other wing.

Cut the primaries (Figure 536) out of 1/32-inch veneer, laying them in line with the grain. Texture or burn them. Fit them into the channel along the primary covert line to make sure it is wide enough and long enough to accommodate all of them. The next to the longest primary, which is the first primary, goes in first; the longest primary goes behind and next to it and so on down to the tenth primary which is the shortest. From the front of the wing, the first primary will be on the bottom, which is a true-to-life detail. (Figure 545) Wrap the complete set of primaries with a rubber band whenever you're not using them.

Sand the top of the wings and sand the trailing edge of the secondaries to a feather edge. Draw on the feather layout. Burn or carve in the layout and raise the quills. Burn or Foredom tool texture the wings. Do not texture the undersides of the wings yet.

Reset the primaries and glue them into the channel with superglue. The primary covert area of the wing is still too thick, so slightly hollow the underside of that area so the wood flows right into the primaries. The leading edge is still sharp, so round it slightly with the Foredom tool sander and then sand by hand.

If you are making the wings-up bird, pencil in the layout of the under-wing coverts (Figure 548) burn or carve it in and texture all over. If the wings are going to be down, detailing only needs to be done where the undersides are visible.

Hold the wings onto the back of the bird and trace around the edges. Make a notch for the wings and tack them in place so you can see how the finished bird will look. You will not permanently attach them yet because they will be in the way when you paint.

Fig. 530. upperside

Fig. 531. underside

Fig. 532. upperside

Fig. 533. underside

Fig. 534. upperside

Fig. 535. underside

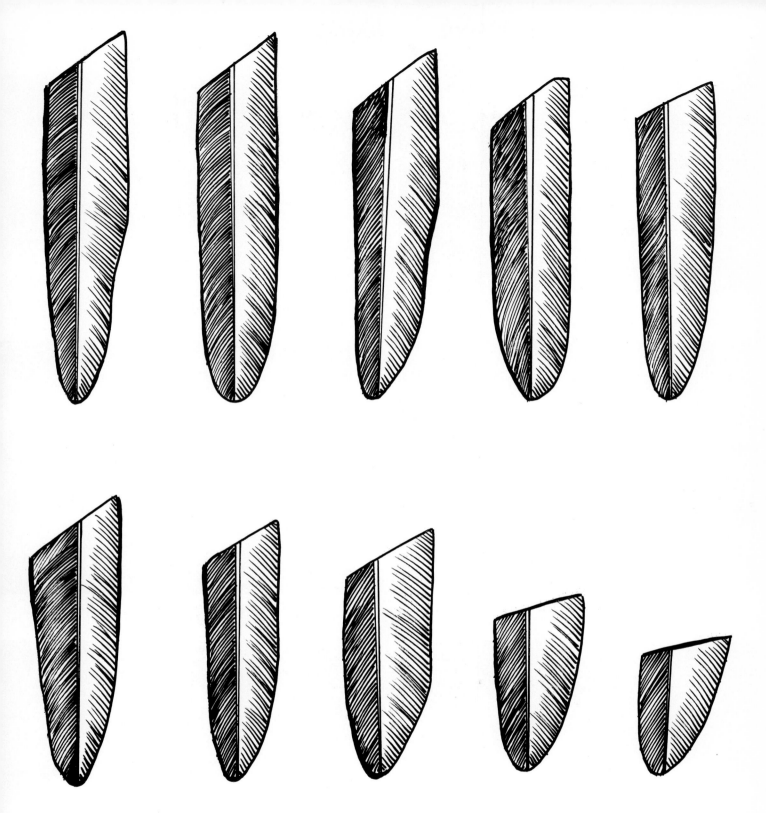

Fig. 536. Patterns for the primaries

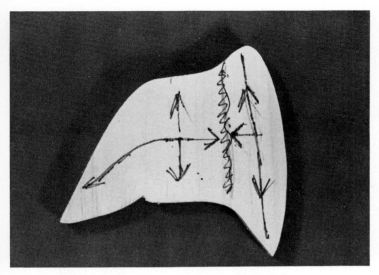

Fig. 537. Mark these guidelines on the wings to help you shape them.

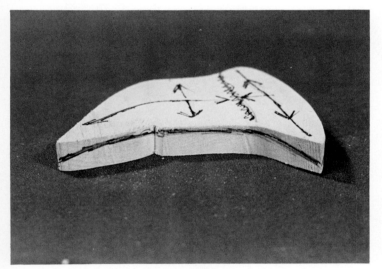

Fig. 538. Trailing edge of wing is tapered to line drawn on edge.

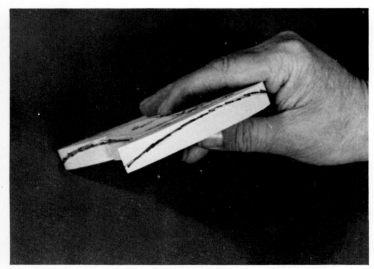

Fig. 539. Roll rasp across tertials to round edge as shown.

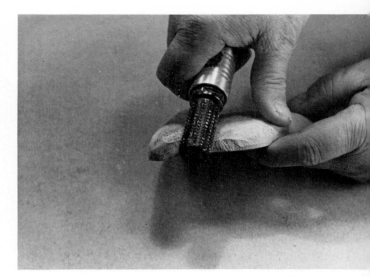

Fig. 540. Use rasp to help in rounding edges of wing.

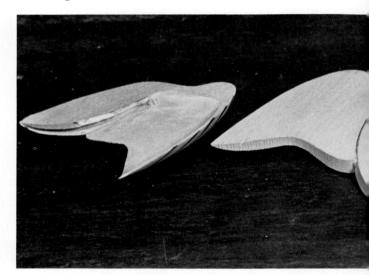

Fig. 541. Underside of wing on left has been finished; wing on right is still too thick.

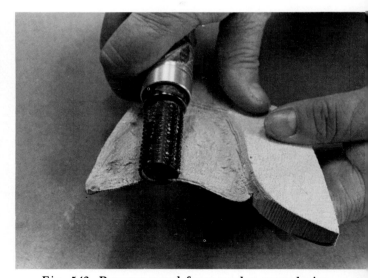

Fig. 542. Remove wood from under secondaries and tertials.

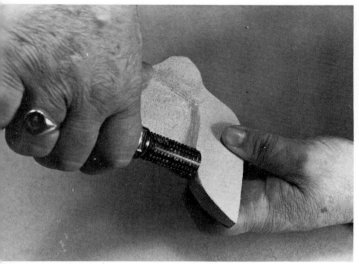

Fig. 543. Create a 90° angle along primary covert line.

Fig. 546. Pencil feather layout (wing on right), burn it in and texture (wing on left).

Fig. 544. Cut a channel along primary covert line for the primaries.

Fig. 547. Primaries are glued into the channel and underside of wing is ready to be slightly hollowed.

Fig. 545. Check that the channel is wide enough and long enough to fit all 10 primaries.

Fig. 548. On the wings-up bird, the under-wing coverts must be laid out, carved and textured.

PAINTING DRAKE

After you apply your preparatory burnt umber and white paint washes, proceed to the base washes, beginning at the tail of the bird.

Paint the top of the wing medium dusky gray, using black, white and burnt umber. Paint the underside of the wing light dusky gray.

Paint the top of the tail, the sides, back and collar around the neck medium dusky gray. Paint the rump and under-rump black, adding some ultramarine blue to the black paint. (See color plate 47)

Paint the belly whitish, using white and a touch of burnt umber. Wet-blend it into the gray paint on the sides and paint a jagged edge where it meets the black rump and under-rump paint. Paint the underside of the tail light dusky gray. Paint the undertail coverts pale yellow, using yellow ochre, white and a dot of burnt umber. (See color plate 48)

The base color for the head is burnt sienna. Apply several thin washes, and then, when the paint is wet, add a tiny amount of yellow ochre to the cheek and wet-blend it in. Also wet-blend a tiny amount of burnt umber into the crown to darken it slightly. (Figure 562) Wet-blend some black about ¾-inch up from the base of the crest, and also under the chin.

With a piece of chalk, outline the area for the green patch around the eye and extending through the edge of the crest. Paint it with thin washes of thalo green and a touch of thalo yellow green. Mix yellow ochre, white and a bit of burnt sienna for the faint line around the green patch. (See color plate 55)

Paint the chest with a mixture of a little raw sienna and white. This makes a buffy color with a pinkish cast. After you apply several washes of this color, paint black spots, 1/8-inch in diameter, at random on it. (See color plate 53) On top of these, apply several more washes of the base color, then repaint about one-third of the black spots. (See color plate 54) (These can be done before or after the vermiculations are painted.)

Paint the vermiculations with successive coats of white and black, using Method 4. (Color plates 50 and 51) Paint cupped feathers on the black rump very faintly with white and a dot of yellow ochre. Edge the tail feathers in white paint with the pull-and-lift method. (Color plate 52) Wash between applications of feather

Fig. 549. These up-wings are completely carved and textured.

Fig. 550. Mark the postition for the wings. The inner marking is for the wings-up bird; the outer line is for the wings-down bird.

Fig. 551. Temporarily tack the wings in place to see how they look.

Fig. 552. Give the bird and its wings two thin washes of burnt umber.

Fig. 555. The top of the wing is painted medium dusky-gray.

Fig. 553. Next, apply two thin white washes.

Fig. 556. Paint top of tail, sides, back and collar around neck a medium dusky gray.

Fig. 554. Underside of wing is painted light dusky gray.

Fig. 557. Paint rump with a mixture of black and a little ultramarine blue.

edgings with ultra-thin burnt umber.(The vermiculations can be painted before the chest is spotted, if you wish. Paint the bill black and coat with gloss medium.

Paint the primaries on the upper side of the wing a little darker than the arm of the wing, using a little more black in the dusky gray mixture. Paint the secondaries thalo green with a touch of thalo yellow green. Add some green iridescent paint powder to them to create the illusion of iridescence. (Color plate 56) Paint a narrow band of white along the trailing edge of the secondaries. Paint the secondary coverts with raw sienna and white mixed to a pale orangish color. Edge them in white.

Paint cupped feathers on the upper arm of the wing using raw sienna and white. Edge the tertials and primary coverts in raw sienna and white, using the flat edge of the brush. Apply the toning wash of ultra-thin burnt umber and re-edge, apply the toning wash and repeat several times. (Color plate 57)

The undersides of the wings are medium dusky gray. The tips of the primaries are a little darker. All the coverts are edged in white.

Paint the feet and legs bluish-gray to olive-gray, using black, white and burnt umber. Paint the webs darker and the nails black.

Fig. 559. Belly is painted whitish and wet-blended into gray sides. Paint a jagged edge at under-rump.

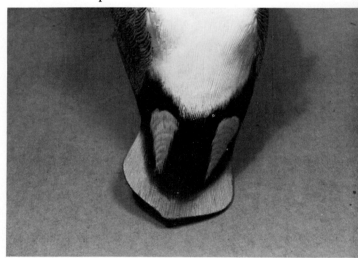

Fig. 560. Paint the under-tail coverts a pale yellow.

Fig. 558. Under-rump is painted with the same black. Tail is painted light dusky gray.

Fig. 561. Paint head burnt sienna and chest a buffy color with a pinkish cast. Also see color plate 49.

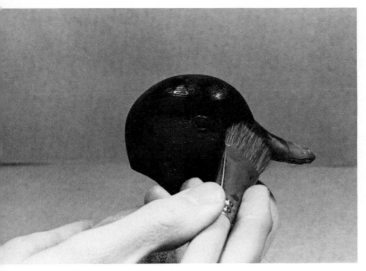

Fig. 562. Wet-blend a tiny amount of burnt umber into crown.

Fig. 563. Wet-blend a tiny amount of yellow ochre into cheek.

Fig. 564. Paint patch around eye with thalo green and thalo yellow-green.

Fig. 565. Paint a narrow yellowish line around the green patch.

Fig. 566. Begin method 4 of vermiculations over back and sides.

Fig. 567. Edge tail feathers in white paint.

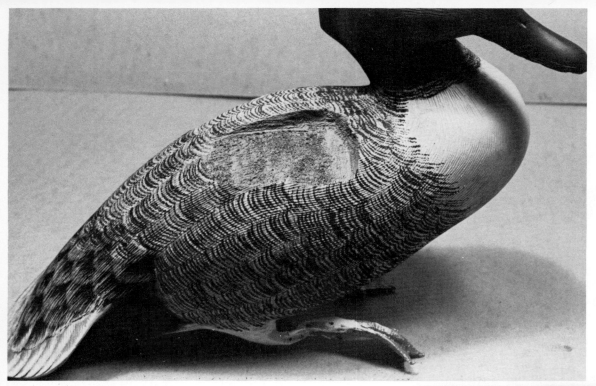

Fig. 568. Black paint is alternated with white in method 4 of vermiculations.

Attach the wings to the body as you've done before. After you've sanded and textured the Wood Dough, repaint the areas that are covered with Wood Dough. Finally, apply a final toning wash of ultra-thin burnt umber over all the gray areas and the vermiculated areas.

PAINTING HEN

Paint the hen the same way you painted the hen in Project Four. Paint the belly whitish. Paint fairly tight cupped feathers over the belly in plain white. Paint the tertials, scapulars and primary coverts on the underside of the wing white with just a touch of raw sienna. The cupped feathers in the area forward of the secondaries and the secondary coverts are painted the same as the drakes. Paint the primaries burnt umber with a touch of white, with the tips slightly darker. Paint the feet and legs bluish-gray with dusky webs.

Fig. 569. Apply a toning wash of ultra-thin burnt umber to vermiculated area.

Fig. 570. Paint 1/8-inch round black spots randomly over chest.

Fig. 571. Spots have been painted on chest.

Fig. 574. Paint bill black and coat with gloss medium.

Fig. 572. Apply several washes of base color over the spots.

Fig. 575. Paint primaries a little darker than the arm of wing.

Fig. 573. Re-paint about one-third of the black spots.

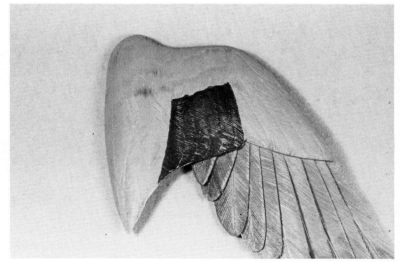

Fig. 576. Paint secondaries green and add iridescent green powder.

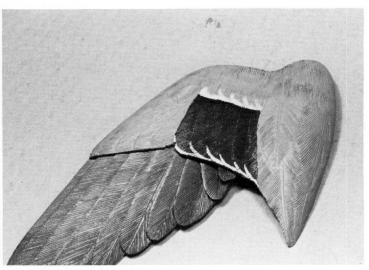

Fig. 577. Edge secondaries with white and paint secondary coverts.

Fig. 578. Edge the feathers on the arm of wing.

Fig. 579. In this project you also can make an extended-wing hen.

Other Types of Waterfowl Carvings

Waterfowl carvings do not have to be textured. Hunting decoys and smooth decorative bird carvings are still being made by many carvers for a variety of reasons.

Fig. 580. Black duck decoy by Taylor Johnson.

Chapter 19
Hunting Decoys

The hunting decoy is the only true American folk art. The Indians made decoys of skins and reeds. As time passed, man's sense of aesthetics caused hunting decoys to evolve to their present state. Some of the most charming and graceful carvings I have ever seen happen to be hunting decoys—the Ward decoys and the Jersey shore, Delaware River, Illinois River, Chincoteague and the Stratford decoys. The lines in some of the decoys are fantastically simple but beautiful. One of my favorites is a Black duck decoy made by Taylor Johnson in Bay Head, N.J. around 1900.

The hunting decoy should not be confused with any other kind of waterfowl carving. It is a working tool, designed for a special set of circumstances, such as for use in a specific body of water. The problem is that carvers keep trying to make hunting decoys more decorative. They add texturing or inserts, eventually turning their hunting decoys into floating decoratives.

If you're going to make a hunting decoy, it will probably be for one of two reasons--for competition in the hunting decoy division of a show or for the special mystique of hunting over your own hand-carved decoys. (I can't think of any other reasons why you'd decide to make one because it has become more expensive to make a wooden decoy than to buy one of some cheaper material than wood.) Whatever your reason, keep it simple! If you add decorative details, they will be a nuisance as far as hunting is concerned, and the carving will be separated from the other hunting decoys in competition.

The hunting decoy is usually larger than lifesize. This is partly because extra width gives it more stability on the water and partly because hunters feel the larger the decoy, the better the ducks will decoy to it.

The head is large and the bill is thick because hunters hold a decoy by the head and bill. The decoy should not be textured anywhere because mud may cake in the grooves. (Combing and stippling to simulate vermiculations are permitted in competition.) Wing tips are generally not raised because they may break off under working conditions. Hunting decoys usually are rigged, meaning that they have a line and anchor. In competition you would not need them, but you would need to make provision for them.

Most important, hunting decoys should be able to float in smooth and rough water. They must be seaworthy-- balanced and stable on the water--so they must be hollowed out. They must be able to self-right when tipped on one side. Diving ducks, which are generally associated with rough water, must be able to self-right from any angle. To do so, the duck needs a lower center of gravity than in a floating decorative; consequently, it has a weighted keel.

MAKING A HUNTING DECOY

Because a hunting decoy is rather large, the body is made out of two blocks of wood rather than one. Hold the two blocks together with several dots of 5-minute epoxy. Rough-out the body on the bandsaw. Do your basic shaping. Then pop the pieces apart. Hollow them on a drill press, leaving about a ½-inch shell of wood on all sides and a ½-inch rim. Be sure both pieces are hollowed evenly. Plane the rims on the piece smooth, then glue them together permanently with 5-minute epoxy. You can fill the seam with Wood Dough if you choose, but it's not critical on a hunting decoy.

Make the keel out of any wood--an inexpensive pine is satisfactory. The keel should never be longer than the decoy and

Fig. 581 & 582. Two hunting decoys made by the
author in the collection of James Dodd.

probably shouldn't be more than 1½-
inches deep. I generally make keels
1¼-inches deep and 2 to 2½-inches wide.
There are no absolutes about keel dimensions; there are probably as many different
keel sizes as there are carvers.

Determine what type of weight you'll
incorporate in the keel. You can use small
pieces of lead poured into drilled holes in
the top or sides of the keel. You can also
use a strip of lead inserted in a hollow in
the top of the keel or attached on the
outside of the keel. Determine the amount
of lead needed by holding the keel and lead
on the decoy with a wide rubber band and
floating it in a tub of water. Add lead as
necessary until the duck is balanced and
able to self-right.

Finally, attach the keel to the decoy
with 5-minute epoxy and drive in two
finishing nails diagonally from the ends of
the keel into the decoy bottom. Drill a hole
through the keel or screw in a little hook
for the rigging provision.

PAINTING WOOD DECOYS

Working decoys need to be repainted
every couple of years, especially if they are
used often. Competition guidelines may
suggest very simple painting of the decoy so
the average hunter will be able to repaint it
easily.

Seal the decoy all over with shellac cut
with alcohol. Apply acrylic or oil paint--
thin washes aren't necessary--so the base
colors meet in a line without wet-blending

or any smooth transition between them.
You can comb modeling paste and gesso on
the vermiculated areas, but it's perfectly
satisfactory to paint them gray. The keel is
generally painted white.

OTHER MATERIALS FOR DECOYS

I prefer the aesthetics of a wood
decoy, but cork decoys are actually more
durable. Cork is light, inexpensive, easy to
work and shape and very buoyant. It needs
to be keeled and weighted so it can
self-right, but does not need to be hollowed
out.

Cork's one disadvantage is that it is
dirty and messy to work with. If you buy
low-cost cork, it will be crumbly and pieces
will chip off easily, so you must glue
½-inch marine plywood to the bottom.
This kind of cork also needs several coats of
sealer.

Consequently, I buy the more expensive, high-density bottle cap or insulation
cork from Wiley Cork Company in
Wilmington, Delaware. It is so tightly
made that it doesn't need sealing and is
virtually indestructible. It is well worth its
higher cost.

Cork can be bought in various
thicknesses. You can buy a piece in the
thickness you require, but that's expensive.
I glue pieces together with contact cement
until the block is the correct thickness.

The head is carved out of wood
because a cork head would break off. You
can also buy plastic heads.

Fig. 583. High density cork, which is in the middle, makes a more durable decoy than lighter cork.

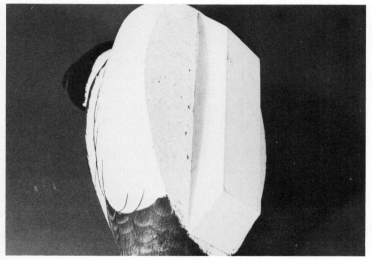

Fig. 584. The keel on hunting decoys should be no larger than bird bottom.

Cut the body out on a bandsaw and shape it with a surform rasp, a rasp on the Foredom tool or a sander. Use a dull rasp because a sharp one cuts into the cork too easily. Cut a channel where the tail goes and slide in a piece of ¼-inch thick fiberboard to be the tail, because a cork tail would break off. Glue it in with any waterproof glue.

Drill a hole up through the cork body and a couple of inches into the head. Insert a 1/8-inch brass screw eye. This will hold the head on the body and the hook will stay on the bottom to serve as the rigging provision.

Seal the cork well with Val oil or full-strength shellac (unless you use high density cork.) Paint with a flat oil or acrylic house paint. Any details, such as the secondary color patch, can be painted with acrylic artist's paint.

Fig. 585. Attach the keel and lead to decoy and hold with rubber band to determine amount of lead needed.

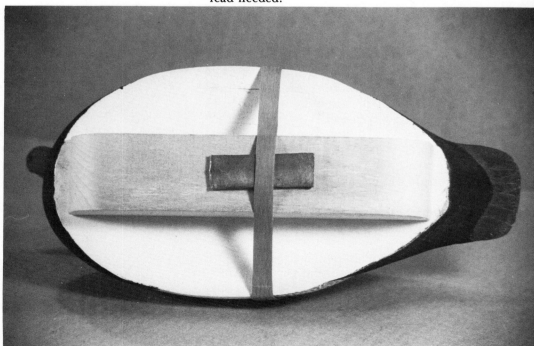

Chapter 20
Smooth Decorative Carvings

Smooth decorative bird carvings became particularly popular about 15 years ago. They are not very common now because of the popularity of texturing, but there's still room for them in the carving world.

Generally, a smooth carving is painted to be decorative. However, it can also have inserts or the feather layout burned in. It can be superbly stylized, as Armand Carney does, with a combing technique and delicately developed painting techniques. Very few carvers are so proficient.

I suggest to my students that they buy smooth machine-made blanks to paint over and over again. If they can do a good job of painting a smooth bird, they certainly will be able to paint a textured bird.

For it is a fact that smooth carvings are more difficult to paint than textured carvings. A textured bird has a definite feather layout that is easy to follow with paint. With a smooth bird you're looking at a smooth, broad expanse. You have to start from scratch.

First, you have to do an outstanding job of sanding--much better than you'd do on a textured carving. As far as I'm concerned, this is the curse of smooth-bird carving because I hate sanding. Then you put on one coat of gesso and sand it. Finally you chalk on the outlines for the paint colors and feather patterns. All colors must have a smooth transition between them. A smooth carving takes a lot of time, care and precision to paint well.

Smooth carvings can be stained instead of painted, and this is a good deal easier to do. Apply a wood stain of your choice directly on the bare wood. Lightly sand and restain if desired. Top it with wax, gloss or satin polyurethane, or any other finish you like.

One problem with staining a carving is that Wood Dough does not take stain the same way wood does, so use as little Wood Dough as possible. After staining the carving, smear burnt umber artist's oil paint lightly over the Wood Dough to blend it with the rest of the wood.

You might decide to do an unpainted smooth-bodied carving just because you like a certain wood. Paulownia, which is readily available in my area, is a beautiful, soft and wide-grained wood that doesn't take detail well, so it's ideal for a smooth carving. White cedar and almost any hard wood like walnut, cherry, or red cedar make good smooth, unstained carvings, but because they are so hard they're more difficult to carve. If you do not stain the wood, just glue the seam, and do not fill it with Wood Dough.

SUPPLIERS OF BLANKS

Machine-made blanks can be bought from the following suppliers:

Bay County Decoys
Oak Hall, VA 23416

Dolington Woodcrafts
Washington Crossing
Newtown Road
Newtown, PA 18940

Elk Creek Decoys
955 Blueball Road
Elkton, MD 21921

Flyway Decoys
RD #2, Box 252C
Wading River Rd.
Egg Harbor City, N.J. 08215

Hutch Decoys
7715 Warsaw Ave.
Glen Burnie, MD 21061

Wildfowler Decoys
56 Park Ave.
Babylon, N.Y. 11702

Your Continued Development

Here are four more carving projects, all of which incorporate additional techniques. By the time you have finished them you will have been at least introduced to many of the basic techniques used in the carving world today. Continue your development as a carver by entering your carvings in shows, seeking a market for them and finally, learning how to develop your own patterns.

Chapter 21
Making Repairs

One thing you should learn as part of your development as a carver is how to repair a carving if anything goes wrong with it.

Sometimes you'll have begun a carving when you discover that the wood is beginning to check or crack. If you're not too far into the carving, the best thing to do would be to throw out the wood and start again. Usually if wood checks once, it is likely to check somewhere else.

On the other hand, if you're well into a carving and want to salvage it, it is worth a try. Cut into the check a little beyond it as well as a little deeper. Pour in 5-minute epoxy to fill the entire cut. Cut a channel, as you do in making a seam, so you can overfill the area with Wood Dough saturated with acetone, and finally sand it smooth.

A honeycomb checks looks like a honeycomb inside the wood. It comes from improper drying of wood. It never can be fixed, so you may as well throw away the wood.

If you find a knot of any size in your block, you will have to get rid of it because if it's loose it will eventually come out, or it may bleed through the paint. Cut out the knot with a Foredom tool or drill. If it's a smooth-bodied bird, fill the hole with auto-body filler and sand smooth. If it's a textured bird, fill the hole almost to the top with auto-body filler. When it is dry, overfill with Wood Dough, sand and texture. If the knot is very small, just drill it out and fill with Wood Dough.

If an insert breaks, it will have to be replaced. With a fishtail chisel, pry down into the channel to break the glue line. You may have to remove several inserts at the same time. Make a new insert and glue it inside the channel.

If a feather tip breaks, replace the feather. If the broken piece is very small, you can try to sculpt a new one out of Wood Dough.

If the texturing gets bumped severely, fill the area with Wood Dough, sand, texture and paint.

If an eye gets scratched, dig it out and replace it with a new eye.

Chapter 22
Carving an Old Squaw Drake

Although the Old Squaw may appear to be very similar to earlier projects, it actually isn't. New and important techniques are utilized in making it.

CARVING THE BODY

The body of the Old Squaw is made from two 2-inch blocks of pine or basswood. It can be made from one block, if you have a piece of 4-inch stock available, but that's expensive to buy. Whatever the size of the blocks, the body must be hollowed even if the carving isn't going to be a floating decorative. Hollowing is necessary when a block of wood is thicker than 3-inch stock (and can be done as a safety measure for blocks three inches or smaller). It was cut closer to the heart of the tree and tends to move a lot, so it may crack or check. When it is hollowed, the internal stresses of the wood are relieved, so there will be less probability of the the wood checking. The 2-inch blocks also should be hollowed because the denser the mass, the more likely they are to check.

Begin by puting together the two blocks with several dots of 5-minute epoxy. Rough out the body as usual, trim it and

Fig. 588. The Old Squaw drake carving project utilizes new and important techniques.

the bottom one more. If it is going to float, hollow the pieces to a ½-inch thickness and leave a ½-inch wide ledge. If it's not going to float, it doesn't have to be hollowed so precisely as balance is not a concern.

Put the pieces back together with 5-minute epoxy and fill the seam.

CARVING THE HEAD

The head is basically shaped the same as other carvings are except that it doesn't have the same cut-in at the culmen. The forehead just flows right down into the bill. The eyes should be hazel and 9 mm. in size.

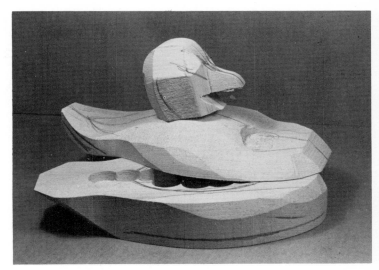

Fig. 589. Body is made in two pieces that must be hollowed.

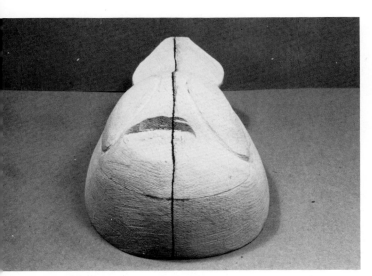

Fig. 590. Centerline helps you shape the body and keep both sides symmetrical.

Fig. 592. Head is carved as other heads are except that there is no cut-in at culmen.

Fig. 591. Head is roughed out and ready to be shaped.

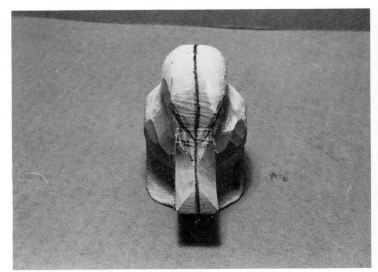

Fig. 593. Head is ready to be textured following figure 596.

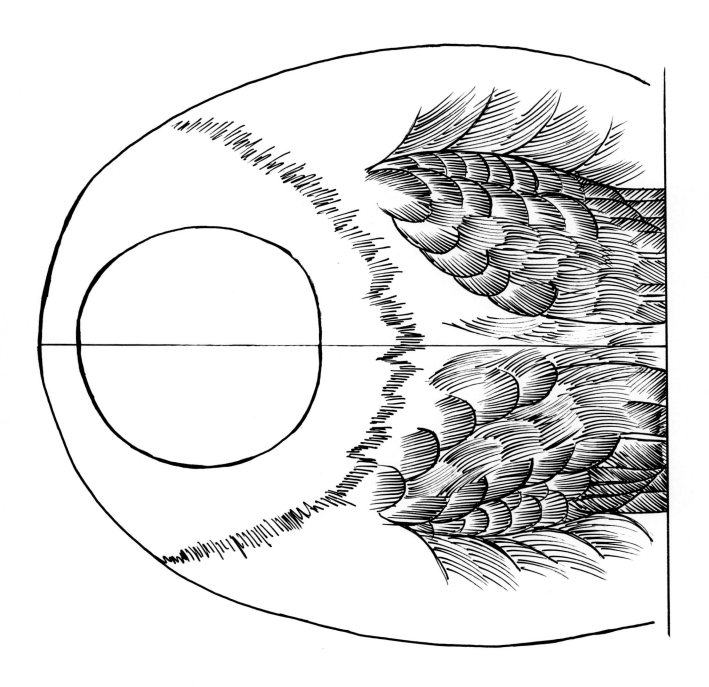

Fig. 594. Plan view and texturing

Fig. 595. Tail feather insert

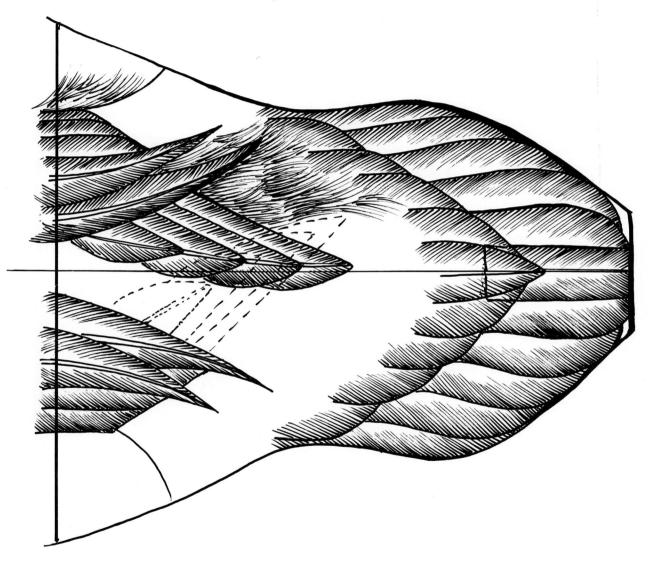

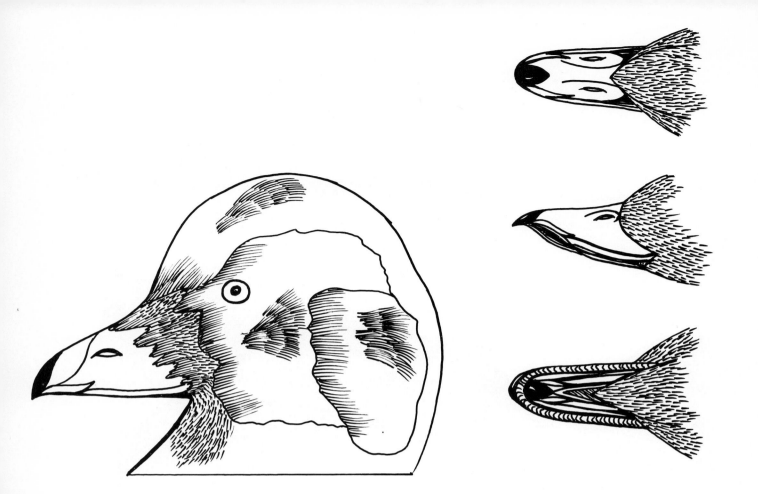

Fig. 596. Head profile

Fig. 597. Bill--top, profile and underside

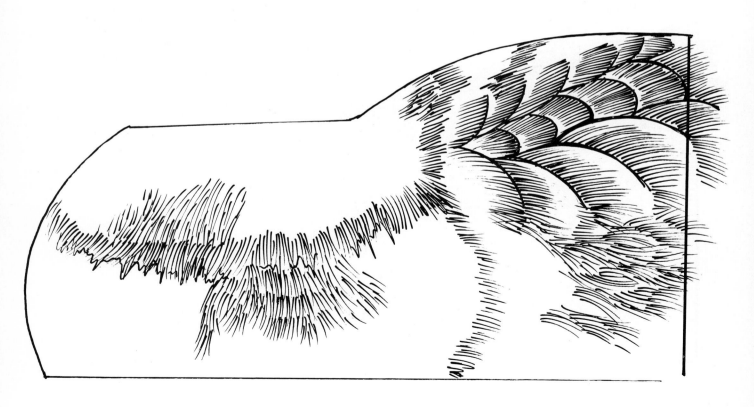

214

Fig. 598. Profile of body

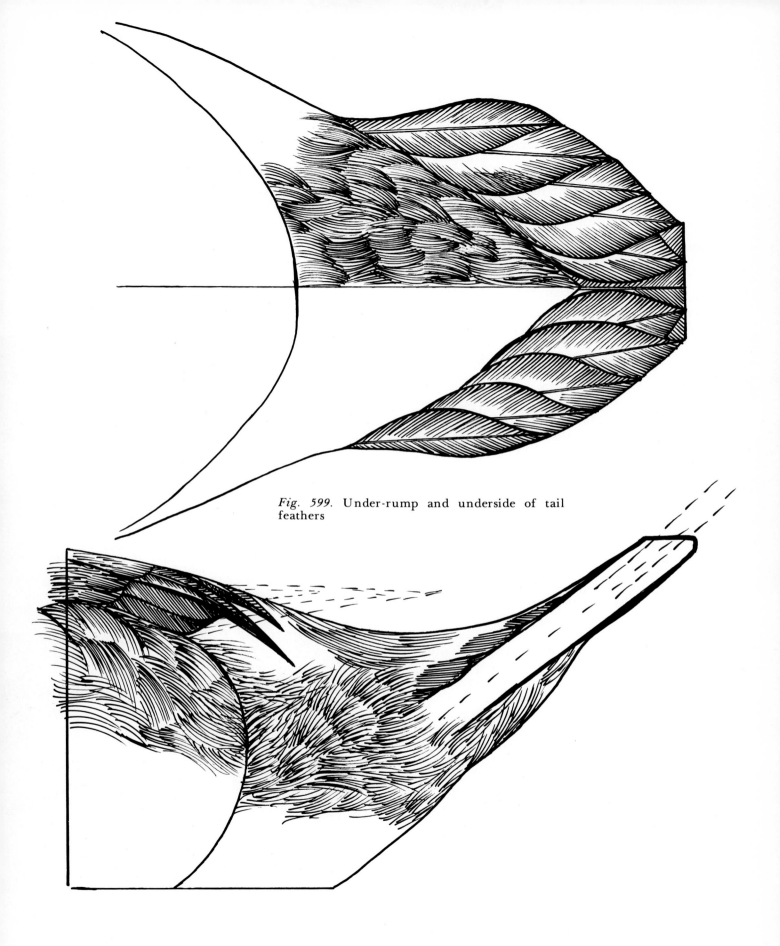

Fig. 599. Under-rump and underside of tail feathers

TEXTURING

On the live bird, the solid expanses of black and white make the feather layout less noticeable than it is on other birds. Therefore, a simple texturing all over the body is all that's necessary to simulate the flow of the feathers. To add interest to the surface I texture part of it coarsely with the stone on the Foredom tool and texture the tail, primaries, secondaries and tertials with the metal discs or dental separating discs. The surface can also be textured with the burning pen.

INSERTS

I use two types of inserts on this carving. On the live bird, when it is floating on the water, the tail is long and pointed and the tips of the primaries are slightly arced. To duplicate the tail feather, I cut a flat insert out of veneer, using the pattern in figure 595, boil it and bend it in a jig to give it a slight curve. Insert the tail feather in a channel cut under the tail coverts. I make the primaries in a solid block, and bend them by cutting them off the block and burning them on the underside. Make a pattern from the dotted lines on the plan view and profile of the body.

PAINTING

The Old Squaw is basically a black and white bird, and therefore, fairly difficult to paint well.

Apply two washes of burnt umber, then two white washes. Next paint the entire bird with 8 to 10 washes of light gray (mix black, white and a little burnt umber).

Paint the center four feathers of the tail, center of the rump, the line between the wings, the collar around the neck and the chest brownish-black (black and burnt umber). The arm of the wings is also painted brownish-black.

Edge the feathers on the sides, rump, tail (not the black feathers), tertials and wing patch forward of the tertials with white. Paint the secondaries a rust color, made of burnt sienna and burnt umber. Paint the primaries burnt umber mixed with a touch of white.

Paint the head, upper chest and neck whitish (white and a touch of burnt umber).

There are two color patches on the cheek. The forward one is burnt umber plus white. The darker one is burnt umber with a touch of black. Put them on at the same time as the white so you can blend them into the white, leaving a jagged edge around them.

Paint around the eye with the whitish color.

Paint the bill black, with a flesh-color patch behind the nail on the forward and top part of the bill (use red, white and raw sienna). Paint the nail black.

Apply an ultra-thin burnt umber toning wash all over the carving except on the black areas.

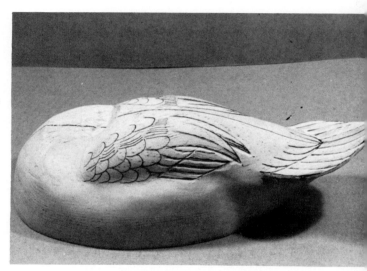

Fig. 600. Carve or burn in feather layout.

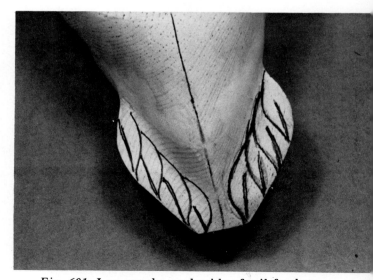

Fig. 601. Lay out the underside of tail feathers.

216

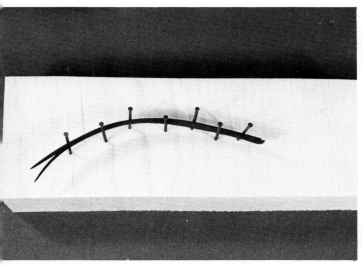

Fig. 602. Bend the center tail feather in a jig.

Fig. 603. Cut a channel under the tail coverts for center tail feather.

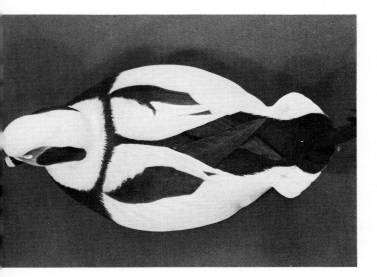

Figs. 604, 605, 606 & 607. Painting details of Old Squaw drake.

217

Chapter 23
Carving a Clapper Rail

Fig. 608. This project originates from a mounted Clapper Rail.

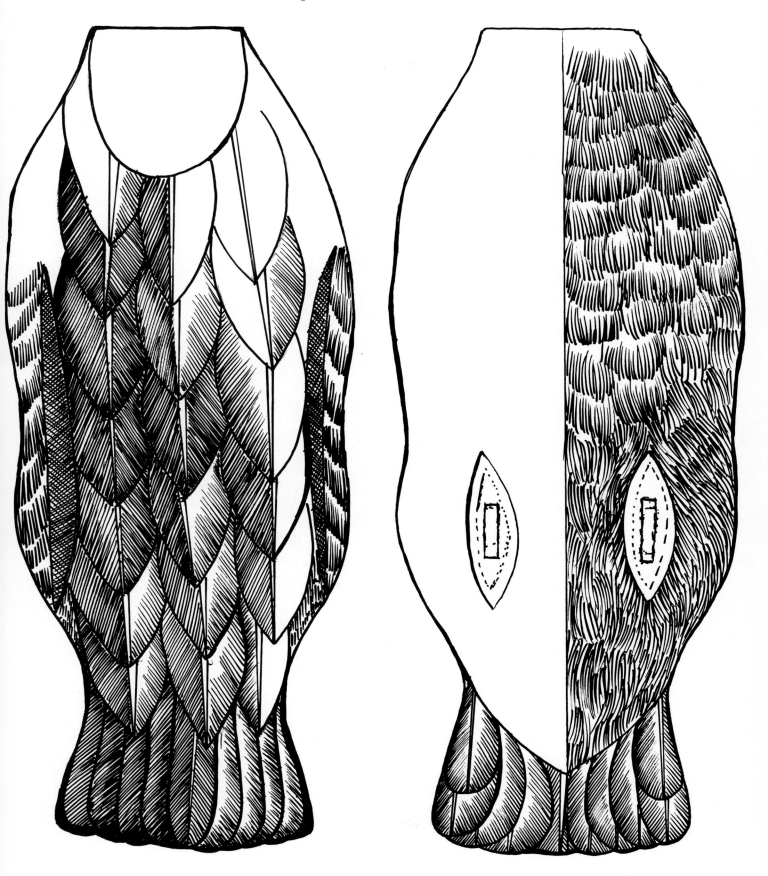

Fig. 609. Back of bird

Fig. 610. Underside of bird

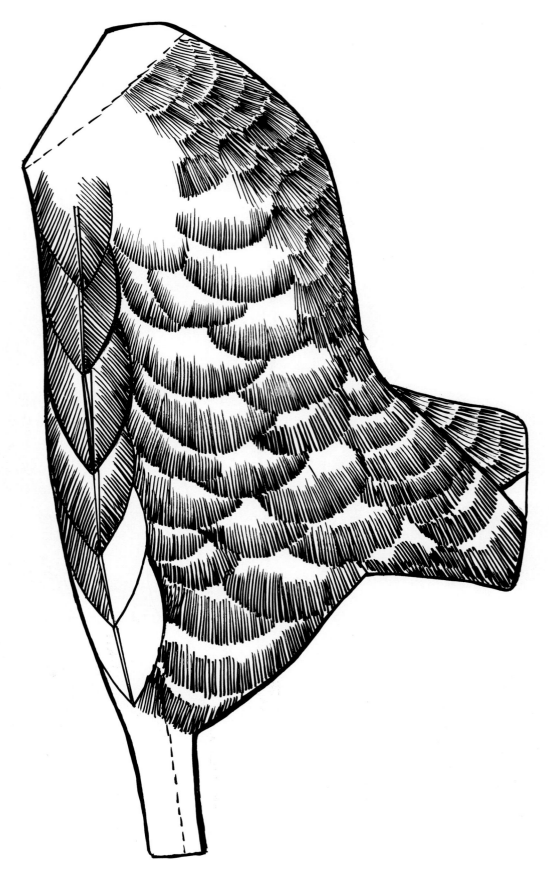

Fig. 611. Profile

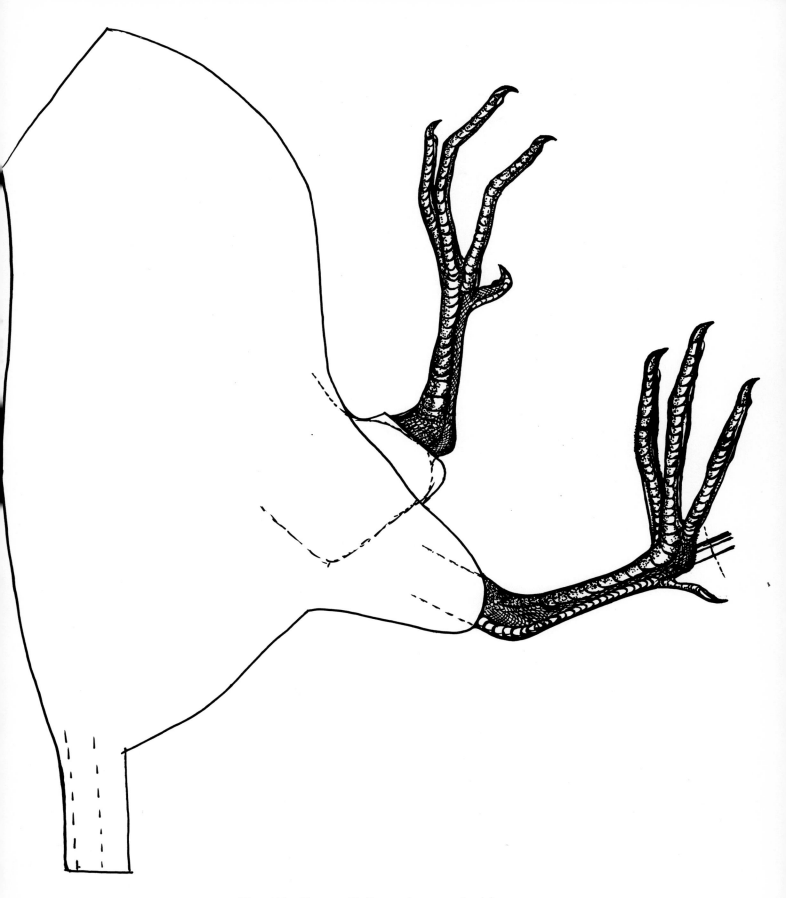

Fig. 612. Clapper Rail can be carved with one
foot up as in mount

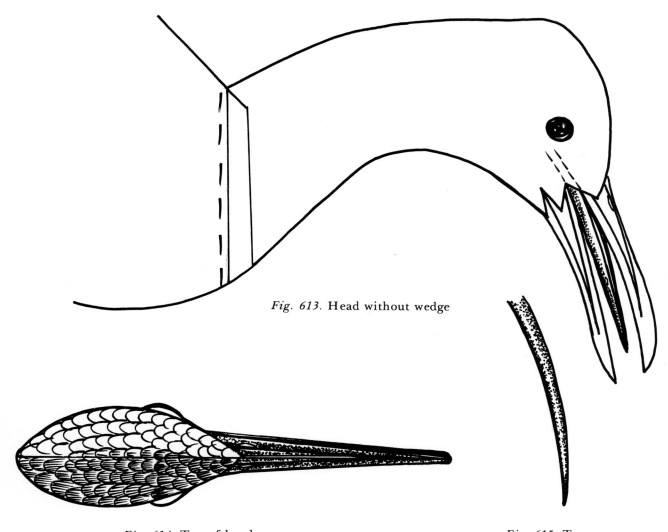

Fig. 613. Head without wedge

Fig. 614. Top of head

Fig. 615. Tongue

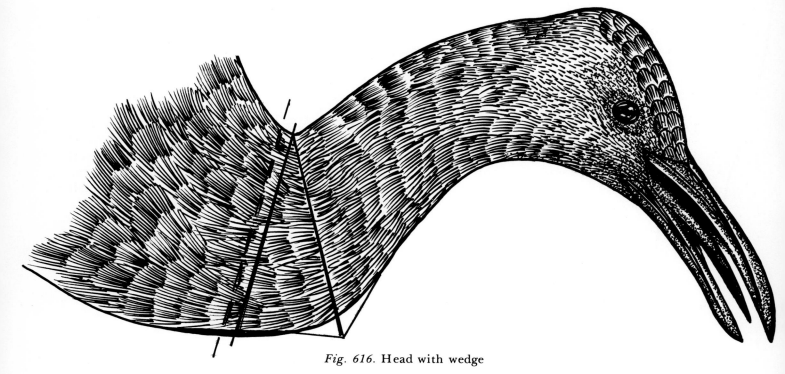

Fig. 616. Head with wedge

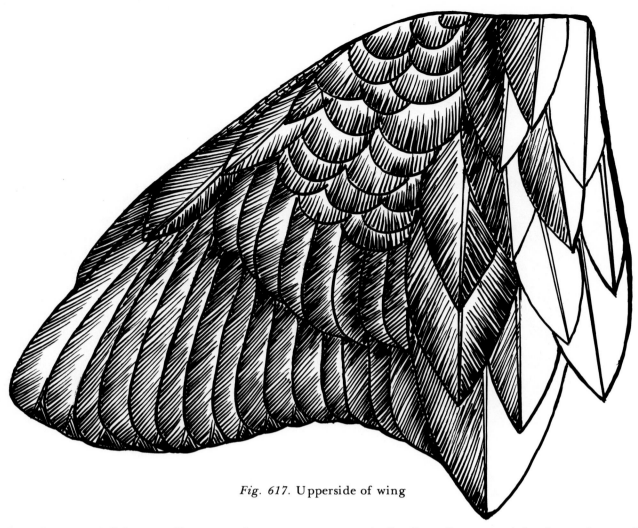

Fig. 617. Upperside of wing

The Clapper Rail is actually a marsh bird and not a waterfowl. It originates from a mount I had made of a road-killed Clapper Rail. A number of my students have used the mount as the source material for carvings; many won blues and two won best of show ribbons in the decorative division. Consequently, I'm particularly fond of this carving project. The bird has a grace and elegance about it that I think is particularly nice to duplicate in a carving. Just as John Scheeler said, "No one is any better than his source material." This Clapper Rail's track record at shows has proven that statement true.

CARVING THE BODY

A Clapper Rail has heavy thighs, much heavier than the tufts on ducks, so they have to be included in the block. When you cut out the body block there will be a wide expanse for the thighs because there's no way to cut them out individually. (Figure 611) With a rasp on the Foredom tool, cut between the thighs so that the belly line flows straight into the under-rump, thus creating two thighs. Cut from the front of one and from the back of the other to offset them, leaving one thigh in front of the other.

The body block also includes the shelf that was used on the extended wing Green-winged Teal. When the head is put on this shelf and turned just slightly, it has a slight angle to it, like the mount has. (Figure 613) The pattern can be adapted by inserting a small wedge of wood between the shelf on the body and the head. The wedge is glued onto the shelf and twisted slightly in either direction. The head is glued on top and twisted a little further, so the bird has a smooth, flowing twist to its head and neck, like figure 616.

Patterns for the head with and without the wedge are included here so you can make a pair of Clapper Rails that are different in attitude from each other. Mount them singly or together in a tableau.

223

Fig. 618. Underside of wing

CARVING THE HEAD

The head itself isn't very different than anything you've done before, but the bill is. Bandsaw the head block, then bandsaw between the mandibles. Basically shape the head and bill with a rasp, and sand. Heat a steel rod red hot and burn a channel in the inside of the lower mandible. Heat the rod again and curve it to fit the shape of the upper mandible. Burn a hollow in the inside of the upper mandible. With the same rod, burn two channels--one for the tongue and one for the lower mandible--under the upper mandible.

Finish shaping the bill with a knife and put in the nostril and other indentations. Sand it smooth.

Make the tongue out of a small piece of basswood or any hardwood carved according to figure 615. You also can make a simple tongue out of a piece of brass rod, 3/16-inch in diameter. Grind one end to a point, curve it slightly and set it in place with 5-minute epoxy.

The eyes are brown and 7 mm. in size.

FEET

Use cast pewter feet and attach them as usual. If you wish to make them, you can't use any of the methods I suggested before because this bird has three distinct toes. Start with 1/8-inch and 1/16-inch brass rods. Put them together with the narrower width in back. Wrap them with fine wire, leaving ½-inch or so at both ends unwrapped to be inserted into the body and the mount. Glue the wire to the rods with superglue or 5-minute epoxy to make them rigid.

Construct three toes with pieces of 1/8-inch brass rod. Solder them or glue them onto the leg. Make nails by sharpening the ends of the rods with files, grinding bits or sanders on the Foredom tool. Cover the leg and foot with dental

224

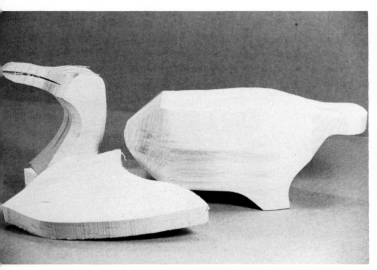

Fig. 619. Roughed-out head, body and wing.

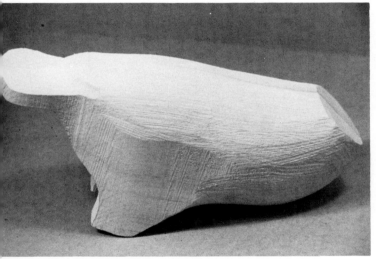

Fig. 620. Body has been shaped but not sanded.

Fig. 621. Wedge is glued to shelf on body to give twist to head and neck.

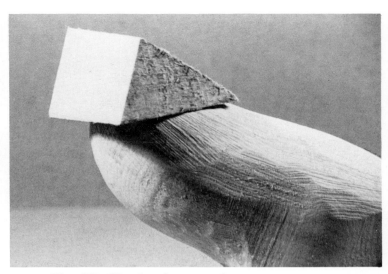

Fig. 622. Glue head onto wedge.

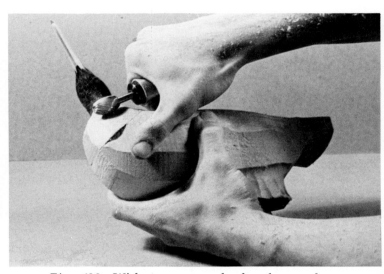

Fig. 623. With rasp, smooth the sharp edges where the pieces join.

Fig. 624. Head has been sanded.

225

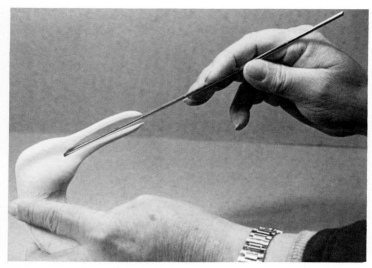

Fig. 625. Burn hollow in lower mandible with heated steel rod.

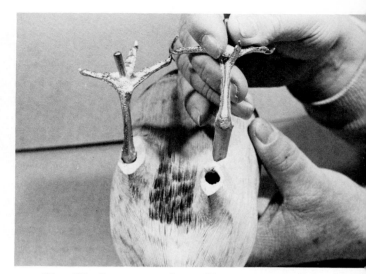

Fig. 628. Cast pewter feet will be able to support body on display base.

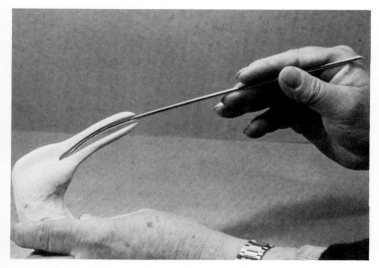

Fig. 626. Curve rod to burn hollow in upper mandible.

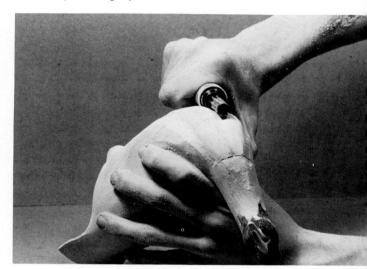

Fig. 629. With rasp, create muscular indentations in chest.

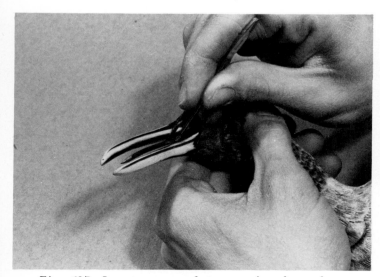

Fig. 627. Insert a carved tongue in channel burned in head.

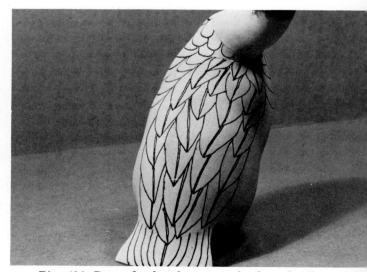

Fig. 630. Draw feather layout on back and tail.

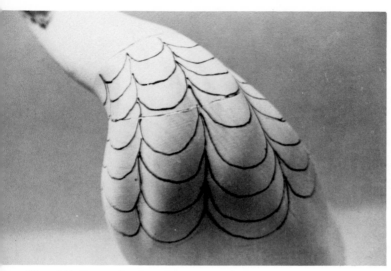

Fig. 631. Draw feather layout on chest.

Fig. 632. Head texture is burned because the head is so prominent.

Fig. 633. Uppersides of wings are textured with burning pen.

acrylic or moldable epoxy, and texture.

There are several reference books listed in the back of this book that thoroughly cover all the details of making feet.

TEXTURING

After the head and neck are attached to the body and everything is shaped, I use a hollow rasp to create muscular indentations in the chest. These give the impression that the bird is really straining. In a way, this is taking artistic license. I'm overemphasizing a prominent point of the bird so it jumps out at you. If you make the bird with its head forward, you should make these indentations to a lesser degree.

I usually burn texture in just the head, wings and tail feathers. On the chest and back I burn the feather layout, and I Foredom tool texture everything else. If I were entering this bird in competition I would burn the texture all over it.

CARVING THE WINGS

The wings are made in two blocks and are glued in notches cut on the back of the bird. They can be set in two different ways. If the head is back, set both wings down, which is true to life. If the head isn't back, the wings can be set any way you like.

PAINTING

Apply the basic burnt umber washes and white washes. Paint the back, tail and upper-wings with several washes of raw umber containing a touch of white. After a soft sheen begins to develop, wet-blend some burnt umber into the centers of the feathers to darken them. Edge the feathers very faintly with a mixture of white, raw sienna and a little Paynes' gray. Wash with ultra-thin burnt umber and re-edge; repeat these steps several times.

Paint the primaries on the under-wings medium brownish-gray. The rest of the under-wing is burnt umber with tiny bars of white. These are done the same way as feather edging, but they are shorter lines than most edgings. Immediately adjacent to the white bars paint dark bars, using burnt umber with a little black.

Paint the sides, under-rump and thighs burnt umber with white edgings.

Paint the chest from the leg joints to the bill with a mixture of raw sienna, white and a little burnt umber. Lighten the paint gradually as you get closer to the bill.

The area extending from the bill to the back of the neck and upward to the edge of the crown is painted dark dusky gray. The chin is painted with the same color as the chest. Extend this color up to the midline of the cheek where it is wet-blended into the gray.

Apply an ultra-thin burnt umber toning wash to the crown and back of neck. With a script brush, paint tiny black streaks through the crown.

There is a faint line along the edge of the crown that extends from the bill to beyond the eye. Paint it with raw sienna and white. Paint a whitish rim following the curvature of the eye.

Undercoat the tongue and the bill inside and out with burnt umber. Paint the center ridge of the bill burnt umber. Wet-blend it on the sides with orange (mix red and yellow to a very subdued yellow-orange). Paint the feet about the same color as the edges of the bill; mix burnt umber and the orange paint. Wash them with burnt umber. Paint the nails burnt umber.

Fig. 634. Undersides of wings are less conspicuous and can be textured by Foredom tool.

Apply an ultra-thin toning wash over the entire carving.

Mount the carving on driftwood or a base. Put a shell in the bird's mouth. For competition purposes, carve a shell out of basswood rather than using an actual shell.

Fig. 635. Note the feather patterns in chest and wings.

Fig. 636. Chin and chest paint are wet-blended into cheek paint.

Fig. 637. Note feather patterns on under-rump and thighs.

Fig. 638. The Clapper Rail is mounted on an attractive piece of driftwood.

Chapter 24
Carving a Whistling Swan and Canada Goose

Fig. 639. The Canada goose and the swan are made in the same way.

Figs. 640 — 643. CANADA GOOSE

Fig. 640. Head profile

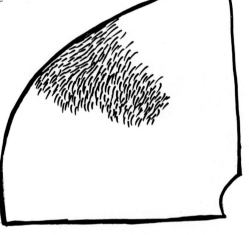

Fig. 641. Back of head piece

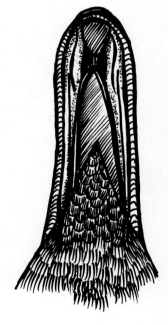

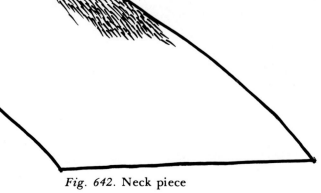

Fig. 642. Neck piece

Fig. 643. Underside of bill

231

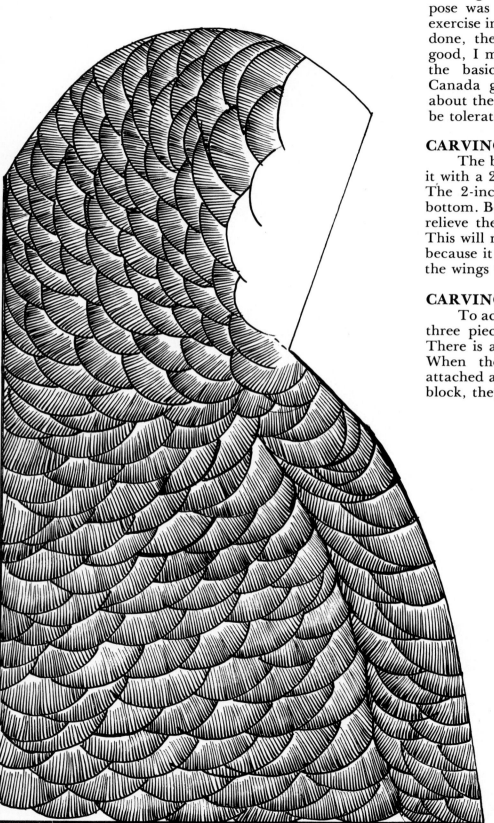

This carving project originated from a commission I once received for a half-life-size swan in a preening pose. I found that creating the gracefully twisted neck for this pose was a challenge and an interesting exercise in problem solving. Once I had it done, the reception to the swan was so good, I made more swans and later used the basic pattern for a lifesize lesser Canada goose and Snow goose. This is about the maximum size carving that can be tolerated in private collections.

CARVING THE BODY

The body is 5-inches thick, so I make it with a 2-inch block and a 3-inch block. The 2-inch piece should be put on the bottom. Both pieces need to be hollowed to relieve the internal stresses of the wood. This will not be a floating decorative bird because it is too cumbersome to float and the wings would be partly underwater.

CARVING THE HEAD AND NECK

To achieve the twisted head and neck, three pieces of 2½-inch stock are used. There is also a ledge on the body block. When the head and neck pieces are attached and shaped and put on the body block, they form a reverse S-shape.

Fig. 644. Goose body--profile

A new technique is used here. The three pieces for the head and neck have to be glued together to be shaped with the rasp before they are textured. But the twisted shape makes it practically impossible to texture some areas on the head and neck. So, when you glue them, put a piece of paper between the head and the back of the head pieces and glue them to the paper. Go on to shape the head and neck, following a centerline drawn through each piece. When you're done, pop the pieces apart. If you had not put the paper there, chances are you'd rip the wood when you pop the pieces apart.

The eyes for both birds are brown, 10 mm. in size.

CARVING THE WINGS

The wings are made of 2-inch stock. Since they are so thick, they must be hollowed on the underside to get rid of the excess wood. The drill press does this quickly. I like the wings to be so well done they jump out at people. Therefore, I carve in the feather layout with the knife and chisel and burn texture into the rest of the wing.

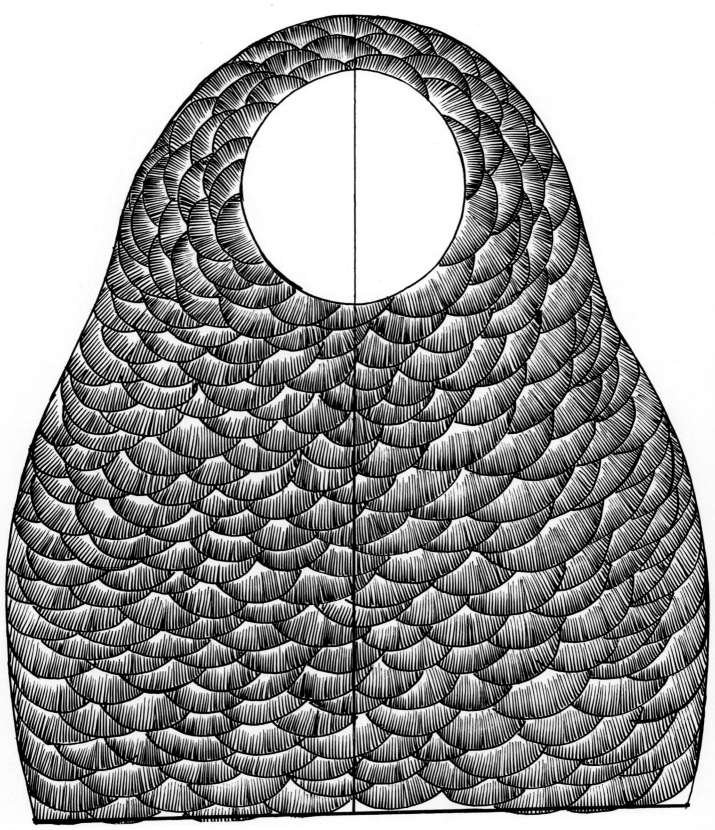

Fig. 645. Goose body--plan view

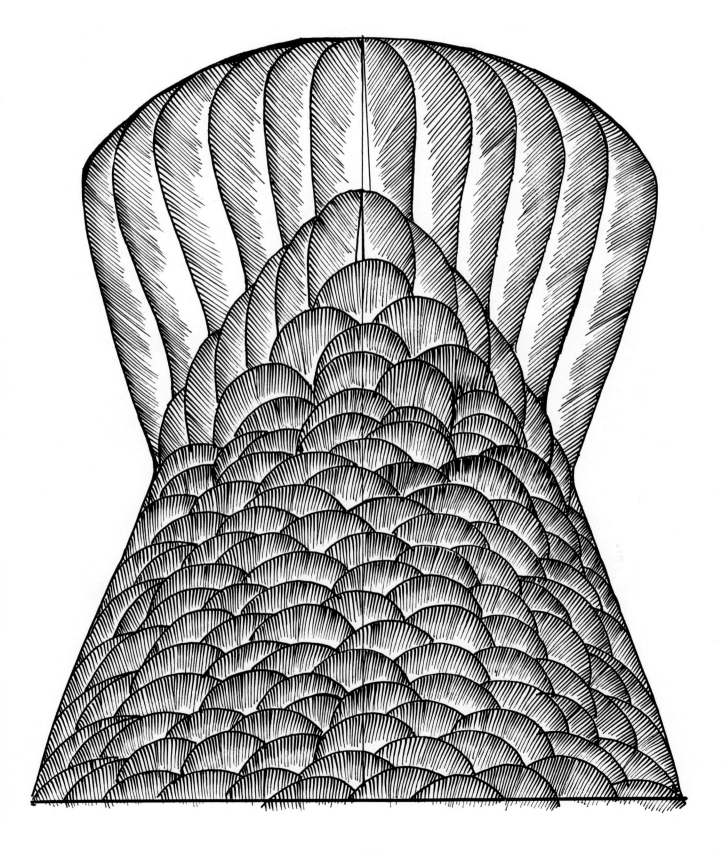

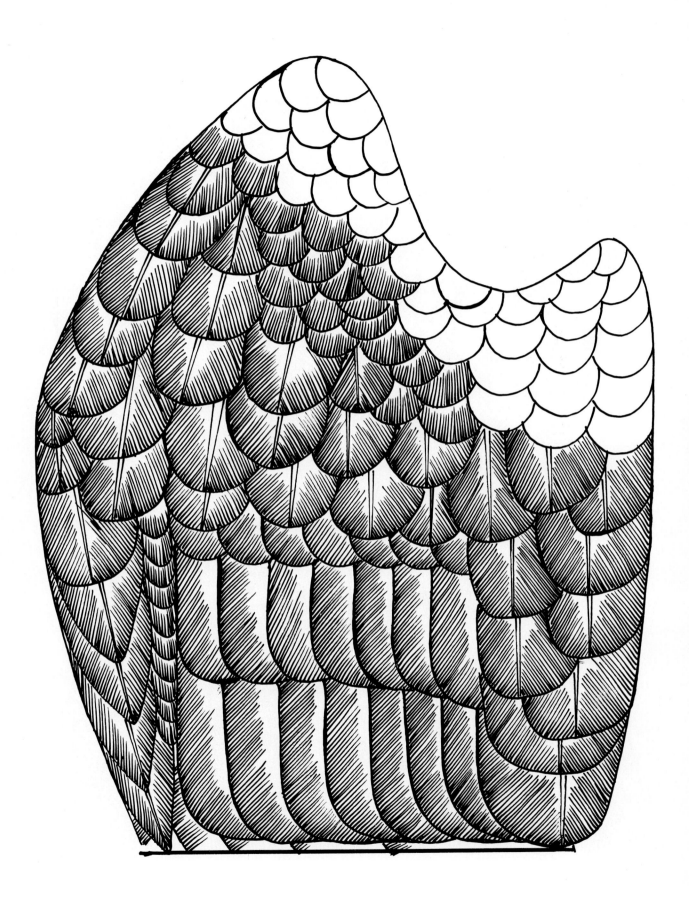

Hold the wings on the body and trace around their edges. Cut notches for them. Do not attach them until the painting is almost finished because it would be impossible to paint the sides of the bird.

TEXTURING

To keep my carving time to a minimum, I burn texture into the head and tail feathers as well as the wings and texture the rest of the neck and body with the Foredom tool. I picked those areas because they are the most prominent ones. If this carving is to be entered in competition, I would burn in texture all over.

PAINTING THE SWAN

After the burnt umber washes and the white washes, mix a pale gray paint using white, a dot of black and a little burnt umber. Apply this mixture to the entire bird, giving it 3 or 4 washes. Edge every feather with white. Where you textured with straight lines, create feathers with the white paint. Apply a very thin wash coat of white paint and re-edge the feathers. Repeat until there is a graduation of tone in each feather. The interior of the feather should be slightly dark, going out to white at the edges. Now the bird will appear chalky because of the white washes. Apply an ultra-thin toning wash of burnt umber

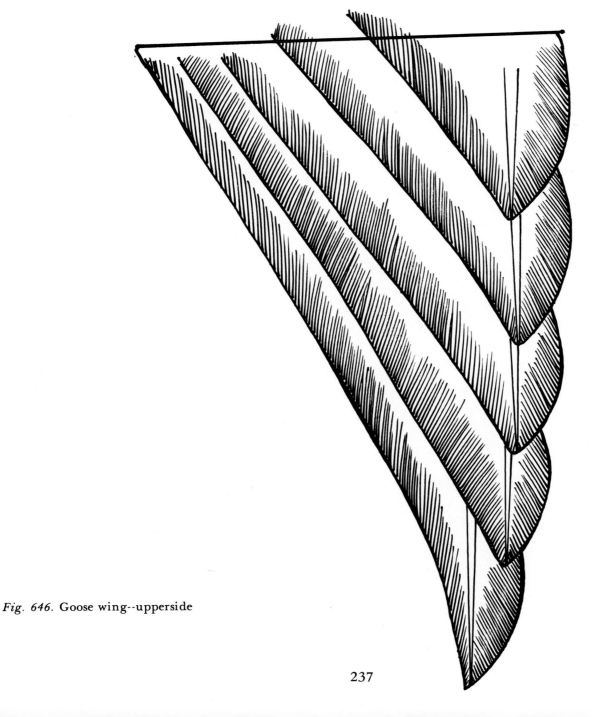

Fig. 646. Goose wing--upperside

237

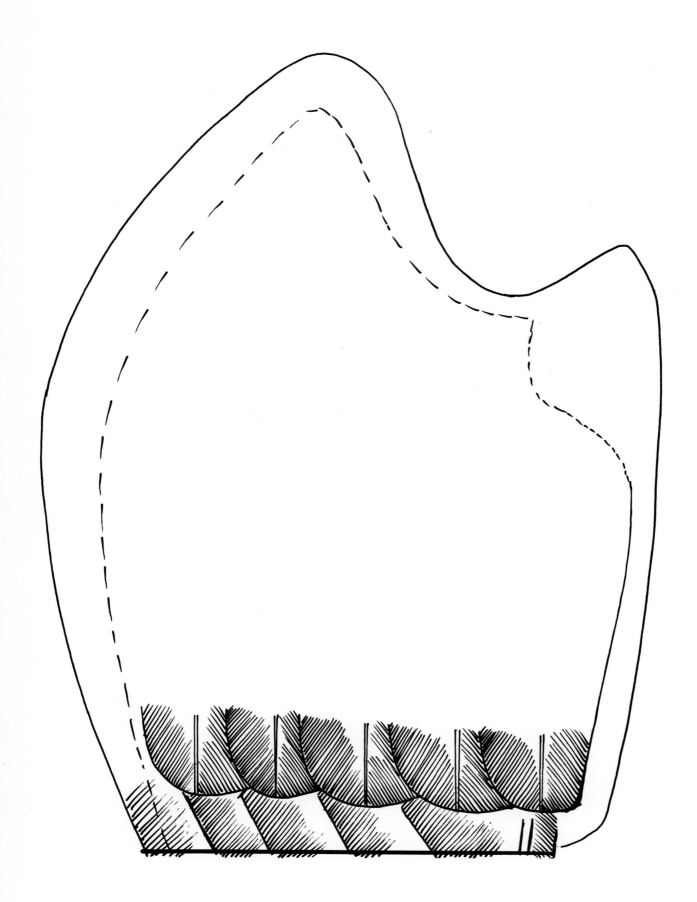

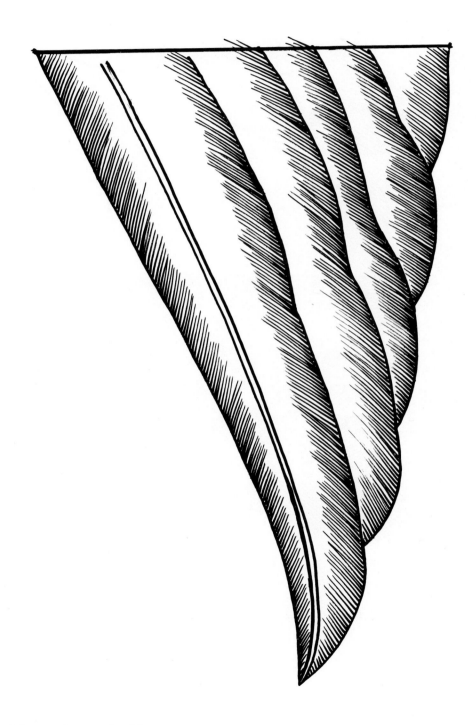

Fig. 647. Goose and Swan wing--underside

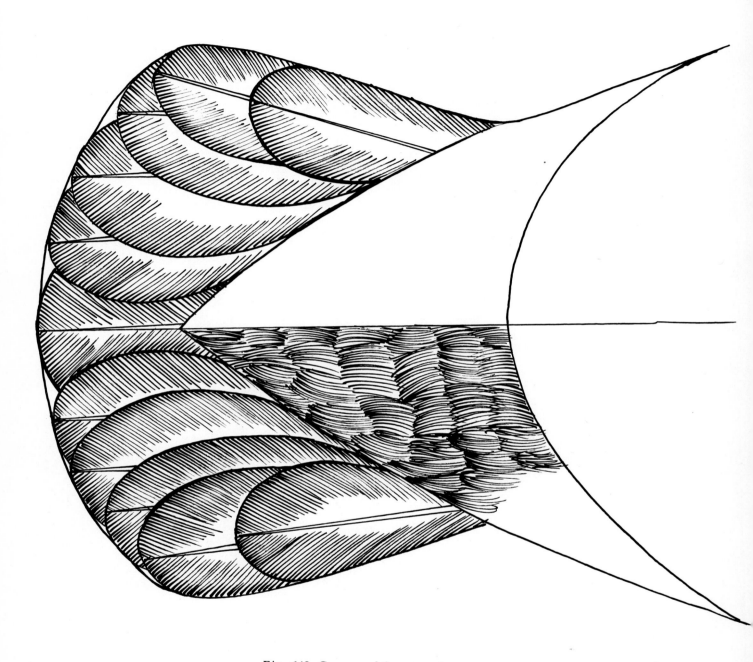

Fig. 648. Goose and Swan under-rump

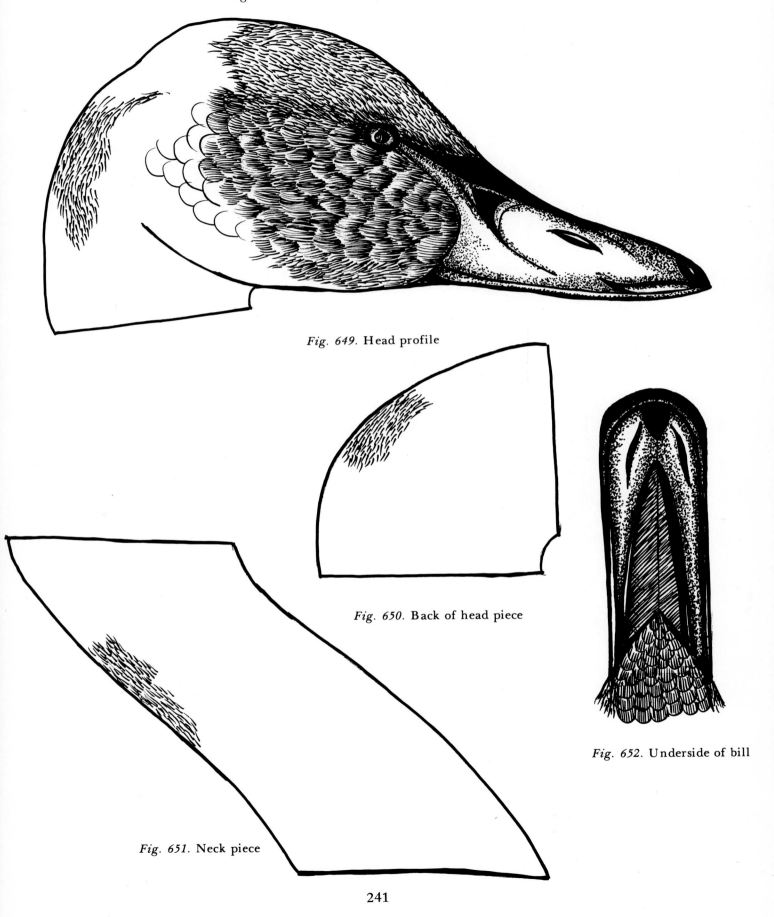

Fig. 649. Head profile

Fig. 650. Back of head piece

Fig. 652. Underside of bill

Fig. 651. Neck piece

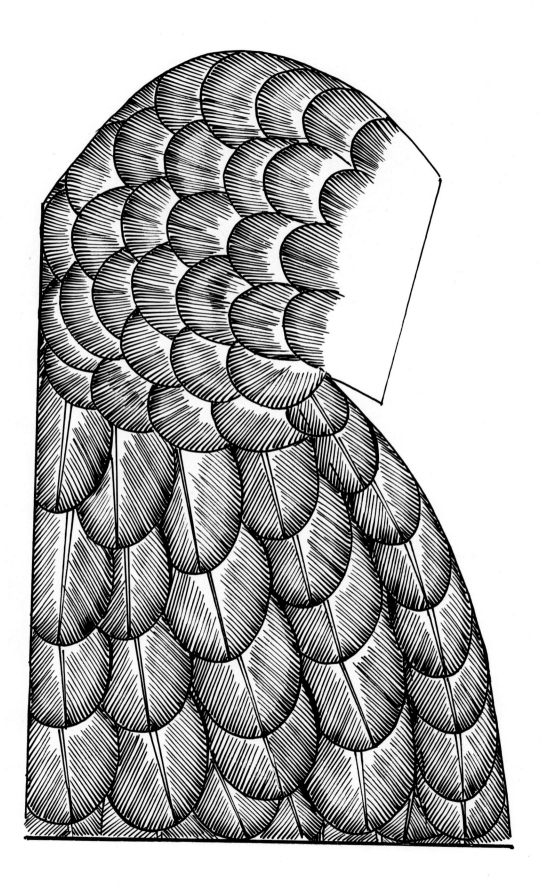

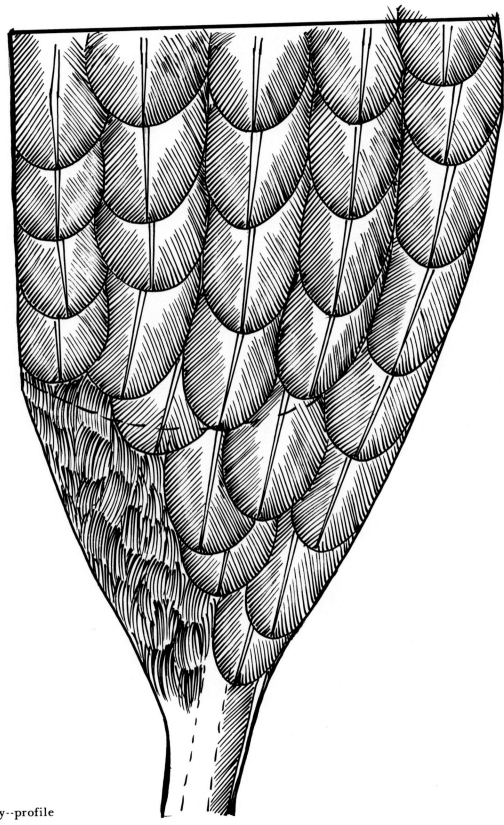

Fig. 653. Swan body--profile

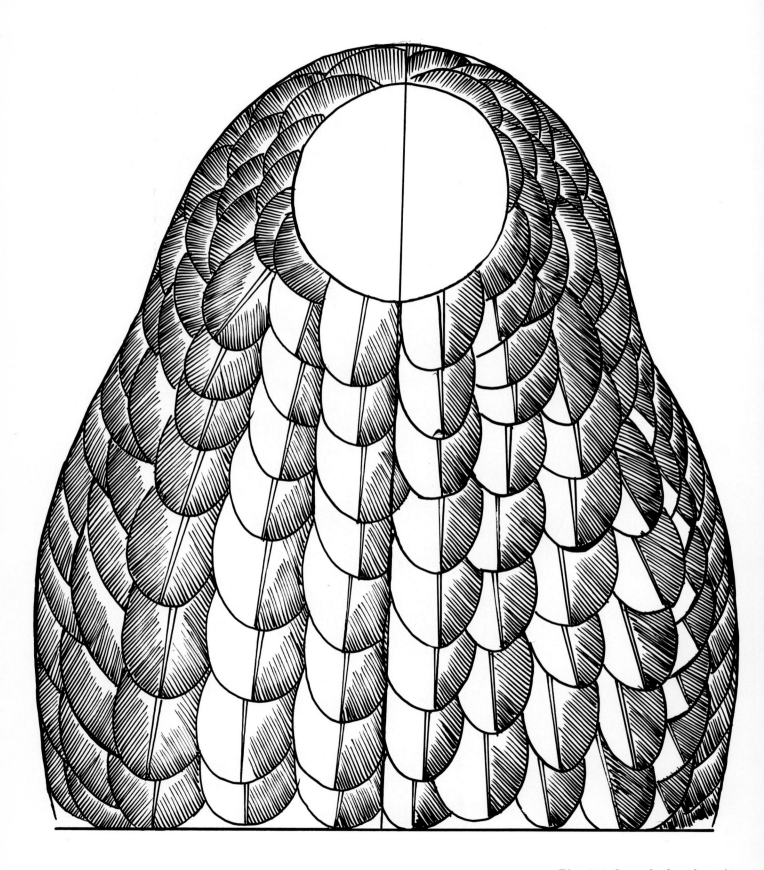

Fig. 654. Swan body--plan view

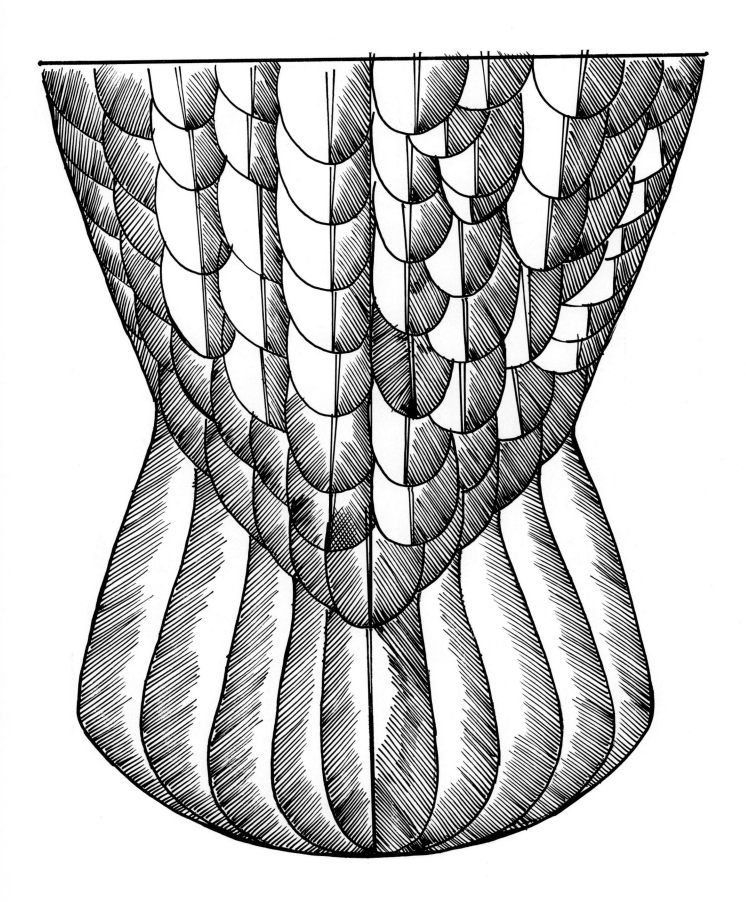

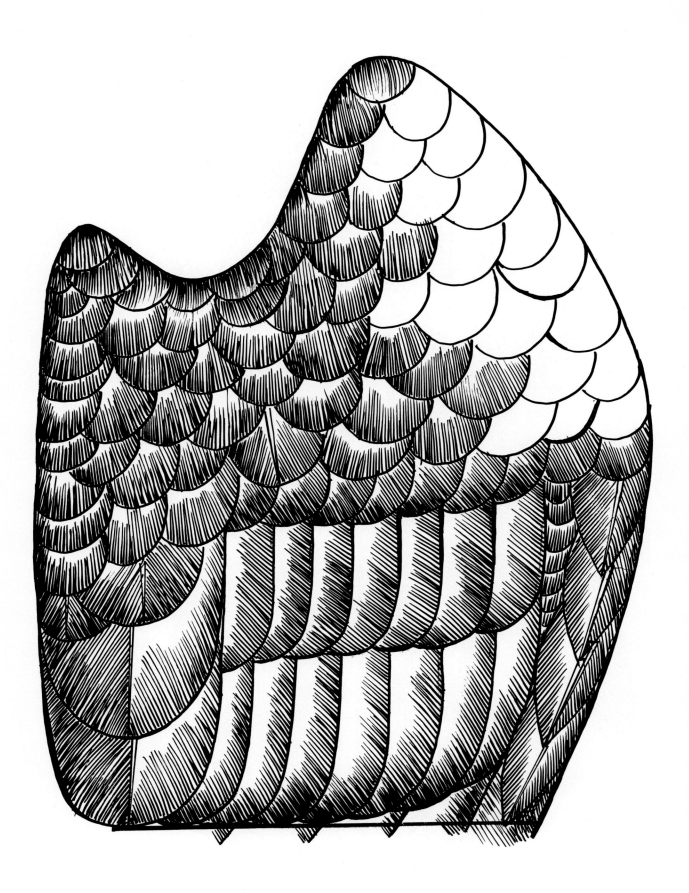

Fig. 655. Swan wing--upper side

all over the body to take away the chalkiness.

Paint the wings the same way. Attach the wings to the body, fill the gaps with Wood Dough, and re-texture as necessary. Touch up the paint.

Paint the bill black with splashes of yellow ochre flaring into the bill from the eye. Apply gloss medium on top. Coat the quills with gloss medium, if you wish, to brighten them and pull them out of the base surface. In life, quills are a little waxy.

PAINTING THE CANADA GOOSE

After the burnt umber and white washes, paint the sides and chest brownish-gray. Edge the feathers with white, apply a thin white wash, re-edge, and so on, just as you did with the swan.

Paint the upper-rump and tail brownish-black using burnt umber and ultramarine blue. Paint the head, neck and bill with the same paint.

Paint the primaries a little more brownish-black by adding a little more burnt umber to the paint mixture. The secondaries and secondary coverts are painted with a mixture of burnt umber and a touch of white. All the feathers are edged with raw sienna and white. Wash the entire area with burnt umber. Wash the secondaries with ultra-thin black.

Paint the under-wings medium dusky gray, growing darker toward the primaries. Attach the wings to the body at this time.

Paint the under-rump whitish--white with a touch of burnt umber--and extend it through the 1-inch wide white band bordering the tail. Paint the patch on the head with this whitish mixture and add flecks of black paint. Apply a tiny patch of whitish paint just under the lower eyelid. Coat the bill with gloss medium.

Fig. 656. Swan head, back of head and neck pieces are roughed out.

Fig. 657. Goose head, back of head and neck pieces are roughed out.

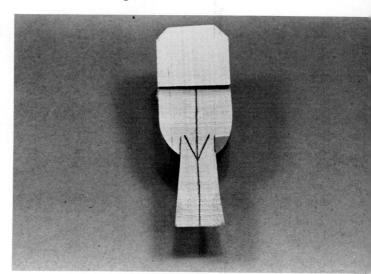

Fig. 658. Underside of head has been trimmed on one side.

Fig. 659. In vise, set back of head piece on neck at a slight angle.

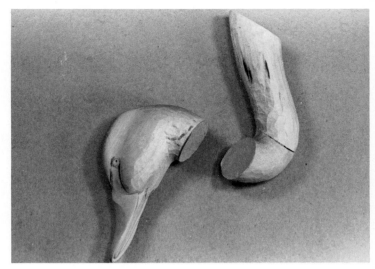

Fig. 662. Paper helps you pop the head off the neck to texture the pieces.

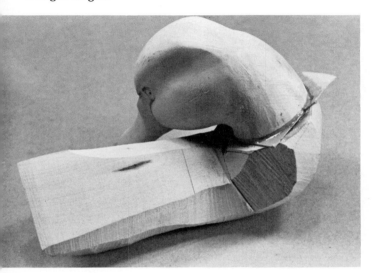

Fig. 660. Glue head onto paper and then onto back of head pieces.

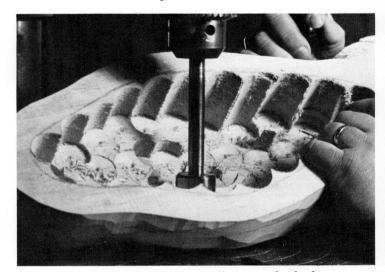

Fig. 663. With drill press, hollow out the body.

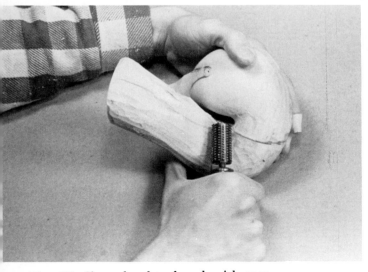

Fig. 661. Shape head and neck with rasp.

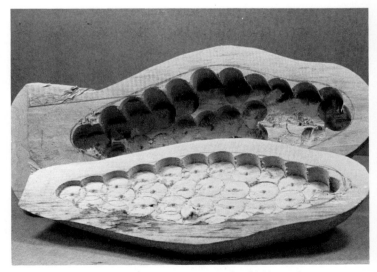

Fig. 664. Both body pieces must be hollowed out evenly.

249

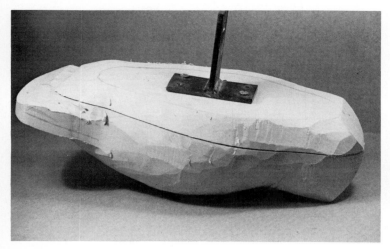

Fig. 665. Put T-bar on bottom of body block to insert into vise for removal of excess wood.

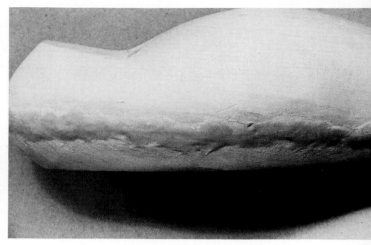

Fig. 668. Fill channel with Wood dough.

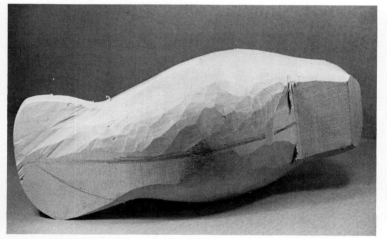

Fig. 666. Excess wood has been removed from body with drawknife.

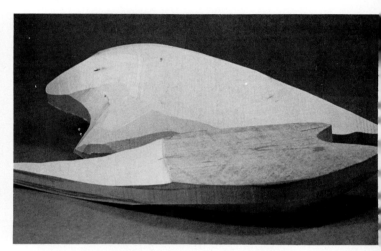

Fig. 669. Swan wings are roughed out. Note underside of wing in front, top of wing in back.

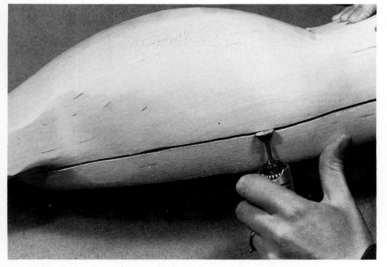

Fig. 667. Cut channel along seam line of sanded body block.

Fig. 670. Wings are hollowed out from underside.

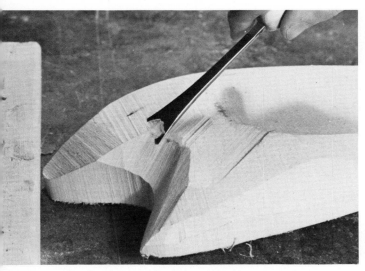

Fig. 671. With fishtail chisel trim excess wood from wing.

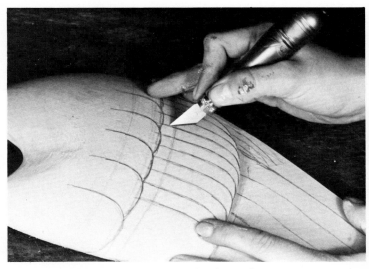

Fig. 674. With knife, trace feather edges.

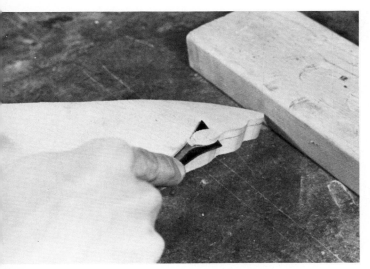

Fig. 672. Block of wood keeps wing from moving as you trim it with fishtail chisel.

Fig. 675. Offset chisel is used to carve feather layout.

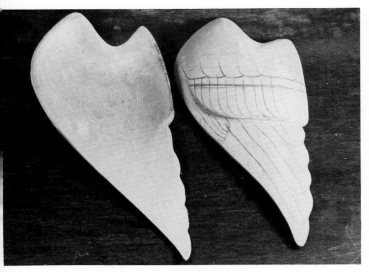

Fig. 673. Wings are sanded and laid out for detailing.

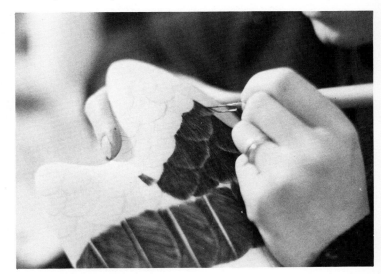

Fig. 676. Texture is burned into wings.

251

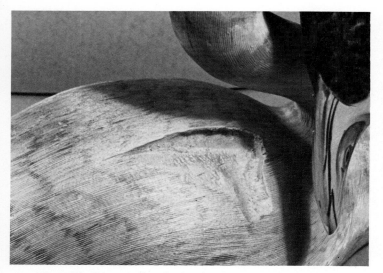

Fig. 677. Cut notches in back of swan for wings.

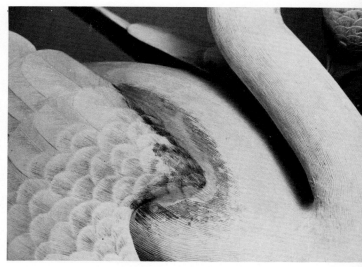

Fig.679. After body and wings are painted, attach wings and texture Wood Dough around seam.

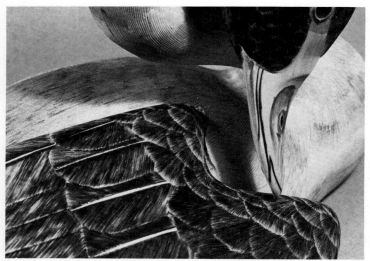

Fig. 678. Check that wings fit into notches but do not attach yet.

Fig. 680. Swan's tail feathers and wings stand out because they were carved with knife and textured with burning pen.

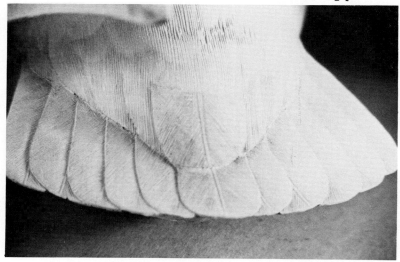

Fig. 681. Note the detail of the swan's tail feathers.

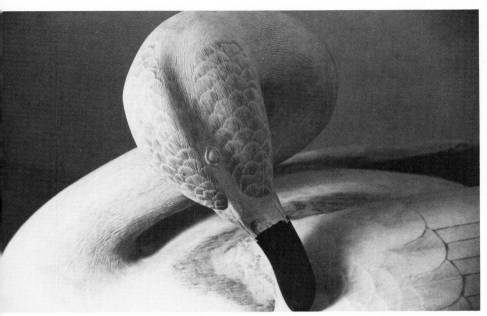

Fig. 682. Note the detail on the swan's head.

Fig. 683. Note the detail on the Canada goose.

Fig. 684. Canada goose has cupped feathers on wings and back painted with raw sienna and white.

Chapter 25
Carving an Antique Swan

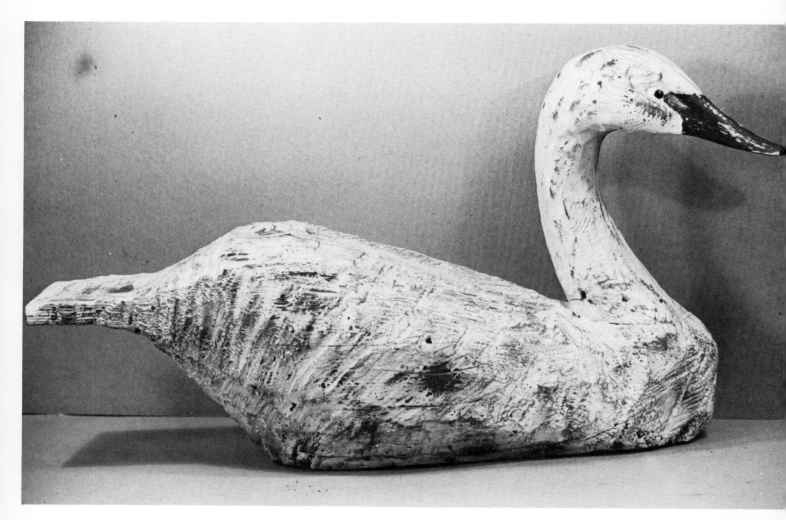

Fig. 685. The Antique swan is a project you can't make a mistake with.

Here is a carving project that you can just zip through because you can't make it look too good. It's impossible to make a mistake with it.

Look for a big chunk of wood that is rough and rustic. Several pieces will also do. The body should be a total of 24-inches long, 7-8-inches high and 9-10-inches wide. (The pattern had to be reduced in size for this book. It is ¼ the size it should be.) Barn beams or an old telephone pole will do very well. Do not use a modern pole because of the creosote in it.

If you use more than one piece of wood, glue them together on the inside of the blocks and then dowel them together. Drive in the dowels at opposing angles to lock the pieces together. Don't worry about any gaps or cracks; they will give the carving the feeling of age and antiquity.

Bandsaw the body block. Put the tail end of the block in a vise, and shape the body with a chain saw. (A hatchet or drawknife will also work.) This will leave the wood very rough. After it is completely shaped, attach the head.

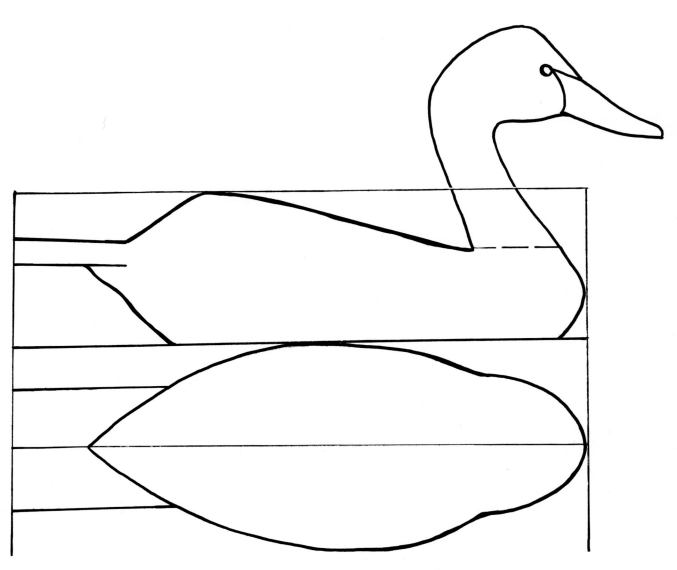

Fig. 686 — 688. Antique Swan's plan view and profile, reduced to ¼ size.

Fig. 689. Old telephone pole has had its edges squared off with chainsaw.

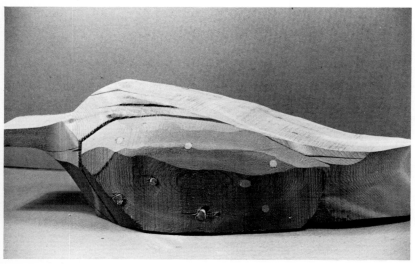

Fig. 690. Attach extra pieces to body, if necessary, with dowels.

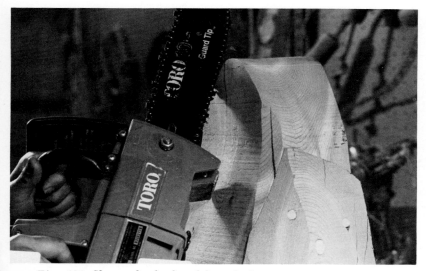

Fig. 691. Shape the body with a chain saw.

CARVING THE HEAD AND NECK

Make the head and neck out of two pieces of 2-inch thick pine and join them down the middle. This adds a feeling of authenticity. If you use a 4-inch block of wood, it won't simulate age as well. Dowel the wood together. Bandsaw the head and shape it with a large bit on the Foredom tool and sand the bill only.

Attach the head and neck to the body with 3/8-inch dowels, inserted diagonally to each other. Because the neck was cut across the grain, it is weak, so also drill 1/8-inch holes straight down through the neck from the back of the head, and drive in a 40-penny nail or a brass or steel rod. You could also drive a few finishing nails along the base of the neck and angle them into the body to strengthen the neck.

The eyes can be fired brown eyes in 10 or 12 mm. This will add to the saleability of the carving, but will not be as authentic as other methods. One method is to drill ½-inch holes, and drive in short pieces of ½-inch dowel. Round them off and paint them black to simulate eyes.

Another method is to drive a large brass tack into the head for each eye and paint it black.

PAINTING

Burn the wood all over with a propane torch. This will make the wood ripple as if it has been weathered. Wire-brush away all the char. This will leave a browned surface. Brush shellac all over. Paint about two coats of flat white acrylic house paint on the head and body. Paint the bill with black paint and add a couple of splashes of yellow. Then go over the paint with a propane torch, hitting it lightly and severely in different areas to bubble up the paint. Brush the bird with a soft suede brush or the denture brush to remove the loose paint. Raw wood will show in some places, but this again simulates the feeling of age. Apply a heavy coat of paste wax to the entire bird. Let it stay overnight and then buff. The antique swan is now finished.

Congratulations on your brand new antique!

256

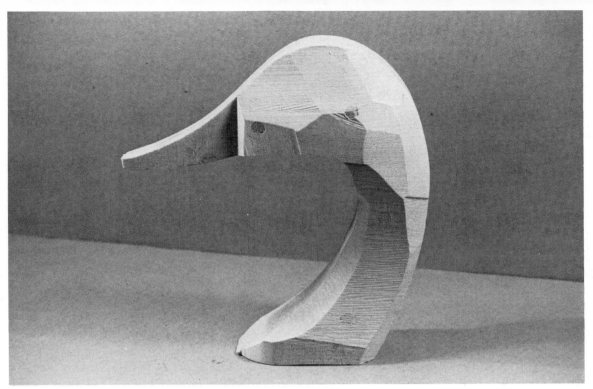

Fig. 692. Shape head with a large bit on Foredom tool and do not sand it.

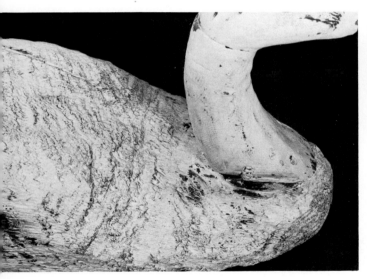

Fig. 693. The swan is roughened to give a feeling of age.

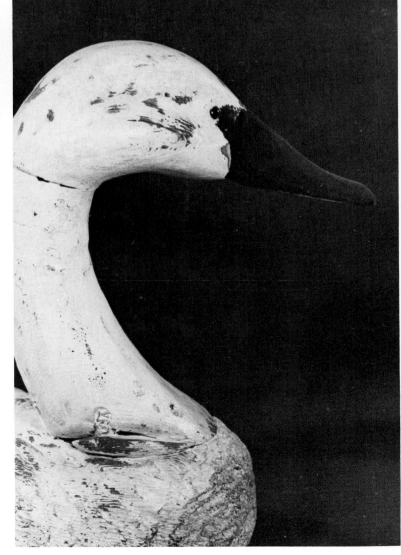

Fig. 694. The bill is the only part that is sanded.

Chapter 26
Competition and Exhibition

When you finish a carving, enter it in a show. Don't be embarrassed or shy. Competition is good for you. It gets your adrenalin pumping and makes you alive. You learn more from going to a show and competing in it than you learn in months of trial and error, for you see your bird in an entirely new light. It will probably look quite different from the way it looked all by itself in your home.

Chances are you won't win a ribbon at your first show. That doesn't make you a loser. The fact that you're competing at all makes you a winner. The more you compete, the more you learn. Study the carvings that win ribbons and objectively compare your work with them. Ask the judges or some of the winning carvers for a critique of your carving and listen to what they have to say.

Competitions and exhibitions are a good way to learn about carving, but don't try to learn everything all at once. Study only one part of a bird's anatomy at a time. At one show study just heads; at another show, study just tails, and so on. If you're interested in growing and developing as a carver you need to learn everything you can. Participate in any classes or seminars offered at the show. The Ward Foundation provides seminars at the World Championships each year. Other shows will probably follow suit as time goes by. These seminars are very worthwhile. Anyone who has been asked to teach one has proved himself as a carver and teacher. You'll pick up information that's often difficult to come by and you'll have the experience of learning under someone who's new to you.

JUDGING

Over the years I've won many ribbons at many shows and I've also been a judge. So I'm always asked, what are the judges looking for? This question is difficult to answer. So much has happened in the last 6 to 10 years that there are very few specific judging guidelines. This leaves almost everything to the discretion of the judges.

A show's entry form states some very general rules. For example: the carving must display likeness to species and animation; the maximum size for miniatures; a carving can not have been entered in that show before; a floating decorative must be balanced on the water. However, too many guidelines are not given to the carvers or the judges. For instance, there's no written rule that a carving with a cast bill will be disqualified, but it always is if the judges catch it. This lack of rules makes it very difficult for the beginning carver to compete.

It also makes it difficult for the judges to do as good a job of judging as they are capable of. Show officials generally assume judges know everything, but they don't. Ideally there should be a specialist in different fields in each group of judges, but this is difficult to arrange. I think there should be a seminar developed for judges so they can agree before a show what constitutes good judging. At present, judges have to judge one carving against another rather than against an ideal. It may be relatively easy to choose a blue ribbon winner, but to select the other winners, judges finally have to judge fault against fault.

Judges are people too. They respond to carvings just as other people do. If they're "grabbed" by something about a carving, they gravitate toward it. The workmanship of a carving is important to them. "Neat and clean" are key words. They assess the artistic concept and content in the decorative division. Judges also respond to a carving that has captured the bird's life quality and sense of movement. They want a carving to be realistic, but a life-like carving that's lacking a small realistic detail is more likely to win than a stiff and perfectly technical carving.

It's not easy to be a judge. There is so much work that goes into a carving that I hate to think of people "losing". I know how it is to "lose". I've felt angry, bitter and terribly disappointed when a carving I've worked hard on doesn't win a ribbon. The mistake some carvers make at such a low point is to give up carving. This is wrong. They should turn their anger and disappointment into a determination to learn why the carving didn't win and go on to use this knowledge to make a better one the next time. Don't just rail at the judges or show officials. They are all volunteers who are doing their jobs for their love of the art. You actually should thank them for giving you the opportunity to show your work and to learn more about carving.

ENTERING A SHOW

Every carving competition has divisions--usually floating decoratives, decoratives and sometimes hunting decoys (called the Gunning Stool division at the U.S. National show). These divisions are often broken down into categories.

In the decorative division there's a miniature category and a lifesize category. The miniature category generally is subdivided into waterfowl, shorebirds, birds of prey and game birds. In the lifesize category are shorebirds, birds of prey, game birds, waterfowl and song birds.

The floating decorative division also is generally divided into categories. For instance, in this year's U.S. National show, there is listed a class for divers, dabblers, geese and confidence (birds that are generally solitary birds--loons, grebes, gulls). Within each of these categories, specific species are listed. This breakdown has come about because there are often a great many floating decoratives in competition. The list may include "other" or "miscellaneous" which implies that all unlisted species will be judged together. If there is no "other" on a list, do not enter any species that is not listed.

The hunting decoy division is generally not broken down into species unless the show is a large one, as determined by the number of entries. At some shows the hunting decoys you enter are your gift to the show. They are auctioned off after the judging is completed, the profit helping to pay the expenses incurred in running the show.

These divisions are the same for each class of carver--juniors, novices, amateurs and professionals (sometimes called junior, novice, intermediate and open). The carver in the junior class is under 16 years of age. The novice is a carver who has never won a blue ribbon at a major show. The amateur or intermediate carver is one who has never won a best of show ribbon in a class. The professional or open class is the only class that a carver who has won a best of show ribbon in the amateur class at any major carving show may enter. It is also the class for a carver whose work represents a very high level of proficiency.

With the exception of the junior class, no one forces a carver to enter a specific class or to move out of a class at a given time. I envision that someday there will be an earned-point system under which everyone will begin as novice. Then, when a carver wins a blue ribbon at a very top show, he will earn, say, 10 points; a blue ribbon at a show of lesser stature will give him 3 or 4 points. When he accumulates a certain number of points, he will move to a new class. Of course this would have to be a computerized system, tied into all the carving shows.

To enter a show, there's an entry fee for each carving you submit--say, $2.50. You can transport the carving yourself or ship it to the show where it will be placed on display for you. To package an entry, use a box with flaps that's larger on all dimensions than the carving. Wrap the carving in a clear plastic bag so you can see it whenever you handle it. Pack shredded paper around all sides inside the box. (I don't use the "popcorn" styrofoam because there's no place to put it at a show when you're repackaging the carving.)

If you ship a carving, put the inner box inside a larger box, with more shredded paper around it for protection.

AWARDS

There are first, second, third, and honorable mention awards for carvings in a given category for each classification of carver. For instance, in the decorative division there are awards for each of the lifesize bird categories. In the floating decorative division, however, there are awards for each species within each category. After the initial judging, all the first-place winners of each of the species within a category are judged to determine the first, second and third-place winners of that category. Now there's one carving that has two blue ribbons. When all the categories have been similarly judged, four carvings have two blue ribbons each. These four are then judged together; first, second and third-place are awarded, and the first-place winner is given best-of-show honors for the entire floating decorative division.

At some shows, such as the World Championships, there are purchase awards for the first-place winners in stated categories, such as the World Class. The show officials or the funding agency purchase the carvings, generally to put them in a public display.

EXHIBITION

You can go to carving and craft shows just to exhibit your carvings for the purpose of sales, but you have to pay a fee to exhibit. Some shows are invitational only, and a "jury" selects who will be permitted to exhibit.

Plan your exhibit well. Take a number of carvings that you haven't exhibited before. Create an attractive display. Keep in mind that most halls have poor lighting, so design your own. Bring plenty of extension cords.

Design a business card, brochure or identifying tags for each carving. You want people to remember your name. Find out if the show permits price tags on exhibited carvings. At some shows, tags are permitted only in sales areas.

CARVING SHOWS TO ENTER

Academy of Natural Sciences "Wildfowl Expo"
19th and the Parkway
Philadelphia, PA 19130
Late November. New, but promises to be one of the major shows; silver medal competition; invitational exhibition; sales area

Artistry in Wood--
Northern Virginia Carvers
120 Cherry St. S.E.
Vienna, VA 22180
Midsummer; small carving show

Bayville Seaside Festival (Chamber of Commerce)
P.O. Box 115
Bayville, N.Y. 11709
Early September; large one-day craft show

Bel Air Show
Hartford Day School
715 Moores Mill Road
Bel Air, MD 21014
Early March; small exhibition

Bizarre Bazaar
321 Greenway Lane
Richmond, VA 23226
Early December; large craft show

Canadian National Exhibition
Toronto, Ontario M6K 3C3
Canada
Late August; competition and exhibition; entry blank an education in itself

Cape May Waterfowl Carving Show
Convention Hall
Beach Drive
Cape May, N. J. 08204
Midsummer; small carving show

Clayton International Hunting Decoy Contest
Clayton Arena
Clayton, N.J. 08312
Mid-summer; exhibition and competition; limited to 1000 hunting decoys

Easton Waterfowl Festival Association
Tidewater Inn
Easton, MD 21601
Early November; most comprehensive wildfowl exhibition in world; 12 to 14 separate show locations; long waiting list for exhibitors

Great James River Decoy Competition
North Side Lions Club
c/o Fred Langshultz
1033 Cheswick Road
Richmond, VA 23229
Mid-February; good competition and exhibition

Great Snow Goose Decoy Contest
Chincoteague Island, VA 23336
Usually late spring; exhibition and competition

Havre de Grace Decoy Festival
P. O. Box 339
Havre de Grace, MD 21078
Mid-May; exhibition

Iowa Carving & Art Show
2815 W. Locust St.
Davenport, Iowa 52804

Early fall; big competition and exhibition

Louisiana Wildfowl Carvers & Collectors
  Guild
615 Baronne Street
Suite 303
New Orleans, LA 70113
  Early fall; major competition and exhibition; big prize money

Mid-Atlantic Waterfowl Festival
P.O. Box 651
Virginia Beach, VA 23451
  Excellent carving show; competition and invitational exhibition; sales area

Midwest Decoy Contest
Pointe Morrille St. Game Area
Route 2
Rockwood, MI 48173
  Early fall; competition and exhibition

Nags Head Waterfowl Weekend
Outer Banks Chamber of Commerce
P. O. Box 90
Kitty Hawk, N.C. 27949
  Early fall; mid-sized carving exhibition

National Nature Art Exhibition
3995 Horseshoe Bend Road
Troy, Ohio 45373
  Early June; exhibition

National Wildlife Art Show
P. O. Box 26130
Kansas City, MO 64196
  March; juried show; about 100 exhibitors; sponsored by Ducks Unlimited

O.D.C.C.A. (Ohio Decoy Collectors &
  Carvers Assn.)
P. O. Box 29224
Parma, OH 44129
  March; exhibition and working decoy competition

Pacific Flyway Decoy Association Wildfowl
  Festival
P.O. Box 201
Arcata, Calif. 95521
  June; exhibition and competition held in Santa Rosa

Pacific Southwest Decoy Competition
731 Beach Avenue
Chula Vista, CA 92010
  Mid-February; competition and exhibition

Salem County Decoy Show
Salem County Sportsman's Club
Salem, N.J. 08079
  Early fall; small exhibition

Somerset County Carving Wildlife Art
  Show
190 Lord Sterling Road
Basking Ridge, N.J. 07920
  Probably fall; exhibition

Stoney Brook Decoy Show
c/o Wildfowler Decoys
57 Park Avenue
Babylon, N.Y. 11702
  Mid-February; small exhibition, principally antique decoys

U.S. National
Great South Bay Waterfowlers Association, Inc.
P.O. Box 36
Brightwaters, N.Y. 11718
  Late March; oldest running decoy show in U.S.; competition and exhibition; money prizes in professional and gunning classes

Ward Foundation Wildfowl Arts Exhibition
P.O. Box 2613
Salisbury, MD 21801
  Mid-October; prestigious; one of best exhibitions in country, by invitation only; sales area

Wildlife Art Show
Newark White Clay Kiwanis
Box 356
Newark, Del. 19711
  Mid-March; mid-sized show; competition and exhibition

World Championships
Ward Foundation
P.O. Box 2613
Salisbury, MD 21801
  Late April; held in Ocean City, MD; finest carvings in world; over 2000 carvings judged each year; total $50,000 prize money; sales area

York Carvers Contest
York College
Country Club Road
York, PA 17405
  Early fall; competition and exhibition

Chapter 27
Marketing Your Carvings

Finding a market for your carvings is accomplished very easily if you are exhibiting and competing at shows. If you win a blue ribbon at a show, someone is sure to want to purchase the carving. This is not to say that you can't sell a carving if you haven't been in a show. Many of my students sold their first four Canada geese as soon as they had finished them.

If you intend to be marketable, you have to be visible. No one is going to seek you out. You have to say, "Hey, here I am!" rather than sit back and wait for potential customers to flock to you. You may have to gain exposure by persuading a local newspaper to do an article about your work. It is my experience that local newspapers are always in need of such features.

If you're involved in organizing a carving show in your area, publicize it well to attract people. The more who come, the more who'll see your work. Consider asking a local company, such as the telephone company, to include a flyer about the show in their regular mailings to customers. Get the Chamber of Commerce involved with the publicity.

Look for a shop that sells crafts on consignment. These are generally delighted to take on good new work. Of course, they subtract a percentage of your selling price; 25 to 35 percent is typical. If the carving doesn't sell after a period of time, take it elsewhere to gain new exposure. What about stores or restaurants that are looking for ways to change their decor? Offer them your carvings for display purposes and include your business card in the display. Perhaps a store wants to buy your carvings outright. If so, they will probably sell them for double what they paid you.

Make a limited edition of a pattern for a carving. This will probably have some impact on selling because people like the idea of getting something particularly special.

Bartering is another way to market your carving, but you won't get any money for it. Instead you'll trade it for an item or service that you need. This may be just as good, if not better, than money. I've bartered for all kinds of services, including dental work, a wood supply and a hunting trip to Europe.

Whatever your market, you must first establish what your work is worth. I believe you shouldn't price your work by the hour because you may make a carving so slowly that the price would be prohibitive. I suggest you just pick a price that seems fair to you. Go to shows to see what other carvers ask for their carvings.

After setting a price, see what happens. If your carvings never sell or no one wants to barter with you, you've probably priced them too high. On the other hand, if they're snapped up immediately and you can't carve them fast enough, you've probably priced them too low. If you're really stymied about finding a price, donate a carving to a charity auction such as one held by the Ward Foundation or your local chapter of Ducks Unlimited. See what price your work brings. Do this several times and you should be able to arrive at a fair market value. Auctioning your carvings is also a good way to gain exposure and pricing knowledge.

There is one important point to remember. If you price your carvings so high that they never sell, you will lose more in potential customers that you will lose if you sell them a little low. If your carving sits so long in a shop that it begins to gather dust, it does nothing for anyone.

Always sign your work. Your customers expect it and your name will become more widely known. Moreover, you should sign it out of your own sense of pride. Use indelible ink on the bottom of a flat-bottomed decoy or the base of a standing bird. Some people use a burning pen to burn in their signature; others brand their carvings with their own logo.

Keep a photograph album of all your carvings and a catalog of your customers. Some day you may have people coming back to you for more of your carvings, and it is helpful to know their preferences.

Fig. 695. Brant by Tom Birch.

Chapter 28
Developing Your Own Patterns

Up to this point you have been developing your expertise as a carver as you mastered the techniques and procedures I've described. Your craftsmanship, therefore, should be excellent.

Now begins the truly creative process. The craft can be turned into an art. As you learn how to develop your own patterns for your carvings instead of following patterns supplied by others, you will truly become an artist. This is not to say that, if you don't create your own patterns, there's no room for you or your work in the carving world. Probably the broadest category of carvers are those who only follow patterns. I am just suggesting that you can grow and develop even further.

Most people insist they can not draw. This simply is not so. Everyone can draw or can be taught to draw sufficiently well to prepare a good workable pattern. You do not need to develop all the subtle shadings an artist wants in a painting. All you have to learn is how to draw a good profile and plan view of a proposed carving.

The key to a good carving is a good pattern. Spend the time working on your pattern until you are completely satisfied with it. Only then should it be turned into a carving.

One important step must be taken in developing a pattern and that is to study extensively the species you plan to carve. This does not mean that you simply study the dimensions and color of the species listed in this book. Those are essential, but they are not enough.

Many bird carvers hunt birds and have them mounted by a taxidermist for study material. This is an excellent way to gather information but has three drawbacks. One is that it is very expensive to have mounts made. Second, you're relying on the knowledge of the taxidermist, and

it's no simple matter for them to know all the facts about every bird's anatomy. Third, while you may attempt to copy a specific mount for your carving, you should also be familiar with the entire species and not with just one bird. One bird will differ from the next as you and I differ. By observing many of them you develop a consensus of what the bird looks like. Then, copy your specimen knowing that variations within the species do occur.

Go to museums, colleges or universities near you. Many have large collections of mounted birds and/or skins which may be borrowed. Look at all the photographs of the species you can find. Build up your own film library. At carving shows a number of people sell fine photographs of live birds under real conditions. Establish your own library of reference books and other materials. Above all, observe the live species and learn about their habitats.

By the time you are ready to draw a pattern you should be sure the position you choose lies within the limits of the bird's anatomy and that the scene in which you place it does not contradict what occurs in nature. Think the pattern all the way through to where the finished carving will be placed, bearing in mind that all sculpture should be viewable from a full 360 degrees. Your carving should not have a "good" side and a "bad" side.

Study the dimensions of your species in the list on page 266.

On a large piece of paper or cardboard, form a rectangle using the width and length dimensions of the bird. This is the plan view. Draw a centerline through the length of the rectangle.

Draw another rectangle above the plan view, using the height and length dimensions. This is the profile.

Utilizing the knowledge you've gleaned about your species, determine where different points of its body are. For instance, if it's a diving duck, you know its tail would be below the center of the profile, so make a dot there. This is a reference point in your drawing. Is it a duck with a short tail? Place a dot denoting the length of the tail. This is now a finite point for the tail. Continue to work on each rectangle, measuring carefully, until you've drawn the bird's plan view and profile.

If the dimensions list does not include your bird, work from a mount. Use calipers and compasses as necessary to measure the mount and use these measurements in the pattern.

On the plan view, figure out which side of the centerline of the drawing is the best. Cut out that side, fold the paper along the centerline, and trace the other side. Thus both sides will be exactly the same. Do the same with the profile.

Now proceed to roughing out the bird, using all the skills you have perfected up to this point.

And, go for the blue.....

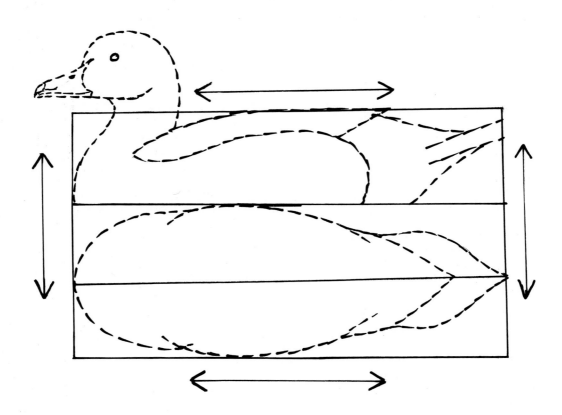

Fig. 696. How to draw a pattern.

DIMENSIONS OF SOME COMMON WATERFOWL

	sex	overall length	wing span	body length	body width	width for carving	body height	stock size for flat-bottomed decoy	head width life	head width carved
Blue-winged	M	16	24½	10	4¼	4½	4	3	1½	1 5/8
Teal	F	15	23½	9¾	4	4¼	3¾	3	1½	1 5/8
Cinnamon	M	16	25	10	4½	4¾	4	3	1½	1 5/8
Teal	F	15½	24	9¾	4¼	4½	3¾	3	1½	1 5/8
Green-winged	M	16	24	10	3¾	4¼	3¾	3	1½	1 5/8
Teal	F	14	23	9½	3¾	4	3½	3	1½	1 5/8
Wood	M	19	29	12½	4¾	5½	4½	3¾	1¾	2
duck	F	17	27	11½	4¼	5	4	3¼	1½	1¾
Baldpate	M	20	33	13	5	6	4¾	4	1¾	2
	F	18½	31	12	4¾	5¾	4½	4	1¾	2
Gadwall	M	21	35	13	5½	6	5	4	1¾	2
	F	19	33	12½	5	5¾	5	4	1¾	1 7/8
Pintail	M	*25	35	*17	5½	6	5½	4	1¾	1 7/8
	F	20½	32	13	5¼	5¾	5	4	1 7/10	1¾
Shoveler	M	20	32	12½	5	5¾	4½	3½	1½	1¾
	F	18½	29½	11½	4½	5½	4	3½	1½	1¾
Mallard	M	23	36	14	5¾	6¼	5½	4¼	1 7/8	2¼
	F	21½	35	13	5½	6	5	4	1¾	2
Black	M	23	36	14	5¾	6¼	5½	4¼	1 7/8	2¼
duck	F	21½	35	13	5½	6	5	4	1¾	2
Ruddy	M	14¾	21	10	4¼	4¾	4	3	1¾	2
duck	F	14	20	9½	4	4½	3¾	3	1¾	2
Canada	M	36	68	22	9	9½	8½	6	2	2¼
goose(common)	F	35	64	20	8½	9½	8	6	2	2¼
White fronted	M	29	59	19	7½	8	7	5½	2	2¼
goose	F	27	55	17	7	7½	6½	5	1¾	2
Lesser Snow &	M	29	58	19	7½	8	7	5½	2	2¼
Blue	F	27	56	18	7	7½	6½	5	1¾	2
Brant	M	25	47	16	6½	7½	6	5	1¾	2
	F	23	45	15	6	7	5½	4¾	1¾	2
Harlequin	M	17½	26½	11½	5	5½	4½	4-3¾	1 5/8	1¾
	F	15½	24	11	4½	5	4	3	1½	1¾
Old Squaw	M	*21	29	*16½	5	5¾	4¾	4	1¾	2
	F	15½	27½	11	4¾	5½	4½	4-3¾	1¾	2
Canvasback	M	22	32	13	5¾	7	5¼	4¼	2	2¼
	F	21	30½	12½	5½	6¾	5	4	2	2¼
Bufflehead	M	14½	23½	10	4¼	4¾	4	3	1¾	2 (hood 2½)
	F	13½	21½	9	3¾	4½	3¾	3	1½	1¾
American	M	19	30½	12½	5¼	6½	5	4	1¾	2 (hood 2½)
Golden-eye	F	17½	28	11½	5	6	4¾	3½	1¾	2
Barrow's	M	20	31	13	5½	6½	5¼	4	1 4/5	2
Golden-eye	F	17½	28	11½	5	6	4¾	3¾	1¾	2
Greater	M	18½	31	11½	5½	6¾	5	4	2	2¼
Scaup	F	17½	30	10¾	5¼	6¾	5	4	2	2¼
Lesser	M	17	29	10½	5	6	4¾	3¾	1¾	2
Scaup	F	16	26½	10	4 9/10	6	4¾	3¾	1¾	2
Redhead	M	19¾	32	12½	5¼	6¾	5	4	2	2¼
	F	19	31	12	5	6½	4¾	4	2	2¼
Ring-necked	M	17	29	10½	5	5½	4¾	3¾	1¾	2
duck	F	16½	27	10	4¾	5	4½	3¾	1¾	2
American	M	25½	36½	16	6	7	6½	5	1¾	2 1/8
Merganser	F	23½	35½	14½	5¾	6¾	5¾	4¾	1¾	2
Hooded	M	18	26	11½	4½	5¾	4 1/3	3¾	1 5/8	2
Merganser	F	17	24½	11	4¼	5½	4	3¾	1½	1¾
Red-breasted	M	23	33	14½	5½	6	5¼	4	1¾	2
Merganser	F	21	30	13½	5¼	6	5	4	1¾	2

Pintail *with pin (2¾" tail feather)
Old Squaw * includes 4½" tail feather

Bull, John and Farrand, Jr., John. *The Audubon Society Field Guide to North American Birds-Eastern Region.* Chanticleer Press, Alfred A. Knopf, Inc.

Burk, Bruce. *Game Bird Carving.* Winchester Press.

Burk, Bruce. *Waterfowl Studies.* Winchester Press.

Clement, Roland C. *The Living World of Audubon.* Grosset & Dunlap.

Coleman, Bruce. *The Color Nature Library of Books.* Crescent.

Gilly, Wendell. *Bird Carving--A Guide to a Fascinating Hobby.* Bonanza Books.

Kortright, Francis H. *The Ducks, Geese and Swans of North America.* Wildlife Management Institute.

LeMaster, Richard. *Wildlife in Wood.* Model Technology, Inc.

Peterson, Roger Tory. *A Field Guide to Birds.* Houghton Mifflin.

Queeny, Edgar M. *Prairie Wings.* Schiffer Publishing Ltd.

Robbins, Chandler S., Bruun, Bertel., and Zim, Herbert S. *A Guide to Field Identification Birds of North America.* Golden Press.

Shourds, Harry V., and Hillman, Anthony. *Shore Bird Patterns.* Brigantine Press.

Tawes, William I. *Creative Bird Carving.* Tidewater Press.

Terres, John K. *The Audubon Society Encyclopedia of North American Birds.* Alfred A. Knopf, Inc.

Todd, Frank S. *Waterfowl--Ducks, Geese and Swans of the World.* Sea World Press.

Tunnicliffe, Charles. *A Sketchbook of Birds.* Holt, Rinehart and Winston.

Walkinshaw, Lawrence. *Cranes of the World.* Winchester Press.

The Audubon Society Field Guide to North American Birds. Alfred A. Knopf, Inc.

There are many publications put out monthly by special interest groups and state organizations. Many states have game news and conservation newsletters. All major show publications are great source material.

"Arizona Highways"
Arizona Department of Transportation
2039 W. Lewis Avenue
Phoenix, AZ 85009
    (published monthly)

"Audubon"
National Audubon Society
950 Third Avenue
New York, NY 10022
    (six issues a year)

"Chip Chats"
National Woodcarvers Association
7424 Miami Avenue
Cincinnati, OH 45243
    (bi-monthly)

"Classic Sportsmen"
P. O. Box 770
Camden, SC 29020
    (quarterly)

"Decoy World"
77 Bakers Street
Aberdeen, MD 21001

"Ducks Unlimited"
P. O. Box 66300
Chicago, Ill. 60666
    (five issues a year)

"Fine Wood Working"
Taunton Press
Newtown, CT 06470
    (bi-monthly)

"Grays Sporting Journal"
1330 Beacon Street
Brookline, MA 02146
    (seven issues a year)

"International Wildlife"
National Wildlife Federation
8925 Leesburg Pike
Vienna, VA 22180
    (bi-monthly)

"North American Decoys"
Hillcrest Publications
P. O. Box 246
Spanish Fork, Utah 84660
    (quarterly)

"Ranger Rick"
National Wildlife Association
1412 16th Street. N. W.
Washington, D.C. 20036
    (monthly)

"Sunshine Artist"
Sun Country Enterprises, Inc.
501-503 N. Va. Avenue
Winter Park, FL 32782
    (monthly)

"Virginia Wildlife"
Va. Commission of Game & Inland fisheries
P. O. Box 11104
Richmond, VA 23230
    (monthly)

"Ward Foundation News"
Ward Foundation
North American Wildfowl Museum
Salisbury State College
Salisbury, MD 21801
    (quarterly)

Index